LIBRARY OF NEW TESTAMENT STUDIES

440

formerly the Journal for the Study of the New Testament Supplement series

A NARRATOLOGICAL READING OF 1 PETER

ABSON PRÉDESTIN JOSEPH

t&t clark

Published by T&T Clark International
A Continuum imprint
The Tower Building, 11 York Road, London SE1 7NX
80 Maiden Lane, Suite 704, New York, NY 10038

www.continuumbooks.com

British Library Cataloguing-in-Publication Data
A catalogue record for this book is available from the British Library

ISBN: HB: 978-0-567-16625-8

Typeset by Free Range Book Design & Production Limited
Printed and bound in Great Britain

*To my wife, Larisa
and my children, Daniella and Sophie*

CONTENTS

PREFACE

This book was written originally as my doctoral dissertation at Brunel University, supervised at the London School of Theology. My interest in 1 Peter goes as far back as the days of my undergraduate studies at Caribbean Wesleyan College when I began to wrestle with the meaning of the message of 1 Peter for its primary audience and the claims it seems to make on my own life. While attending a seminar on 'The Death of Jesus in the New Testament', as part of a Research Methods in New Testament Interpretation course at Asbury Theological Seminary, I submitted a paper on the death of Jesus in 1 Peter. There I looked at the ways the author of 1 Peter uses Christ's suffering as an illustration of God's vindication of his children. The conversations and reflections that ensued with Dr Joel Green and other professors at Asbury Seminary on the subject became the foundation for my doctoral dissertation. My reading and understanding of the message of 1 Peter has also benefitted from my interaction with Dr Paul Holloway of the University of Glasgow regarding the affinities between the way(s) the author of 1 Peter appropriated the Old Testament and the modes of interpretation practised at Qumran.

My intention was to find a way to explain the relationship between the Old Testament and 1 Peter and the interpretive implications of the author's dependence on the Old Testament in crafting his message. I have sought to propose a methodology that takes into account and keeps in tension the narrative elements present in the non-narrative text of the epistle of 1 Peter. At an early stage in my research, I realized that many scholars emphasized the need for methodological clarifications regarding the way narrative analysis was being applied to epistolary studies. So, in this book I lay out a methodology that addresses some of the questions that were raised vis-à-vis the suitability of using narratology in the study of an epistle. The method I propose builds on previous proposals advanced in Pauline studies, for example, Richard Hays and Norman Petersen, and more recent work in Petrine scholarship, for example, Eugene Boring, J. de Waal Dryden and Joel Green. The application of narratology to the study of epistolary literature is a recent development in the study of 1 Peter. It is my hope that this book will advance the discussion on the matter.

In addition, it is evident that the author of 1 Peter is concerned about the character formation of his audience. The suffering the audience faces and the solutions the author puts forward are both socially located and theologically motivated. Yet, the author of 1 Peter notes that this is a shared experience for members of the family of God (1 Pet. 5.9). It begs the question of 1 Peter's relevance to the other parts of the world the author had in mind and by extension its relevance to audiences in the world today who may face similar issues. It is my intent that this book will contribute positively to the present conversation vis-à-vis the meaning of 1 Peter's message to its first-century audience on the Anatolian peninsula as well as its relevance for the church today.

ACKNOWLEDGEMENTS

Living in community is inherent to the divine nature: God is Father, Son and Holy Spirit. Consequently, that human beings are created in the image of God has to do, in part, with the fact that God places us in community. This present study is the fruit of my labour, yet I could not have completed it successfully without the support of others who are part of the community within which God has placed me.

I owe a debt of gratitude to my wife, Larisa, who cheered me on during the difficult parts of the process, helped me focus on the task at hand, and cared for the family especially on those days when the writing process took priority over other aspects of life; and to my children, Daniella and Sophie, for the sacrifice they made as I spent long hours and days away from them in order to complete this work. I am grateful to my parents who instilled in me the love for God and a deep desire to pursue the things of God. I am also indebted to Dr Joel B. Green, the supervisor of my doctoral studies, a friend and a mentor whose devotion to God and commitment to scholarship have been an inspiration to me. This book would not have been the same without his guidance. I am also thankful to Dr Stephen Motyer, London School of Theology, and Dr Paul Holloway, the University of Glasgow. The questions they raised and comments they made during the process have helped in improving the quality of this work.

In addition, I am thankful to Global Partners, the mission hand of the Wesleyan Church, to World Hope International, and to Steve and Vicki Brown who gave abundantly and unselfishly so that I could finance my studies. I am grateful for the many people throughout the years who have contributed in one way or another to shaping me as a person and my understanding of the Bible. I have met them along the way in my home church, the Wesleyan Church of Haïti; during the course of my undergraduate studies and subsequent work as a faculty member and Academic Dean at Caribbean Wesleyan College in Jamaica; and during my graduate studies at Asbury Theological Seminary, USA. Finally, I am grateful to Caribbean Wesleyan College for allowing me the time to complete this project.

Above all, I thank God for his enabling presence. To him be all glory and honour!

ABBREVIATIONS

1 Clem.	*First Epistle of Clement*
1 En.	*1 Enoch (Ethiopic Apocalypse)*
1-2 Macc.	1-2 Maccabees
1QH	Thanksgiving Hymns
1QpHab	Commentary on Habakkuk
1QS	Rule of the Community
2 Bar.	*2 Baruch (Syriac Apocalypse)*
4Q504-506	Words of the Luminaries
AB	Anchor Bible
ABD	David N. Freedman (ed.), *Anchor Bible Dictionary* (New York: Doubleday, 1992).
ACCSNT	Ancient Christian Commentary on Scripture, New Testament
ALBO	Analecta Lovaniensia Biblica et Orientalia
AnBib	Analecta biblica
ANRW	Hildegard Temporini and Wolfgang Haase (eds), *Aufstieg und Niedergang der römischen Welt: Geschichte und Kultur Roms im Spiegel der neueren Forschung.* Berlin: de Gruyter, 1972–84.
ANTC	Abingdon New Testament Commentaries
ASNU	Acta seminarii neotetamentici upsaliensis
AsSeign	*Assemblées Du Seigneur*
b. Yeb.	Babylonian Talmud Yebamot
BA	*Biblical Archeologist*
BBR	*Bulletin for Biblical Research*
BCOT	Baker Commentary on the Old Testament
BDAG	Walter Bauer, William F. Arndt, William Gingrich and Frederick W. Danker, *A Greek-English Lexicon of the New Testament and Other Early Christian Literature* (Chicago: University of Chicago Press, 3rd edn, 2000).
BDB	Francis Brown, S. R. Driver and Charles A. Briggs, *The New Brown-Driver-Briggs-Gesenius Hebrew and English Lexicon: With an Appendix Containing the Biblical Aramaic* (Peabody: Hendrickson, 1979).
BECNT	Baker Exegetical Commentary of the New Testament
BETL	Bibliotheca ephemeridum theologicarum lovaniensium
Bib	*Biblica*
BIS	Biblical Interpretation Series

BSac	*Bibliotheca Sacra*
BZ	*Biblische Zeitschrift*
CBQ	*Catholic Biblical Quarterly*
CBQMS	Catholic Biblical Quarterly Monograph Series
CC	Continental Commentaries
cf.	Compare
ConcJ	*Concordia Journal*
ConNT	*Conienctanea Neotestamentica*
CTJ	*Calvin Theological Journal*
DB	F. Vigourouz, (ed.), *Dictionaire de la Bible* (Paris: Letouzey et Ané, 1895–1912).
DLNTD	Ralph P. Martin and Peter H. Davids (eds), *Dictionary of the Later New Testament and Its Development* (Downers Grove, IL: InterVarsity, 1997).
DTIB	Kevin J. Vanhoozer (ed.), *Dictionary for Theological Interpretation of the Bible* (Grand Rapids: Baker Academic, 2005).
ECC	Eerdmans Critical Commentary
EDNT	Horst Balz, Gerhard Schneider (eds), *Exegetical Dictionary of the New Testament* (Grand Rapids: Eerdmans, 1990–93).
EKK	Evangelisch-katholischer Kommentar zum Neuen Testament
ErIsr	*Eretz-Israel*
ETSS	Evangelical Theological Society Series
ExAud	*Ex Auditu*
FilNT	*Filologia Neotestamintaria*
FM	*Faith and Mission*
FRLANT	Forschungen zur Religion und Literatur des Alten und Neuen Testament
HCOT	Historical Commentary of the Old Testament
HeyJ	*Heythrop Journal*
Hist. eccl.	*Historia Ecclesiastica* (Eusebius)
HNT	Handbuch zum Neuen Testament
Holladay	Holladay William L. (ed.), *A Concise Hebrew and Aramaic Lexicon of the Old Testament* (Grand Rapids: Eerdmans, 1988).
HTS	Harvard Theological Studies
HUCA	*Hebrew Union College Annual*
IDB	G. A. Buttrick (ed.), *Interpreter's Dictionary of the Bible* (Nashville: Abingdon, 1962).
Int	*Interpretation*
IVPNTC	InterVarsity Press New Testament Commentary
JAAR	*Journal of the American Academy of Religion*
JBL	*Journal of Biblical Literature*
JPSTC	Jewish Publication Society Torah Commentary
JSJSup	Journal for the Study of Judaism, Supplement Series
JSNT	*Journal for the Study of the New Testament*

JSNTSup	Journal for the Study of the New Testament, Supplement Series
JSOT	*Journal for the Study of the Old Testament*
JSOTSup	Journal for the Study of the Old Testament, Supplement Series
JTS	*Journal of Theological Studies*
LD	Lection Divina
LHHC	Letters and Homilies for Hellenized Christians
LP	*Living Pulpit*
LSG	Louis Second (French Translation of the Bible)
LSJ	Liddell, H. G., R. Scott, H. S. Jones (eds), *A Greek-English Lexicon* (Oxford: Clarendon, 9th edn, 1996).
LXX	Septuagint
MSR	*Mélanges de Sciences Religieuses*
mss	manuscripts
MT	Masoretic Text
NABPRSS	National Association of Baptist Professors of Religion Special Series
NAC	New American Commentary
NBD[2]	J. D. Douglas and N. Hillyer (eds), *New Bible Dictionary* (Downers Grove, IL: InterVarsity, 2nd edn, 1982).
NCB	New Century Bible
NIB	The New Interpreter's Bible
NICNT	New International Commentary on the New Testament
NICOT	New International Commentary on the Old Testament
NIDB	*New Interpreter's Dictionary of the Bible*
NIDOTE	W. A. VanGemeren (ed.), *New International Dictionary of Old Testament Theology and Exegesis* (Grand Rapids: Zondervan, 1997).
NIVAC	The New International Version Application Commentary
NovT	*Novum Testamentum*
NovTSup	Novum Testamentum Supplements
NRSV	New Revised Standard Version
NT	New Testament
NTS	*New Testament Studies*
NTT	Norsk Teologisk Tidsskrift
OT	Old Testament
OTL	Old Testament Library
OTP	James H. Charlesworth (ed.), *Old Testament Pseudepigrapha* (New York: Doubleday, 1983).
Paed.	*Paedagogus* (Clement of Alexandria)
Pss. Sol.	*Psalms of Solomon*
QR	*Quarterly Review*
RCT	*Revista catalana de teología*
ResQ	*Restoration Quarterly*
RevScRel	*Revue des sciences religieuses*
RNTS	Reading the New Testament Series

RSR	*Recherches de sciences religieuses*
RVV	Religionsgeschichtliche Versuche und Vorarbeiten
SB	Sources Bibliques
SBEC	Studies in Bible and Early Christianity
SBL	Society of Biblical Literature
SBLDS	SBL Dissertation Series
SBLMS	SBL Monograph Series
SBLRBS	SBL Resources for Biblical Study
SBS	Stuttgarter Bibelstudien
SCS	Septuagint and Cognate Studies
SFC	Selections from the Fathers of the Church
SHBC	Smith & Helwys Biblical Commentary
Sib. Or.	*Sibylline Oracles*
Sir.	Sirach
SJT	*Scottish Journal of Theology*
SNTS	Society for New Testament Studies
SP	Sacra Pagina
Strom.	*Stromata* (Clement of Alexandria)
SUNT	Studien zur Umwelt des Neuen Testaments
T. Ash.	*Testament of Asher*
T. Job	*Testament of Job*
T. Levi	*Testament of Levi*
T. Mos.	*Testament of Moses*
TDNT	G. Kittel and G. Friedrich (eds), *Theological Dictionary of the New Testament* (trans. G. W. Bromiley; Grand Rapids: Eerdmans, 1964–76).
TDOT	G. J. Botterweck and H. Ringgren (eds), *Theological Dictionary of the Old Testament* (trans. J. T. Willis, G. W. Bromiley, and D. E. Green; Grand Rapids: Eerdmans, 1974–).
Tg	Targum
Them	*Themelios*
THNTC	Two Horizons New Testament Commentary
TNLT	Ceslas Spicq (ed.) *Theological Lexicon of the New Testament* (Peabody: Hendrickson, 1994).
Tob	*Tobit*
TREN	Theological Research Exchange Network
TynBul	*Tyndale Bulletin*
TZ	*Theologische Zeitschrift*
VT	*Vetus testamentum*
WBC	Word Biblical Commentary
Wis.	Wisdom of Solomon
WUNT	Wissenschaftliche Untersuchungen zum Neuen Testament
WW	*Word and World*
ZAW	*Zeitschrift für die alttestamentliche Wissenschaft*
ZNW	*Zeitschrift für die neutestamentliche Wissenchaft und die Kunde der älteren Kirche*

Chapter 1

A SURVEY OF LITERATURE

1.1. Introduction

The purpose of this book is to bring to light the significance of 1 Peter's christological understanding of God's actions on behalf of Israel for its audience vis-à-vis the proper response toward suffering. It is evident that the person and work of Jesus Christ play a major role in the way the author crafts his message.[1] Before I lay out my proposal, I will survey contemporary literature on 1 Peter, focusing mainly on the ways scholars have understood (1) the nature and function of the epistle's christology, (2) the epistle's relationship to the Old Testament, and (3) the epistle's suitability to a narratological approach. I will then be able to propose how this monograph will contribute to the ongoing discussion.

Much of the discussion on the christology of 1 Peter has centred more on the form in which the christology is presented in the letter than on the content itself.[2] This can be explained by the fact that scholarly interest in 1 Peter is still on the rise. In addition, whereas there is general consensus on the centrality of the Old Testament to 1 Peter because of the author's extensive use of Scripture in crafting the letter, views differ on the way the author of 1 Peter has appropriated the Old Testament. Further, there are avenues yet to be explored regarding the relationship between 1 Peter and the Old Testament.

---

1. The issue of the authorship of 1 Peter is contested and there is no consensus among scholars. For a discussion see, e.g., Paul Achtemeier, *1 Peter* (Hermeneia; Minneapolis: Fortress, 1996), pp. 1–14, 39–43; John H. Elliott, *1 Peter: A New Translation with Introduction and Commentary* (AB, 37; New York: Doubleday, 2000), pp. 118–20; and Karen H. Jobes, *1 Peter* (BECNT; Grand Rapids: Baker, 2005), pp. 5–19. The authorship issue is not determinative for my thesis.

2. See Steven R. Bechtler, *Following in His Steps: Suffering, Community, and Christology in 1 Peter* (SBLDS, 162; Atlanta: Scholars, 1998), pp. 1–22. In his monograph, Bechtler surveys the literature from Harnack to Feldmeier, covering the period from 1897 to 1992. See also Jacob Prasad, *Foundations of the Christian Way of Life According to 1 Peter 1, 13-25: An Exegetico-Theological Study* (AnBib, 146; Rome: Pontificio Istituto Biblico, 2000); and Sharon C. Pearson, *The Christological and Rhetorical Properties of 1 Peter* (SBEC, 45; Lewiston: Edwin Mellen, 2001), pp. 1–48; her survey of the different ways in which 1 Peter has been understood is especially commendable.

Finally, several proposals have been put forward recently with regards to the application of narratology to the study of 1 Peter, yet this is an area of study that is not fully explored. Narratological studies of 1 Peter can be said to be still in an infancy state. In sum, it can be said that the rehabilitation process of 1 Peter in New Testament scholarship is complete,[3] however, views on how the content and form of the epistle are understood continue to evolve.[4]

1.2. *A survey of literature*

This survey will be divided into three major sections. The first section, beginning in 1946, will deal with representatives from the period of so-called relative obscurity of Petrine scholarship.[5] Contemporary study of 1 Peter takes its point of departure from the 1946 publication of Edward Selwyn's commentary.[6] Selwyn was the first to identify 1 Peter primarily as an epistle, thereby positioning himself over against the understanding that 1 Peter was a baptismal homily.[7] This period ranges from 1946 to 1976, the time of the publication of Elliott's study, 'The Rehabilitation of an Exegetical Step-Child: 1 Peter in Recent Scholarship'. The second section focuses on representatives from the rehabilitation period, 1976 to 1986, during which we find renewed interest in Petrine scholarship. Beginning in 1986, New Testament scholarship began to pay more attention to 1 Peter as evidenced by the number of

---

3.   I am alluding to John H. Elliott's famous comment about 1 Peter's being an exegetical stepchild. See, 'The Rehabilitation of an Exegetical Step-Child: 1 Peter in Recent Research', *JBL* 95 (1976), pp. 243–54. Ten years later, Earl Richard talks about the rehabilitation process being on the way. See, 'The Functional Christology of First Peter' in Charles H. Talbert (ed.), *Perspectives on First Peter* (NABPRSS, 9; Macon, GA: Mercer University Press, 1986), p. 122.

4.   See the commentaries by Achtemeier, *1 Peter*; Peter H. Davids, *The First Epistle of Peter* (NICNT; Grand Rapids: Eerdmans, 1990); Elliott, *1 Peter*; Jobes, *1 Peter*; Earl Richard, *Reading 1 Peter, Jude, and 2 Peter: A Literary and Theological Commentary* (RNTS; Macon, GA: Smyth & Helwys, 2000); Donald P. Senior, *1 Peter, Jude and 2 Peter* (SP, 15; Collegeville, MN: Liturgical, 2003); and monographs by Bechtler, *Following in His Steps*; Barth L. Campbell, *Honor, Shame, and the Rhetoric of 1 Peter* (SBLDS, 160; Atlanta: Scholars, 1998); Pearson, *Christological and Rhetorical Properties*; Lauri Thurén, *The Rhetorical Strategy of 1 Peter with Special Regard to Ambiguous Expressions* (Åbo: Pargas, 1990); Philip L. Tite, *Compositional Transitions in 1 Peter: An Analysis of the Letter-Opening* (San Francisco: International Scholars Publications, 1997); Prasad, *Foundations of the Christian Way of Life*. Such publications as these indicate that 1 Peter has captured the attention of many. They also provide evidence for a wide range of options vis-à-vis the approaches and understanding of the message of the letter.

5.   Richard, *Reading 1 Peter*, p. 9. There, Richard talks about 1 Peter being rescued from relative obscurity by recent scholarship.

6.   Edward G. Selwyn, *The First Epistle of St. Peter* (London: Macmillan, 1946).

7.   See, e.g., Richard Perdelwitz, *Die Mysterienreligion und das Problem des I. Petrusbriefes: Ein literarischer und religionsgeschichtlicher Versuch* (RVV, 11.3; Giessen: Töpelmann, 1911); Hans Windish, *Die katholischen Briefe* (HNT, 15; Tübingen: Mohr Siebeck, 2nd edn, 1930).

dissertations and articles that began to appear, as well as commentaries that incorporated that new appreciation of 1 Peter. Section three will deal with representatives from recent scholarship, 1986 to the present.

1.2.1. *Relative obscurity: 1946–1976*

During the period of relative obscurity, scholarship on 1 Peter was not so much concerned with the christology of the epistle as it was with ascertaining the authenticity of the epistle, the form in which the epistle was handed down to the church, and the sources behind its composition.[8] There was a clear sense of the importance of the author's use of the Old Testament in the redaction of the epistle; however, there was no consensus on the manner in which it was appropriated. During this period the discussion about the application of a narratological approach to 1 Peter was non-existent.

In 1946, Edward Gordon Selwyn proposed that 1 Peter was an epistle that contained traces of baptismal and catechetical materials.[9] Against the compositional unity of 1 Peter were scholars like Richard Perdelwitz, Hans Windish, Rudolf Bultmann, who argued that 1 Peter was made up of traditional hymnic material that originated from a baptismal liturgy.[10] For example, Perdelwitz argued that 1 Peter was made up of two independent sections composed separately by the same author to the same audience at different times for different purposes. One section, 1.3–4.11, was given as baptismal homily, the other 1.1-2; 4.12–5.14 written to exhort the audience vis-à-vis the persecutions they were facing.[11] However, there is no consensus as to the sources of the hymns, how many were present in 1 Peter, or the structure of individual hymns.[12] Further, Selwyn points out that the author of 1 Peter was deeply steeped in the Jewish Scriptures which he quotes directly and alludes to. He also suggests that the vocabulary of 1 Peter contains echoes of apocryphal texts like Wisdom, Ecclesiasticus, and the four books

---

8.   Eduard Lohse, 'Parenesis and Kerygma in 1 Peter', in Charles H. Talbert (ed.), *Perspectives on First Peter* (NABPRSS, 9; Macon, GA: Mercer University Press, 1986), pp. 37–59.

9.   Selwyn, *First Epistle of St. Peter*, pp. 17–25, 363–4. Selwyn proposes that there are four main types of sources underlying 1 Peter: liturgical, a persecution fragment, catechetical, and verba Christi.

10.   Perdelwitz, *Die Mysterienreligion*; Windish, *Die katholischen Briefe*; Rudolf Bultmann, 'Bekenntnis- und Liedfragmente im ersten Petrusbrief', *ConNT* 11 (1947), pp. 1–14. See Lohse, 'Parenesis and Kerygma', p. 38. See also, Martin, 'The Composition of 1 Peter', pp. 29–42.

11.   Perdelwitz, *Die Mysterienreligion*.

12.   Ralph P. Martin, 'The Composition of 1 Peter in Recent Study', in Ralph P. Martin (ed.), *Vox Evangelica: Biblical and Historical Essays by Members of the Faculty of the London Bible College* (London: Epworth, 1962), pp. 29–42, (30–4). The discussion about the plan and structure of 1 Peter continues. See, e.g., Charles H. Talbert, 'Once Again: The Plan of 1 Peter', in Charles H. Talbert, *Perspectives on First Peter* (NABPRSS, 9; Macon, GA: Mercer University Press, 1986), pp. 141–51.

of the Maccabees and other Jewish apocalyptic texts like the Book of Enoch and the Testaments of the Twelve Patriarchs.[13]

In addressing the content of the epistle and its doctrinal framework Selwyn deems 1 Peter's christology to be undeveloped, as it reflects a pattern of thought that is thoroughly primitive.[14] In the same vein he shows how 1 Peter is markedly theocentric. He argues that God and his dealings with humanity are the central theme of the letter.[15]

In 1954, Eduard Lohse published a study of the christology of 1 Peter in which he sought to emphasize the epistolary framework of 1 Peter. He follows Selwyn in arguing that the paraenesis in 1 Peter is compiled from various elements. He notes, 'Old Testament quotations, particularly Wisdom psalms and proverbs, Palestinian and hellenistic conceptions and traditions, and isolated sayings of our Lord stand side by side and are adduced according to the specific needs of the moment'.[16] However, Lohse does not go so far as to find a fixed catechetical schema within 1 Peter. He underscores the christological nature of the rationale that 1 Peter offers his audience for the ethical admonitions present in the letter.[17] He also points out that 1 Peter, particularly 1.3–2.10, appropriates Scripture in a similar fashion to what we find in texts from Qumran. He proposes that the points of similarity between this section and material from Qumran 'are not to be traced to a direct appropriation by 1 Peter. Instead, 1 Peter refers to traditional material that is appropriated in already christianized form'.[18]

Marie É. Boismard's 'Une Liturgie Baptismale dans la Prima Petri' appeared in 1956.[19] There she compares the text of 1 Peter with other epistles to demonstrate the presence of a baptismal liturgy in 1 Peter. She follows Selwyn and treats 1 Peter as an epistle, but argues, with Perdelwitz, that 1 Peter has at least partially reproduced a baptismal liturgy.[20] Although limited in scope, Boismard's treatment shows how the Old Testament is integral to the author's message. For example, she highlights the importance of the author's use of Exodus as a type of Christian baptism; discusses, for example, how the themes of covenant and obedience rest in the background. Boismard states, 'The intention of the author of 1 Peter is perfectly clear: he wants to

---

13.　Selwyn, *First Epistle of St. Peter*, pp. 24–5.

14.　Selwyn, *First Epistle of St. Peter*, pp. 73–5.

15.　Selwyn, *First Epistle of St. Peter*, p. 75. Francis W. Beare also talks about the theocentric nature of 1 Peter. See, *The Epistle of First Peter* (repr. 1961, Oxford: Blackwell, 2nd edn, 1958), p. 33.

16.　Lohse, 'Parenesis and Kerygma', p. 55. See also Ceslas Spicq, *Les Épîtres de Saint Pierre* (SB; Paris: Gabalda, 1966), pp. 14–18.

17.　Lohse, 'Parenesis and Kerygma', p. 57.

18.　Lohse, 'Parenesis and Keryma', pp. 49–50.

19.　Marie É. Boismard, 'Une Liturgie Baptismale dans la Prima Petri', *RB* 2 (1956), pp. 182–208; idem, *Quatres Hymnes Baptismales dans La Première Epître de Pierre* (LD, 30; Paris: Cerf, 1961).

20.　Boismard, 'Liturgie Baptismale', pp. 183, 205. Boismard advances that a weakness in Selwyn's work is his refusal to admit the presence of a baptismal homily or liturgy rehearsed by the author of 1 Peter.

demonstrate that Christians constitute the new Israel; it is with them that God has established the new covenant, a reissuing of the covenant established at Sinai, after the exodus out of Egypt'.[21]

John H. Elliott's *The Elect and the Holy: An Exegetical Examination of 1 Peter 2:4-10 and the Phrase basileion hierateuma* was published in 1966.[22] In this book Elliott carries out an in-depth study of the relationship between 1 Peter and the Old Testament, but also the possible influence of the Jewish tradition of interpretation on 1 Peter. The study came as a reaction to the lack of exegetical examination of the scriptural basis of the doctrine of the priesthood of believers. According to Elliott, treatments on the subject did not do justice to the text of 1 Peter. He argues against the notion that 1 Pet. 2.4-10 conveys ideas about the universal priesthood of believers, and urges that this pericope has to do with the elect and holy nature of the believing community and its relationship with Jesus. Elliott highlights how the language of 1 Pet. 2.4-10 reflects 'a combination of separate bodies of OT passages having the elect messianic/eschatological λίθος and the chosen People of God as their subjects'.[23] He proposes that a λίθος tradition similar to what is at work in 1 Peter and in the larger New Testament corpus can be found in the Qumran and in the *Targumim* and Rabbinic literature. He notes, 'This image traces its origin to the OT, especially the Psalms, prophetic, and apocalyptic literature. Early LXX, apocalyptic, Qumranic, Targumic and Rabbinic interpretation point to the pre-Christian origin of its messianic-eschatological associations'.[24] Elliott discusses the christological thrust of the λίθος image and shows how a midrash in vv. 4-5 attests to the fact that the audience participates in the life and experience of Jesus. In sum, according to Elliott, 'The λίθος complex has not been cited merely to make a christological statement but to provide the basis for a description of the believing community'.[25]

In 1969, Ernest Best published a study on 1 Pet. 2.4-10. There, he inquires about the relationship of the Old Testament texts to the text of 1 Peter.[26] Best argues against Selwyn and Elliott that 1 Pet. 2.4-5 constitutes a midrashic statement on the Old Testament texts that follow in vv. 6-7, 9.[27] His examination of the text leads him to conclude that the author of 1 Peter uses Old Testament quotations 'either to confirm an argument already stated or to advance the argument he is making'.[28] He argues that 1 Pet. 2.4-5 serves that same purpose and, therefore, is not a preparatory midrash to the Old Testament texts in that section. Best does well to survey the author's use of

21.   Boismard, 'Liturgie Baptismale', p. 191, (author's translation).

22.   John H. Elliott, *The Elect and the Holy: An Exegetical Examination of 1 Peter 2:4-10 and the Phrase basileion hierateuma* (NovTSup, 12; Leiden: Brill, 1966).

23.   Elliott, *The Elect and the Holy*, p. 219.

24.   Elliott, *The Elect and the Holy*, pp. 26–33.

25.   Elliott, *The Elect and the Holy*, p. 38.

26.   Ernest Best, 'I Peter II: 4-10 – A Reconsideration', *NovT* 11 (1969), pp. 270–93.

27.   Best, 'I Peter II: 4-10', p. 271. See Elliott, *The Elect and the Holy*, pp. 20, 36–8; Selwyn, *First Epistle of St. Peter*, p. 269.

28.   Best, 'I Peter II: 4-10', p. 293.

the Old Testament in other parts of the epistle, but his treatment is minimal as his focus is on 2.4-10. Best also argues that the author of 1 Peter is heavily dependent on primitive Christian tradition because his mind is not creative. The author's treatment of christological themes present in the passage shows his dependence not only on other parts of the New Testament but also on ideas developed at Qumran.

In 1974, Max-Alain Chevalier published an article, 'Condition et Vocation des Chrétiens en Diaspora', in which he discusses the understanding of the role of Christians in a non-Christian society evident in the epistle.[29] Chevalier suggests that the key to understanding the attitude and role of Christians in society is in the author's own understanding of the 'people of God'. According to Chevalier, the author of 1 Peter organizes his thoughts around three main concepts: the people of God, diaspora, and election. He shows the ways in which the author of 1 Peter integrates the Old Testament in the way he describes the audience. He states, 'The epistle presents the Christian community as the heir of the people of Israel'.[30] Chevalier sees in the audience's designation as 'residents' and 'strangers' an indication of their marginal status, which is characteristic of the condition of all Christians. This designation is dependent on the audience's election, another Old Testament concept, which is made possible through Christ's election. Election brings about the audience's new birth in diaspora. The elect are to live out their faith in the midst of society. According to Chevalier, the author of 1 Peter 'has discovered a fundamental theological theme; namely, the election of a people belonging to God in the midst of the nations. This theme has allowed the author of 1 Peter to see the Christian diaspora, in continuity with the Jewish diaspora, not as a contingent or deplorable condition, but as a necessary and wonderful vocation'.[31] Chevalier has thus demonstrated that the author's understanding of its audience is dependent on the Old Testament's description of the people of God. He has also shown that the theological realities the letter evokes and that the audience faces are socially located.

In this period, one finds discussion of the significance of Christ's sufferings, the prominence of the Old Testament, and the theocentric nature of 1 Peter. These concepts are mentioned primarily in arguments for or against the unity of the composition of the epistle or its dependence and relationship to other sources.[32] However, the understanding of how Peter appropriates the Old Testament is varied. Further, treatments of the text of 1 Peter tend to be very selective, limited in scope, and focused primarily on a given pericope or theme.[33] Yet, these treatments offer valuable insights on the christological

29.   Max-Alain Chevalier, 'Condition et Vocation des Chrétiens en Diaspora: Remarques Exégétiques sur la 1ère Epître de Pierre', *RSR* 48 (1974), pp. 387–400.

30.   Chevalier, 'Condition et Vocation des Chrétiens en Diaspora', p. 391, (author's translation).

31.   Chevalier, 'Condition et Vocation des Chrétiens en Diaspora', p. 398, (author's translation).

32.   E.g., Boismard, 'Liturgie Baptismale'.

33.   E.g., William Dalton, *Christ's Proclamation to the Spirits: A Study of 1 Peter 3:18-4:6* (AnBib, 23; Rome: Pontifical Biblical Institute, 1965).

properties of the epistle and its relationship to the Old Testament and other Jewish literature.

1.2.2. *The rehabilitation process: 1976–1986*

The year 1976 marked a turning point in Petrine studies. The call sounded by John Elliott was heard and the next twenty years saw a rise of interest in the study of 1 Peter. Elliott led the charge himself with the publication of several works on 1 Peter.[34]

In 1980, Jacques Schlosser published a study in which he looked at the relationship between the Old Testament and the christology of 1 Peter.[35] According to Schlosser, the author of 1 Peter crafts his message through concepts and language borrowed from the Old Testament.[36] Schlosser sees this at work in the author's designation of the church as a 'spiritual house', in his development of the concept of election, and in the exodus motif. In addition, he suggests that the exhortation to Christian women denotes a patriarchal theme.[37]

For Schlosser, 1 Pet. 1.10-12 is the basis of the author's christological use of the Old Testament.[38] He demonstrates how certain christological themes present in 1 Peter are read back into the Old Testament, focusing on three particular pericopes: 1.22-25; 2.4-8; and 2.21-25, and comparing the text of 1 Peter with the MT and LXX in the process. He then outlines the major theological themes of the epistle: Christ as Lord and word of God in 1.22-25; Christ as stone in 2.4-8; and Christ as Servant in 2.21-25. For each, he looks at the Old Testament source that the author of 1 Peter draws from and the christological impact of 1 Peter's message.[39]

Schlosser's treatment of the relationship between the Old Testament and the christology of 1 Peter is of importance to the present conversation.

---

34. E.g., John H. Elliott, *1 Peter: Estrangement and Community* (Chicago: Franciscan Herald, 1979); idem, 'Backward and Forward "in His Steps": Following Jesus from Rome to Raymond and Beyond: The Tradition, Redaction, and Reception of 1 Peter 2:18-25', in Fernando F. Segovia (ed.), *Discipleship in the New Testament* (Philadelphia: Fortress, 1985), pp. 184–209; idem, *A Home for the Homeless: A Sociological Exegesis of 1 Peter, Its Situation and Strategy* (Philadelphia: Fortress, 1981).

35. Jacques Schlosser, 'Ancient Testament et Christologie dans La Prima Petri', in Charles Perrot (ed.), *Études sur la Première Lettre de Pierre* (LD, 102; Paris: Cerf, 1980), pp. 65–96. More recently, Schlosser discussed the importance of the resurrection in 1 Peter. He demonstrates how this theme underlines the importance of God's action on behalf of Jesus in the mind of the epistle's audience. It is the basis of their hope. See, 'La Résurrection de Jésus d'Après la *Prima Petri*', in R. Bieringer *et al.* (eds), *Resurrection in the New Testament* (Festschrift J. Lambrecht; BETL, 165; Leuven: Leuven University Press, 2002), pp. 441–56 (445).

36. Schlosser, 'A.T. et Christologie', p. 65.

37. Schlosser, 'A.T. et Christologie', p. 66.

38. Schlosser, 'A.T. et Christologie', pp. 65-7; idem, 'La Résurrection de Jésus', p. 448.

39. Schlosser, 'A.T. et Christologie', pp. 68-96.

He helpfully discusses examples of the author's christological reading of Scripture, taking time to show the different nuances that the author uses from one passage to another. In one place, Scripture is used as proof or argument for the gospel; in another, Scripture is assimilated and becomes the gospel.[40] In other words, the prophetic proclamation and the gospel have the same source of inspiration and are similar in content. I will push this argument further by claiming that in assimilating the Old Testament prophetic proclamation to the gospel, the author of 1 Peter does not so much work with promise/fulfilment category as he deals with ontological identification. In his commentary on Isaiah, for example, Brevard Childs rightly notes,

> The canonical shape of the book of Isaiah shows a suffering servant figure who was not simply viewed as a figure of the past, but assigned a central and continuing theological role in relation to the life of the redeemed community of Israel. Thus, there was a coercion exerted by the biblical text itself, as authoritative scripture, that exercised pressure on the early church in its struggle to understand the suffering and death of Jesus Christ. The theological category used for its interpretation was not primarily that of prophecy and fulfillment. Rather, an analogy was drawn between the redemptive activity of the Isaianic servant and the passion and death of Jesus Christ. The relation was understood 'ontologically', that is to say, in terms of its substance, its theological reality.[41]

In other words, the author sees in the life of Jesus Christ the embodiment of what God desired of the servant of Second Isaiah, of Israel, and of humanity as a whole.

Absent from Schlosser's work is any sustained discussion of the exodus motif in 1 Peter and its christological implications. Schlosser recognizes the presence of the exodus motif in 1 Peter, but his focus is elsewhere.[42] Although it is obvious that the author of 1 Peter discusses the sufferings of Christ through the servant song of Isaiah in 2.21-25, I will show that he has the sufferings of the Christ in view already in 1.2. Subsequently, I will demonstrate that the greeting section of the letter informs us about the author's christological hermeneutic of the Old Testament as much as the other sections of the letter, where the christological implications are more explicit. I will also argue that the language of salvation, sprinkling, and inheritance, all understood as integral to the exodus motif, carries with it the implication of Israel's own sufferings and the outworking of God's salvation on their behalf.

The year 1981 witnessed the publication of several important studies on 1 Peter. Paul E. Deterding published a study on the 'Exodus Motifs in First Peter' in which he compares 1 Peter to Paul's use of exodus motifs in the first letter to the Corinthians.[43] He suggests that 1 Peter contains no such typological presentation of the exodus but allusions to the event are scattered throughout. He argues that the epistle uses at least five different

40. Schlosser, 'A.T. et Christologie', pp. 92–3.
41. Brevard S. Childs, *Isaiah* (OTL; Louisville: Westminster, 2001), pp. 422–3.
42. Schlosser, 'A.T. et Christologie', p. 66.
43. Paul E. Deterding, 'Exodus Motifs in First Peter', *ConcJ* 7 (1981), pp. 58–67.

concepts to explain what God has done in Jesus Christ as a new exodus: redemption, salvation, election, rebirth, and calling.[44] He surveys the text of 1 Peter and discusses how the language there is connected to the exodus.[45] Further, Deterding shows how the author's depiction of the audience's life is undergirded by motifs taken from Israel's wilderness wanderings. He argues that, 'The life of the Christian church in this life corresponds to Israel's wanderings in the Sinai Peninsula'.[46] This implies that the author of 1 Peter sees a connection between his audience's sufferings and that of Israel. Deterding also argues that the epistle's treatment of a heavenly inheritance is reminiscent of the Old Testament description of the land of Canaan which was inherited as a gift from Yahweh.[47] According to Deterding, the way the author of 1 Peter 'interprets the exodus throughout his epistle indicates that he viewed salvation history as the recapitulation of God's mighty acts'.[48]

Deterding's treatment of the exodus motifs in 1 Peter is valuable to the present study. He may be guilty of approaching the text in a piecemeal fashion,[49] yet his treatment has adequately shown the way in which exodus motifs permeate the epistle.

John H. Elliott's seminal study *A Home for the Homeless* was published that same year. There, Elliott carries out a sociological exegesis of 1 Peter focusing primarily on 'the circumstances of its origin, composition and socioreligious strategy, and its contribution to the consolidation, theology and ideology of the early Christian movement in Asia Minor'.[50] Elliott opens his sociological-exegetical analysis of 1 Peter with a study of the terms πάροικος and οἶκος. He argues that the strategic use of these terms in the epistle implies that 'they constitute important indicators of the social as well as religious circumstances concerning the document and its purpose ... [they] are not merely linguistic but also sociological and theological correlates'.[51] For example, Elliott examines the use of πάροικος in the Old Testament, compares it with its use in Asia Minor in the Hellenistic period and argues that its meaning and use are consistent with its secular environment. That is, it designates 'the situation and the political, legal, and social religious condition of living abroad as resident aliens'.[52] For Elliott, this was the reality of Abraham among the Hittites, of Moses in Midian, Israel in Egypt, and Israel in exile. He suggests that the same is true for the use of the term in other Jewish literature, in the New Testament and in 1 Peter in particular. Therefore, the addressees of 1 Peter were living as resident aliens in a foreign environment. He adds, 'It is

---

44. Deterding, 'Exodus Motifs', p. 59.
45. Deterding, 'Exodus Motifs', p. 60.
46. Deterding, 'Exodus Motifs', p. 60.
47. Deterding, 'Exodus Motifs', p. 63.
48. Deterding, 'Exodus Motifs', p. 64.
49. E.g., the presence of a single word can be used as evidence for the presence of an underlying motif.
50. Elliott, *Home*, p. 1.
51. Elliott, *Home*, p. 23.
52. Elliott, *Home*, pp. 24–9.

also clear that the political, legal and social limitations of πάροικος status were understood to constitute the conditions according to which union with and fidelity toward God were tested, relinquished or affirmed'.[53] Elliott acknowledges that there are instances in the Old Testament where πάροικος carries a figurative religious connotation; however, his discussion conveys the view that in 1 Peter πάροικος attests to the social situation of the addressees. Another term used in 1 Peter, διασπορά, which also has affinities with its use in the LXX, conveys the religious connotation.[54]

In his study of the significance of the term οἶκος Elliott builds on his previous work, *The Elect and the Holy*, and shows how 1 Peter's treatment of the concept has some affinities with Philo's treatment of the same and how both approaches are rooted in the Old Testament.[55] He argues that the term οἶκος 'throughout the strata of the Old Testament tradition serves as a prime expression of communal identity and organization and of social, political and religious solidarity'.[56] He then offers a discussion on the relevance of the Old Testament material on οἶκος for the interpretation of 1 Peter. For Elliott, the concept οἶκος τοῦ θεοῦ serves as the root metaphor and organizing image in 1 Peter.[57]

Elliott has helpfully underscored the ways in which a sociological exegetical approach can be brought to bear upon one's understanding of the social, legal, political, and religious realities surrounding the text of 1 Peter. His treatment takes seriously 1 Peter's relationship to the Old Testament, other Jewish literature, and the Hellenistic environment in which the epistle was produced and is valuable to this study.

In 1981 Thomas P. Osborne's 'L'Utilisation de l'Ancient Testament dans la Première Épître de Pierre' also appeared.[58] Osborne conducts a systematic study of the epistle's use of Old Testament quotations. First, he identifies six Old Testament quotations in 1 Peter that contain an introductory formula and compares each quotation to the LXX and the MT in order to ascertain the way in which the author of 1 Peter appropriates the Old Testament text. Then, he repeats the same process for the Old Testament quotations used without an introductory formula. Finally, Osborne offers some general remarks on the use of the Old Testament in 1 Peter. He notes the following:

---

53.   Elliott, *Home*, p. 35.
54.   Elliott, *Home*, p. 38.
55.   Elliott, *Home*, pp. 170–2. See also, *The Elect and the Holy*, pp. 96–101.
56.   Elliott, *Home*, p. 182.
57.   Elliott, *Home*, pp. 165–266. In 1992, Reinhard Feldmeier published a similar study on the significance of πάροικος and παρεπίδημος in 1 Peter. However, he arrived at a different conclusion than Elliott. He advances that the theme of strangerhood as the organizing metaphor of the message of 1 Peter. See, *Die Christen als Fremde: Die Metapher der Fremde in der antiken Welt, im Urchristentum und im 1. Petrusbrief* (WUNT, 64; Tübingen: Mohr Siebeck, 1992).
58.   Thomas P. Osborne, 'L'Utilisation de l'Ancient Testament dans la Première Épître de Pierre', *RTL* 12 (1981), pp. 64–77.

- The comparison of the Old Testament texts in 1 Peter with the MT and the LXX reveals that the author of 1 Peter has undoubtedly used the LXX and not the MT.
- Although the author of 1 Peter draws from all three divisions of the Hebrew Bible (the Law, the Prophets, and the Writings), he shows some preference for Isaiah, Psalms, and Proverbs.
- Where the introductory formulas are well developed, the author refers to the Old Testament as *written* and not *said*.[59]
- The author of 1 Peter appropriates the Old Testament freely in order to make it relevant to the experiences of the communities addressed in the epistle.
- The Old Testament quotations and allusions used play a significant role in the structure of the epistle. They occur at the end of a section and are either preceded by verbal allusions to the quotation or reiterate the main thoughts of the preceding section.
- The majority of the Old Testament quotations have some bearing on the theme of suffering developed in 1 Peter, specifically, the Christian attitude toward suffering.

Osborne also notes that the use of Isa. 53 helps the author of 1 Peter craft the way in which Christ suffered. He suggests, 'Christ's sufferings serve therefore as a model for the sufferings Christians may endure'.[60]

Osborne's study is a brief yet very helpful treatment of the use of the Old Testament in 1 Peter. He has highlighted some important aspects of the epistle's relationship to the Old Testament and the reason for the numerous uses of Old Testament quotations and allusions by the author of the epistle. He proposes that the purpose is to 'understand the context of suffering, explain how to suffer, and encourage the community to remain faithful to a righteous way of life that is an outworking of its election as the people of God'.[61]

Leonhard Goppelt's *Typos: The Typological Interpretation of the Old Testament in the New* was published in 1982, the English translation of his 1939 work, *Typos: Die typologische Deutung des Alten Testaments im Neuen*.[62] He is concerned with explaining the relationship of the Old

---

59.   Osborne explains that this approach distances 1 Peter from the Mishnah because there the more frequent formulas are those that contain the word 'אמר'; however, it rapproches 1 Peter to the Qumran literature where the forms of 'כתב' are used more often. See, 'Utilisation de l'AT', p. 74. See further, Bruce M. Metzger, 'The Formulas Introducing Quotations of Scripture in the New Testament and the Mishnah', *JBL* 70 (1951), pp. 297–307. Joseph A. Fitzmyer, 'The Use of Explicit Old Testament Quotations in Qumran Literature and in the New Testament', in Joseph A. Fitzmyer (ed.), *Essays on the Semitic Background of the NT* (London: Chapman, 1971), pp. 3–58.

60.   Osborne, 'Utilisation de l'AT', p. 76, (author's translation).

61.   Osborne, 'Utilisation de l'AT', p. 77, (author's translation).

62.   Leonhard Goppelt, *Typos: The Typological Interpretation of the Old Testament in the New* (trans. Donald H. Madvig; Grand Rapids: Eerdmans, 1982).

Testament to Jesus Christ.[63] He proposes that 'typology is the method of biblical interpretation that is characteristic of the NT'.[64] He suggests that there is a unity between the salvation the Old Testament bears witness to and that which is preached in the New Testament. In discussing 1 Peter, he writes, 'In 1 Peter and in the NT as a whole, OT salvation, OT redemptive history, and the blessings of the OT salvation are not placed in a direct relationship to Christian salvation, as prophecy is, but are related to it typologically'.[65] He surveys several key passages in 1 Peter and shows how the language used to describe Israel has been transferred to the church.[66] A major weakness in Goppelt's treatment is its brevity. In fact, he treats 1 Peter as an appendix to his discussion of typology in the Pauline epistles. Yet his proposal is a valuable contribution to the discussion of the relationship of 1 Peter to the Old Testament.

Elsewhere, in *A Commentary on 1 Peter*, Goppelt reiterates and develops some of these points. There he argues that the author of 1 Peter uses traditional materials gathered not only from the Old Testament, but also from Qumran and the Essene tradition. He also discusses the christology of the epistle and argues that the christology of 1 Peter is limited to three pericopae: 1.18-21; 2.21-25; 3.18-22. These are regarded as formulaic christological statements and/or Christ-hymns the author uses to motivate his readers. The understanding of soteriology, eschatology, and Christ's suffering share some affinities to traditional material rehearsed within the Qumran community, which 1 Peter uses to shape his readers' behaviour.[67]

During this period, discussions of the sources behind 1 Peter continue to abound. One finds several helpful treatments on the relationship between 1 Peter and the Old Testament, and treatments on the affinities between 1 Peter and Qumran literature. The views concerning the author's appropriation of the Old Testament continue to evolve. In addition, discussion of the christology of the epistle is sustained to a lesser or greater extent, depending on the scope of a given study. There is general consensus on the importance of the christological properties of the letter, and their role in shaping the behaviour of the suffering audience. Also, under the initiative of Elliott, social-scientific criticism is now applied to the study of 1 Peter.

---

63.   Goppelt, *Typos*, p. 1.
64.   Goppelt, *Typos*, p. 4.
65.   Goppelt, *Typos*, p. 153.
66.   Goppelt, *Typos*, pp. 154–6; see also, *A Commentary on 1 Peter* (ed. Ferdinand Hahn; trans. John E. Alsup; Grand Rapids: Eerdmans, 1993), p. 35.
67.   Goppelt, *1 Peter*, pp. 74–5, 80–3, 114; See also, *Theology of the New Testament* (ed. J. Roloff; Vol. 2; Grand Rapids: Eerdmans, 1982), pp. 161–78. It is worth noting that others have adopted Goppelt's structure regarding the amount and location of the christological pericopae in 1 Peter with little modification. E.g., Andrew Chester and Ralph Martin, *The Theology of the Letters of James, Peter, and Jude* (NTT; Cambridge: Cambridge University Press, 1994), p. 107; Pearson, *Christological and Rhetorical Properties*, p. 11; Georg Strecker, *Theology of the New Testament* (Louisville: Wesminster, 2000), pp. 628–34. For an assessment of Goppelt, see Achtemeier, *1 Peter*, pp. 71–2.

1.2.3 Recent scholarship: 1986–present

Beginning in 1986 one notices a rise in treatments that focus on the christology of 1 Peter. In addition, several methodological approaches, including narratology, are put forward as scholars show more and more interest in the study of 1 Peter. Within these studies, one finds valuable discussions of 1 Peter's dependence on the Old Testament and on the affinities between the text of 1 Peter with Qumran literature, and Greco-Roman culture.

In one of the major contributions to Petrine studies published in 1986, *Perspectives on First Peter*, Earl Richard presented an essay entitled 'The Functional Christology of 1 Peter'.[68] Richard reviews some basic issues current in discussion on 1 Peter, examines the author's use of the christological hymn tradition, and discusses the function of 1 Peter's christology. He acknowledges the author's use of a well-defined and particular christology and his extensive use of Old Testament passages and images.[69] He also argues that the author of 1 Peter is dependent upon the hymnic tradition for both the pattern of his christological vision and the basis of his soteriological exposition, claiming that any attempt at reconstructing those hymns is futile.[70] According to Richard, from the hymnic pattern presumed in the letter, one can find six elements that the author uses in varying degrees to make up the core of the epistle's christology:

- 'destined' – concerning the divine plan and humanity's response;
- 'manifested' – in which Richard finds some type of lower, exaltation Christology, since, he believes, 1 Peter does not seem to be interested in the concept of preexistence;
- 'suffering';
- 'resurrection' – with suffering and resurrection derived from a common source: the early apostolic kerygma;
- 'domination over cosmic powers'; and
- 'glorification at God's right hand'.[71]

Implicit in all of these elements is the centrality of God's action. Christ's manifestation, his suffering and death, his resurrection, dominion, and glory have one agent – God.[72] Further, the themes suffering/death and glory/right hand serve as the basis for the christological schema of 1 Peter. He writes,

> The themes of suffering and glory, representing the contours of the Christ-event, offer the framework for the author's understanding of the Christian life in the world.

68. Richard, 'Functional Christology', pp. 121–39.
69. Richard, 'Functional Christology', pp. 121–3; idem, *Reading 1 Peter*, p. 16.
70. Richard, 'Functional Christology', pp. 127–9.
71. Richard, 'Functional Christology', pp. 130–3.
72. According to Richard, although God did not cause Jesus to suffer and die, his suffering and death were according to God's will.

Christ suffered, has gone to share in the Father's glory, and will return at the end-time to bestow glory upon those 'chosen by the foreknowledge of God the Father' (1.1-2) and whose faith has been tested by the fire of suffering (1.5-7).[73]

The basis of the community's new life, its code of conduct, and its hope find their source through the soteriological, ethical, and eschatological functions of the epistle's christology, whose main function is to set the pattern for Christian life.[74]

Richard's outline of the functional christology of 1 Peter is helpful. His focus on the content of the christology of the epistle makes his contribution valuable to our discussion. Though Richard talks about the use of the Old Testament in 1 Peter, however, he credits most of 1 Peter's dependence on hymnic traditional materials. Therein lies a significant weakness of his work.

Although the particulars of the author's indebtedness, or the nature of his indebtedness, to traditional hymnic or confessional material are important, I will demonstrate that it is enough to say simply that the author of 1 Peter knew the story of Christ's advent, death, and resurrection; and that, having immersed himself in that story, he has brought it together in the process of composing his letter. Further, *pace* Richard, although it is clear that Christ's suffering and glory play a very important role in the christology of 1 Peter, I will show that it is also important to highlight Christ's attitude in suffering, which the author holds as an example for the audience to emulate. In addition, the sufferings of Christ are only part of a larger scheme that includes his election, his faithful response, and vindication by God. The epistle's christology is God-centred. One of the purposes of the christology of 1 Peter is to present to its audience a pattern of how God deals with his people and to encourage them to live as God's own people by writing the story of their lives into that of Israel.

In 1989 William L. Schutter published his study *Hermeneutic and Composition in 1 Peter*.[75] Schutter approaches 1 Peter from the standpoint of literary analysis. He compares the structure of 1 Peter to that of the Pauline epistle and suggests that '1 Peter reflects most of the major elements generic to the Pauline letter'.[76] He discusses the compositional devices and techniques used by the author of 1 Peter based on the conviction that their study offers a better understanding of the way the author has used his source-materials. Schutter argues that 1 Peter is dependent on several formal Christian, oral and written, sources besides the Old Testament. He then describes 1 Peter's literary dependence on Old Testament materials and claims that 1 Peter contains as many as forty-six quotations and allusions to the Old Testament. For Schutter, the most significant aspect of formative use of the Old Testament

73.   Richard, 'Functional Christology', p. 134.
74.   Richard, 'Functional Christology', pp. 134–8; idem, *Reading 1 Peter*, pp. 18–20.
75.   William L. Schutter, *Hermeneutic and Composition in 1 Peter* (WUNT, 2.30; Tübingen: Mohr Siebeck, 1989), pp. 19–35.
76.   Schutter, *Hermeneutic and Composition*, p. 27.

in 1 Peter is 'the variety of ways those materials have been handled'.[77] He claims that the author's use of the Old Testament and his hermeneutic have suffered virtual neglect and that his study makes it possible 'to draw with sharper lines the literary context in which the OT has been used and the degree to which it has been formative'.[78]

Schutter is of the opinion that Jewish interpretive presuppositions and methods were decisive in shaping the author's hermeneutic and suggests that the body-opening of the letter, 1.14–2.9, is the best starting place for a reconstruction of the hermeneutic of the author of 1 Peter. He compares several genres[79] to the text of 1 Peter and proposes that the *Gattung* of homiletic midrash is better suited for a comparison with this section of 1 Peter.[80] He supports his claim by showing the ways in which 1 Peter demonstrates some of the characteristics of midrashic composition; namely, the author's belief in the authority of Scripture and the contemporaneity of Scripture which allowed it to be applied to concrete situations. Later on it is expressed in the transference of characteristic concepts used for Israel to his audience.

Schutter goes on to argue that 1.10-12 is the only passage in the entire epistle where one can find explicit information about the author's hermeneutic. Therefore, 1.10-12 constitutes a hermeneutical key to understanding the message of the letter as a whole because this passage gives us unmatched insight into a major aspect of the author's hermeneutical stance. He wrestles with the exegetical problems posed by the text vis-à-vis, e.g., the identity of the prophets, their preaching, and the sufferings of Christ, and proposes that 'the contrast of "sufferings" and "glories" functions as a kind of schema which helps the author to organize the Scriptural foundations implied by the reference to the prophets whether they were OT or NT'. [81] Further, he argues that, the 'sufferings/glories' schema allows for convenient access to the author's use of the Old Testament in other places irrespective of their *Gattung*. Further, Schutter advances that 1.10-12 shares some affinities with pesher hermeneutic practised at Qumran, then proceeds to show the ways in which the pesher-like hermeneutic of the author is at work in the epistle.

Schutter has conducted a thorough inquiry into the role of the Old Testament in the composition of 1 Peter. He helpfully demonstrates how the lordship of Christ has been ascertained by the author through the Old Testament and embedded in his message.[82] However, the fragmentary, jigsaw-puzzle approach he uses is problematic. Schutter pushes his argument too far at times; namely, the use of a single preposition or a word may be evidence for compositional twist, or lack thereof may reflect a lack of

---

77. Schutter, *Hermeneutic and Composition*, p. 43.
78. Schutter, *Hermeneutic and Composition*, p. 81.
79. E.g., missionary preaching; communal discipline, diatribe, and homiletic midrash.
80. Schutter, *Hermeneutic and Composition*, pp. 92–3, 100.
81. Schutter, *Hermeneutic and Composition*, pp. 100–9 (108).
82. Schutter, *Hermeneutic and Composition*, pp. 123–68.

literary integrity on the part of the author.[83] Schutter is right to find in 1.10-12 a hermeneutical key to understanding the way the author uses the Old Testament in constructing the message of the letter. He rightly argues that the hermeneutic of 1.10-12 reflects the influence of modes of exegesis like those at Qumran. His discussion of the affinities between pesher hermeneutic practised at Qumran and the hermeneutic of the author of 1 Peter is helpful to the present study.

I will add that the hermeneutic of 1 Peter is also located in his christological understanding of the role of the Old Testament and his understanding of the person of Christ which the author has in view in the opening section of the epistle. I will show that the composition of 1 Peter is interwoven with stories of God's actions on behalf of Israel, in which the author is so immersed that it becomes second nature for him to rehearse and interpret these actions as he crafts the message for his audience. The author of 1 Peter brings together Old Testament stories of righteous sufferers' faithfulness to God in trials and of God's protection and care of righteous sufferers, which have shaped his understanding of who God is in a coherent fashion. Those individual stories in themselves fit into a larger narrative which contains patterns of God's dealings with his people. It is this larger narrative the author is calling the audience to inhabit. The nature of the author's theological hermeneutic and the extent to which he uses the Old Testament make it possible, therefore, to read 1 Peter narratively

In 1998 Steven R. Bechtler examined the ways in which the author's references to Christ's suffering and glorification were intended to function as integral parts of the letter's response to the suffering of the communities addressed. Bechtler uses the social sciences in his exegesis, based on the conviction that 1 Peter is primarily addressing a social problem. On the one hand, he argues that the author's use of the language of honour and dishonour is key to understanding the problem of suffering. He writes, 'The essence of the problem addressed in 1 Peter is the pervasive threat to honor inherent in the relentless verbal attacks of non-Christians against the letter's addressees'.[84] Bechtler argues that Christ is the key to the letter's response to the suffering it addresses. The christology of 1 Peter functions eschatologically as the Christ event marks the limits both of world history and of the suffering of the readers: their suffering will not last indefinitely, and God's vindication awaits them in the immediate future. The epistle's christology functions soteriologically as 'Christ's death and God's subsequent resurrection/glorification of Christ provided their [the addressees] means of salvation'.[85] This pattern, suffering and glory, is one that can be applied to the addressees' situation as the letter superimposes Christ's experience onto that of his followers. The christology of 1 Peter functions sociologically in shaping group identity, and defining group membership. Those who have a

---

83. See, e.g., Schutter, *Hermeneutic and Composition*, pp. 49–50, 129.
84. Bechtler, *Following in His Steps*, p. 103.
85. Bechtler, *Following in His Steps*, pp. 179–80.

relationship with Christ will receive honour, those who do not will be put to shame. Christians live in a symbolic universe centred on Christ. But in that universe, 'God is both the arbiter of claims to honor and the source of honor for God's people'.[86] If they participate in the sufferings of Christ God will vindicate them as he vindicated Christ and give them honour. Therefore, Christ's experiences serve as a pattern for the community members to follow. Throughout his discussion, Bechtler acknowledges that the author uses the language drawn from early-Jewish and early Christian traditions, and images and metaphors that evoke LXX Israel to describe the liminality of the audience's Christian experience.

Bechtler has made an important contribution to Petrine scholarship with his treatment on the suffering, community, and christology of 1 Peter. He offers a valuable discussion of the author's use of different metaphors to describe the audience. Also important in Bechtler's treatment is the emphasis on God as the main actor and the arbiter of honour in the liminal world in which early Christians lived. His discussion of the concept of honour and shame is important to this study as bestowal of honour from God is the ultimate reward granted to the one who responds faithfully to suffering. Bechtler's treatment helpfully highlights the socio-political realities that gave rise to the sufferings of the audience and the centrality of Christ's experience in shaping and defining the behaviour of 1 Peter's audience.

In 1999, Paul J. Achtemeier published a study on the christology of 1 Peter in which he shows points of similarity between 1 Peter's christology and the rest of the New Testament corpus.[87] He suggests that the language the author uses to illustrate certain christological points reveals that he is operating from the background of Israel as God's chosen people as opposed to Greco-Roman cultic ideas. For Achtemeier, the author of 1 Peter is aware of Israel's Scriptures and deliberately draws from it to craft his message. He maintains, however, that 1 Peter's audience was almost certainly not Jewish.[88]

Achtemeier demonstrates the uniqueness with which the author of 1 Peter appropriates the Old Testament to craft the christology of the letter. In the author's mind Israel in its totality has become synonymous with the Christian communities which form the epistle's audience. As such Israel is the controlling metaphor which the author uses to express not only the christology but the entire theology of the epistle.[89] In 1 Peter, 'the language and reality of Israel pass without remainder into the language and therefore

---

86. Bechtler, *Following in His Steps*, pp. 188–92.

87. Paul J. Achtemeier, 'The Christology of First Peter', in Mark A. Powell and David R. Bauer (eds), *Who Do You Say That I Am? Essays on Christology* (Louisville: Westminster, 1999), pp. 140–54. For Achtemeier, the christology of 1 Peter serves as support for the ethical admonitions that are promulgated in the correspondence (*1 Peter*, p. 37).

88. Achtemeier, 'Christology', pp. 140–1; idem, *1 Peter*, p. 71.

89. Achtemeier, 'Christology', p. 142; idem, 'Newborn Babes and Living Stones: Literal and Figurative in 1 Peter', in M. P. Horgan and P. J. Kobelski (eds), *To Touch the Text: Biblical and Related Studies in Honor of Joseph A. Fitzmyer, S.J.* (New York: Crossroad, 1989), pp. 207–36.

the reality of the Christian community, who now constitutes the new people of God'.[90] In 1 Pet. 2.9-10, the author describes the Christian community as being founded on Christ, the living stone. Drawing from Isaiah and Psalms, he addresses and speaks of his audience in ways that imply that his audience has assumed without remainder the role that Israel once played.

Achtemeier finds in 1.10-12 the reason why the author of 1 Peter feels justified in the way he appropriates the language of the Old Testament in relation to his audience. This passage points to the continuity of God's purpose, and the unity of the witness of the Old Testament and the Christian community. This is consistent with the way the author formulates his christology as shown explicitly in 1 Pet. 2.21-25, where the author uses Isaiah in a unique way to talk of the passion.[91] For Achtemeier, through this Christ-centred reading of the Old Testament, one finds the contribution of 1 Peter's christology to later Christian theological reflection.

Achtemeier's treatment helpfully highlights the way the author appropriates the Old Testament to craft his christology. His argument about the role of 1.10-12 will contribute later to our discussion of 1 Peter's theological hermeneutic of the Old Testament. A weakness in Achtemeier's work consists in his failure to locate the christology of the epistle within the larger theological framework that constitutes 1 Peter's message. I will urge that the author's Christ-centred reading of the Old Testament does not constitute, in and of itself, the crux of the epistle's message. The author of 1 Peter locates his understanding of the person and work of Christ within the larger framework of who God is, what he has done, and what he is doing for his people. Therefore, it is not enough to speak of how 1 Peter's christology helps one understand Christ's work in the Old Testament. Rather, one must further show how it helps 1 Peter's audience to become more aware of God and his activities on their behalf. Further, Achtemeier is not clear on his understanding of how the author of 1 Peter views Israel and the Christian communities that form the readership of the letter. On the one hand, he suggests that there is unity between the witness of the Old Testament and the Christian community;[92] on the other hand, he argues that for 1 Peter 'the Christian community has supplanted Israel as chosen people'.[93] I propose that to the extent the witness of the Old Testament was borne by the community of Israel, this implies a certain unity and continuity between the community of Israel and the Christian community. Also, I will demonstrate that in pointing out the continuity of God's purpose in 1 Pet. 1.10-12, the author of 1 Peter is not replacing Israel

90.   Achtemeier, 'Christology', p. 143.
91.   Achtemeier, 'Christology', pp. 147–8. Elsewhere, Achtemeier discusses the relationship between 1.10-12 and 2.21-25 in more detail. See, 'Suffering Servant and Suffering Christ in 1 Peter', in A. J. Malherbe and W. A. Meeks (eds), *The Future of Christology: Essays in Honor of Leander E. Keck* (Minneapolis: Fortress, 1993), pp. 176–88.
92.   Achtemeier, 'Christology', pp. 142–4.
93.   Achtemeier, 'Newborn Babes', p. 225.

with the Christian community; rather, he is inviting the latter to embody the story of the former, so that God's purpose can be worked out in their lives.

That same year, Eugene Boring published a commentary on 1 Peter where he argued for the suitability of a narrative approach to 1 Peter.[94] Boring uses the work done in Pauline studies by Norman Petersen and Ben Witherington and the work of Peter Berger and Thomas Luckmann as a springboard to draft the narrative world of 1 Peter.[95] For Boring, the author of 1 Peter is not so much concerned with teaching theology as he is with addressing the experiences of the audience from within the narrative world presupposed by the letter: a world determined by God; a world that is comprehensively defined by Christ as its source, goal, and revelatory midpoint; a world that is socially constructed and projected by the letter as the real world.

In a 2007 essay, 'Narrative Dynamics in 1 Peter: The Function of Narrative World',[96] Boring seeks to lay out the methodology behind his earlier proposal that '1 Peter projects a narrative world composed of all the events it assumes to be real – compelling serious readers/hearers to examine their own understanding of reality, and indirectly inviting them to live their lives in the world projected by the letter'.[97]

First, Boring explains his understanding of narratology by (1) providing some definitions for the crucial terms that are relevant to the concept; namely, event, story, generic narrative, narrative world, story world, and letter; and (2) formulating some methodological theses. He advances that narratological insights gained from the studies of biblical documents that are essentially narrative in nature cannot be applied wholesale to 1 Peter. For Boring, the principal contribution of this approach is the concept of narrative world. He outlines the steps involved in drafting the narrative world of an epistle, then, applies them to the text of 1 Peter as a case in point, before offering an evaluation of the methodology he proposes. He suggests that a narrative approach to 1 Peter:

- may provide an additional basis for rhetorical analysis;
- illuminates the phenomenon of pseudepigraphy;
- allows us to see the distinctive way in which letters reflect the narrative mode of theological thought that pervades the canonical scriptures;

---

94.   Eugene Boring, *1 Peter* (ANTC; Nashville: Abingdon, 1999), pp. 183–201.

95.   Norman Petersen, *Rediscovering Paul: Philemon and the Sociology of Paul's Narrative World* (Philadelphia: Fortress, 1985); Ben Witherington III, *Paul's Narrative Thought World: The Tapestry of Tragedy and Triumph* (Louisville: Westminster, 1994); Peter L. Berger and Thomas Luckmann, *The Social Construction of Reality: A Treatise in the Sociology of Knowledge* (Garden City, NY: Doubleday, 1966).

96.   Eugene Boring, 'Narrative Dynamics in 1 Peter: The Function of Narrative World', in Robert L. Webb and Betsy Bauman-Martin (eds), *Reading First Peter with New Eyes: Methodological Reassessments of the Letter of First Peter* (London: T&T Clark, 2007), pp. 7–40.

97.   Boring, 'Narrative Dynamics in 1 Peter', p. 8.

- lets us see paraenesis functioning as challenging us with an alternative vision of reality rather than a list of commands; and,
- illuminates 1 Peter's view of the way Christ speaks to the readers.[98]

Boring's proposal has opened a new array of possibilities for Petrine scholarship. It offers a helpful and innovative way of approaching the text of 1 Peter. This present study is also convinced of the fruitfulness of a narratological approach to 1 Peter. However, the methodology that guides this study differs from what Boring is proposing. This study focuses on the narrative substructure created by the events rehearsed in the letter, whereas Boring's methodology focuses on the narrative world projected, which happens at the surface structure.

In 2001 there appeared Sharon C. Pearson's monograph, *The Christological and Rhetorical Properties of 1 Peter*, in which she approaches 1 Peter from a tradition-historical standpoint to show how the sufferings/glories pattern in 1 Peter comprises the method and message of the letter.[99] Pearson proposes that the christology of 1 Peter is to be found essentially in 1.3-12, 18-22; 2.4-8, 21-25; and 3.18-22.[100] For Pearson, the sufferings/glories pattern is dependent on the Old Testament concept of humiliation/vindication found in Isa. 53, which Pearson understands to be central to 1 Peter.

Pearson structures her discussion of 1 Peter around what she considers to be the major christological pericopae in the letter. She argues that the introduction of the christology of 1 Peter is established in 1.3. The theme sufferings/glories appears in many places in 1 Peter and most often in the christological formulae. For example, in 1.3-12, the sufferings/glories pattern is used to hold the different traditional materials the author is using to present, in hymn-like fashion, a distinctive christology and a well-developed soteriology, theodicy, eschatology, and ethic. In 1.18-22, christology is used as the basis for the call to holiness and obedience to God. There, Christ is the authoritative expression of God's justice. That Christ has been vindicated offers hope to those who trust God that God can do the same for them in due time. In 2.21-25, the concept of suffering binds together antithetical couplets like sin/righteousness, dying/living, and persecution/entrusting. This pericope is a tightly woven piece based on Isa. 53, which adds the dominant theme of Christ's suffering as atonement. In 3.18-22, the vindication, exaltation, and triumphant rulership of Christ hold everything together. Pearson finds in this pericope the fullest statement of the christology of 1 Peter. She argues that the major christological passages serve to identify Jesus Christ with Old Testament themes held together by the sufferings/glories, and humiliation/vindication themes of Isa. 53. In 1 Peter 1.19, Jesus Christ is portrayed as the paschal lamb; he is identified as the servant of Yahweh in 2.21-25; and in 3.18-22, one finds a narration of his atoning work and exaltation.

---

98. Boring, 'Narrative Dynamics in 1 Peter', pp. 34–7.
99. Pearson, *Christological and Rhetorical Properties*, p. 11.
100. Pearson, *Christological and Rhetorical Properties*, p. 3.

Pearson's study is one of the most important treatments of the christology of 1 Peter in recent scholarship. Her survey of the literature on the subject is wide-ranging and informative, addressing the various options that have been the subject of conversations about the form and content of 1 Peter.

Although Pearson has focused on the content of the christology of 1 Peter, her method in approaching the text constitutes a weakness of her work, for Pearson's ability to see the richness of the author's christological treatment has been hampered by her source-critical agenda. Pearson's exploration of the sources behind the christological concepts present in the letter provides no impetus for an examination of their implications for the letter and its recipients. Pearson does well to attend to the traditional deposits that may be present in 1 Peter. However, she goes too far in finding remnants of hymns and traditional elements behind almost every christological statement, and tends to force sources upon the text. Though Pearson acknowledges the importance of the other Old Testament texts in the composition of 1 Peter, her treatment focuses almost exclusively on the impact of Deutero-Isaiah on 1 Peter. Apparently for Pearson, traditional deposits, sufferings/glories, and Deutero-Isaiah are the elements that undergird the christological and rhetorical properties of 1 Peter. Though each of these may play an important role, other themes require attention in order to do justice to the letter's christology, as do other Old Testament passages that seem to play crucial roles in the document.

J. Ramsey Michaels, in 2004, published an article, 'St. Peter's Passion: The Passion Narrative in 1 Peter', in which he focuses on 1 Peter's discussion of the sufferings of Christ and compares the treatment of Christ's passion in 1 Peter with the passion narratives in the Gospel of Mark and in the non-canonical *Gospel of Peter*.[101] Michaels believes that this comparison is warranted on two counts: (1) Although 1 Peter is not essentially narrative, it can be thought of as the author's passion narrative because it seeks to give an account of the author's testimony to the sufferings of Christ; (2) issues of authorship notwithstanding, 1 Peter 'intends to view the passion of Christ through Peter's eyes. In doing so, it invites comparison with two other possibly "Petrine" passion narratives, the canonical Gospel of Mark and the non-canonical *Gospel of Peter*'.[102] Michaels argues that 1 Peter's primary focus rests on the 'sufferings' of Christ because in his sufferings Christ set an example for the audience. He discusses the author's description of the passion of Christ and concludes that the author of 1 Peter 'knows that the story ended with Christ's death and resurrection, but his interest here is in the "sufferings" that preceded the death, because these he believes are portents of what is in store for his readers'.[103]

Michaels' treatment is very limited in scope yet his approach offers an impetus for narratological studies in 1 Peter. It recognizes and assumes that

101. J. Ramsey Michaels, 'St. Peter's Passion: The Passion Narrative in 1 Peter', *WW* 24 (2004), pp. 387–94.
102. Michaels, 'St. Peter's Passion', p. 388.
103. Michaels, 'St. Peter's Passion', p. 392.

narratological categories can be applied to the non-narrative text of 1 Peter. Further, Michaels' treatment offers valuable insights on the christology of the epistle, and particularly on the role the sufferings of Christ played in the author's portrayal of Christ's passion.

In 2005, Michaels suggested that 1 Peter has a rich and very developed christology.[104] He follows Larry Hurtado in arguing that in 1 Peter Christ enjoys a high status which is set within God the Father's supremacy. God is the main actor. All is from God, yet in or through Jesus Christ, or through his resurrection.[105] Meanwhile, there seems to be some intentional ambiguity at work in 1 Peter. The epistle interchangeably ascribes the same qualities to Father and Son, presenting Jesus to the readers in ways and functions that God the Father is portrayed to the children of Israel in the Old Testament. The christology of the letter also establishes a certain relationship between Jesus and the readers. Jesus Christ is God's lamb through/by which the readers' redemption was procured. His death also frees them from the power of sin and empowers them to live for God. The epistle's christology presents its readers with the eschatological hope that their redeemer, though now invisible, will return to lead and care for them. To that end, and for those who want to follow the Chief Shepherd, 1 Peter's christology draws on the gospel tradition for the notion of discipleship to set the human Jesus as the model for Christian behaviour. For Michaels, 'Christology in 1 Peter is the key not only to individual salvation but also to life in community'.[106]

Michaels has highlighted some of the main features of the christology of 1 Peter: the supremacy of God the Father, the ambiguous language with which the author addresses God the Father and Jesus Christ, the status of the audience as a covenant people like Israel of old, and the human Jesus as the model for Christian behaviour. By focusing on the human Jesus, Michaels' treatment presents a helpful contribution to the discussion as scholars have had to differentiate between the nature of Jesus' sufferings and that of 1 Peter's audience, and set limits around the extent to which one can follow Jesus' example, because Jesus' experience was unique in many ways.

While giving credit to Michaels' approach, I will demonstrate that the focus of Jesus as a model for Christian behaviour as portrayed by the author of 1 Peter resides in the fact that Jesus acts in a way that is consistent with what God expects of those who live in covenant relationship with him. Following in his steps may bring about suffering, but more importantly, it requires obedience to and dependence on God in everyday life. For those who

104. J. Ramsey Michaels, 'Catholic Christologies in the Catholic Epistles', in Richard N. Longenecker (ed.), *Contours of Christology in the New Testament* (Grand Rapids: Eerdmans, 2005), p. 274. Michaels was comparing the christology of 1 Peter to that of James and suggested that 1 Peter's christology was richer and more fully developed.

105. Michaels, 'Catholic Christologies', p. 275; see Larry Hurtado, 'Christology', in Ralph P. Martin and Peter H. Davids (eds), *DLNTD* (Downers Grove, IL: InterVarsity, 1997), pp. 170–84; see also 'Jesus: One and Many: The Christological Concept of New Testament Authors', *JBL* 108 (1989), pp. 710–12.

106. Michaels, 'Catholic Christologies', p. 279.

fit their lives according to this pattern, God's deliverance and vindication are both present and future.

Joel B. Green has offered a scheme of the narrative of 1 Peter in his article, 'Narrating the Gospel in 1 and 2 Peter', which was published in 2006 in which he makes a case for applying a narratological approach to 1 Peter.[107] He states, 'The narrative of 1 Peter comes into focus especially in 1 Pet. 1.13-21 where the apostle's instruction is set within and determined by a temporal map'. [108] This map is comprised of events by which the author of 1 Peter orders the lives of his audience. Green explains that by this scheme the author of 1 Peter purports to introduce and induct his audience 'further into a particular way of construing their history that is deeply rooted in the eternal plan of God and that takes seriously the formation and nurture of God's people, Israel, through Passover, exodus, and the pattern of reconciliation through sacrifice'.[109]

Here again, one finds a study that is limited in scope but very helpful in that it offers valuable insights vis-à-vis the way(s) in which narratological principles can be applied to the study of 1 Peter.[110]

That same year, J. de Wall Dryden published his monograph, *Theology and Ethics in 1 Peter*, in which he demonstrates how narrative plays an integral part in theology and ethics, and, particularly the impact of a narrative worldview on one's theology and ethics.[111] Approaching 1 Peter from a primarily social-rhetorical criticism perspective, Dryden builds on the work of W. T. Wilson on Colossians in which he argues that Greco-Roman paraenetic epistles, like 1 Peter, were not confined to the use of typically 'paraenetic elements', but also incorporated the use of narratives, among other things, to accomplish exhortative goals.[112] Dryden reads 1 Peter against the background of the nature and function of Greco-Roman paraenetic epistles. In the process, he explores five paraenetic literary strategies (narrative worldview, conversion, social identity, moral instructions, and example) and discusses how they function in 1 Peter.[113]

Dryden proposes that 'narrative is a powerful way to communicate worldview in a concrete form that embodies both beliefs and ethos'.[114] He uses the work of Berger and Luckmann as a springboard to suggest that 1 Peter weaves together a story of what the world is like. This story, in turn, becomes the context for the audience's own stories both as individuals and as a community. According to Dryden, there are two ways in which a

---

107. Joel B. Green, 'Narrating the Gospel in 1 and 2 Peter', *Int* 20 (2006), pp. 262–77.

108. Green, 'Narrating the Gospel', p. 269.

109. Green, 'Narrating the Gospel', p. 274.

110. Green has elaborated on his proposal and applied this perspective to 1 Peter in a commentary published in 2007. See, *1 Peter* (THNTC; Grand Rapids: Eerdmans, 2007).

111. J. de Waal Dryden, *Theology and Ethics in 1 Peter: Paraenetic Strategies for Christian Character Formation* (WUNT, 2.29; Tübingen: Mohr Siebeck, 2006).

112. Dryden, *Theology and Ethics in 1 Peter*, p. 7.

113. Dryden, *Theology and Ethics in 1 Peter*, pp. 8–9.

114. Dryden, *Theology and Ethics in 1 Peter*, p. 56.

narrative world is presupposed by 1 Peter: (1) the author only refers to key elements of the story of salvation to evoke an entire narrative worldview that is familiar to both author and readers; (2) although 1 Peter is not a narrative, it is governed by a narrative substructure. He states, 'Thus, while non-narrative in genre, 1 Peter utilizes an *implied* narrative that unifies all the "salvation-historical" events it references. It describes a world that is governed by a story – the story of God's salvation'.[115] Dryden shows how this story is introduced in the epistle's prescript (1.1-2) and suggests that the author is mapping the experiences of the audience onto the grand narrative of salvation. For Dryden, the story of salvation is the organizing principle around which the author builds his message. It functions as an integral tool in the paraenetic enterprise of moral formation, and provides the context of ethical instruction.[116]

Dryden's work is a great example of how insights from narratology can be used to help our understanding of 1 Peter's message and how narratology can be integrated with other methods in the study of 1 Peter. Dryden's view on the presence of a narrative substructure in 1 Peter and the presence of an organizing principle is similar to this study.

1.2.4. *Summary*

This survey of the literature on 1 Peter, beginning from 1946 to the present, has highlighted the contributions of representatives from the three periods of the development of Petrine scholarship. I have focused mainly on the way scholars have understood (1) the nature and function of the christology of 1 Peter, (2) the epistle's relationship to the Old Testament, and (3) the suitability of a narratological approach to 1 Peter. During the first period, although one finds discussions about the christology of 1 Peter, these were secondary to the issues surrounding the genre of 1 Peter, the form in which it was transmitted to the church, the sources behind its composition, and its relationship/dependence on other epistles. During the second period, ushered in at the urging of John Elliott, scholars began to pay closer attention to the epistle. During that period, Jacques Schlosser highlighted the relationship between Peter's christology and the Old Testament and the key role 1.10-12 played in Peter's christological use of the Old Testament; John Elliott made a case for the application of social-scientific criticism to 1 Peter; and Leonhard Goppelt argued for 1 Peter's dependence on Qumran literature from the Essene tradition. Starting with 1986, discussions of the christology of 1 Peter and its relationship to the Old Testament began to flourish. Whereas most scholars admit to the importance of the Old Testament to 1 Peter, opinions vary vis-à-vis the author's appropriation of that source. One also finds

---

115. Dryden, *Theology and Ethics in 1 Peter*, p. 66.
116. Dryden, *Theology and Ethics in 1 Peter*, pp. 80–2.

discussion of the author's dependence on traditional materials and arguments about the affinities between Petrine and Qumranic modes of interpretation. In the process, different methodological approaches have been applied to the study of this epistle in view of making sense of its message. This study builds on the foundation already laid in previous studies on 1 Peter, but also contributes to the ongoing discussion in the following areas.

First, given Peter's extensive use of the Old Testament, this study will focus primarily on the relationship between 1 Peter and the Old Testament, more specifically, Peter's appropriation of the Old Testament guided by his christological understanding of God's actions on behalf of Israel. I will also highlight the importance of 1.10-12 as key to Peter's christological appropriation of the Old Testament and establish that it provides insights into Peter's theological hermeneutic. However, I will take this argument further by showing that the hermeneutical principles identified in 1.10-12 are already at work since the opening verses. I will demonstrate that Peter's theological hermeneutic warrants a narratological approach to the study of the epistle. Therefore, one of the major contributions of this study is its methodology, in which I lay out the characteristics of a narratological approach to understanding the message of 1 Peter. Although Petrine studies have benefited much from other methods previously applied to the study of 1 Peter, there are other avenues yet to be explored that can contribute to the advancement of Petrine scholarship.

Second, it has been argued that the sufferings/glories pattern is the organizing principle for the way Peter reads Scripture. Whereas this is helpful, I will demonstrate that this fails to take into account the larger picture of God's relationship with and actions on behalf of Israel and Jesus which the author uses as a springboard to craft his message to his audience. I will show that the lens through which the author of 1 Peter reads Scripture and encourages his audience to makes sense of their situation comprises four elements: election, suffering, steadfastness, and vindication. I will demonstrate that these four elements constitute the fabula of 1 Peter and are common to the experiences of Israel, Jesus and the epistle's audience.

Third, social-scientific criticism has helped us understand many concepts that are characteristic of the Greco-Roman milieu from which the epistle originated and in which its recipients lived. I will demonstrate that whereas the author's awareness of sociological factors characteristic of Greco-Roman culture is evident in the letter, he encourages his audience to find fresh ways to interact with their social environment. Their problems originate in society and the solution is to be played out within this society, yet the author parses the problems his audience face and their response to them primarily in theological terms. In this sense, the social and theological realities that the audience experience exert a mutual influence on each other.

1.3. Preliminary issues

Before I lay out my proposal, I need to attend to two preliminary issues. First, I will address the issue of 1 Peter's audience in order to clarify my position on the matter. Second, I will offer a brief definition of 'theological hermeneutics'. It is worth noting that my primary agenda is that of pursuing how narratology can be applied in the study of an epistle. Matters that pertain to 'theological hermeneutics' *per se* are important to this endeavour because of the relationship between the two concepts, but they are secondary in terms of the focus of this study.

1.3.1. The audience of 1 Peter

The discussion about the audience of 1 Peter usually centres on the question of whether the audience was made up primarily of Jews or primarily of Gentiles. There is general agreement that the audience was mixed but opinions vary vis-à-vis which ethnic group was in the majority. For example, Édouard Cothenet, Elliott, Goppelt, and Spicq argue for a predominantly Gentile audience.[117] J. Ramsey Michaels goes so far as to argue that the author of 1 Peter simply ignores the Jewish Christian community and that 1 Peter is not addressed to them.[118] However, Ben Witherington argues that 1 Peter's audience was primarily, and perhaps entirely, made up of Jewish Christians; thereby, aligning himself with Eusebius and Calvin among others.[119] The evidence from the letter itself is ambiguous at best.[120] First, in the address section of the letter – 'ἐκλεκτοῖς τοῖς παρεπιδήμοις διασπορᾶς Πόντου, Γαλατίας, Καππαδοκίας, Ἀσίας καὶ Βιθυνίας' (1.1) – the places mentioned cover a vast geographical area of the Anatolian peninsula. This suggests an audience of diverse backgrounds because the geo-socio-political situation of these regions was not homogeneous.[121] Second, there is evidence in the epistle to support the presence of both ethnic groups as part of the audience. The author's overwhelming use of the Old Testament, the identification of his

---

117. Édouard Cothenet, 'Les Orientations Actuelles de l'Exégèse de la Première Lettre de Pierre', in Charles Perrot (ed.), *Études sur La Première Lettre de Pierre* (LD, 102; Paris: Cerf, 1980), p. 19; John H. Elliott, *Conflict, Community, and Honor: 1 Peter in Social-Scientific Perspective* (Eugene, OR: Wipf & Stock, 2007), p. 16; Goppelt, *1 Peter*, p. 6; Spicq, *Épîtres*, p. 13.

118. J. Ramsey Michaels, *1 Peter* (WBC, 49; Waco, TX: Word, 1988), p. xlix.

119. Ben Witherington III, *A Socio-Rhetorical Commentary on 1-2 Peter* (LHHC, 2; Downers Grove, IL: InterVarsity, 2007), pp. 27–34; Eusebius, *Hist. eccl.* 3.4; John Calvin, *Commentaries on the Catholic Epistles* (Grand Rapids: Eerdmans, 1948), p. 25.

120. So also Achtemeier, *1 Peter*, p. 50.

121. See, e.g., Achtemeier, *1 Peter*, pp. 50, 83; Elliott, *1 Peter*, pp. 84–9; Claude Lepelley, 'Le Contexte Historique de la Première Lettre de Pierre', in Charles Perrot (ed.), *Études sur la Première Lettre de Pierre* (LD, 102; Paris: Cerf, 1980), pp. 43–64 (52–8); Schutter, *Hermeneutic and Composition*, pp. 8–9.

audience with Israel, and the traditional view that Peter was the apostle to the Jews have been used to support the view that the audience is predominantly Jewish.[122] Scholars who argue for a predominantly gentile audience have appealed to some of the language that Peter uses throughout the epistle [e.g., ταῖς πρότερον ἐν τῇ ἀγνοίᾳ ὑμῶν ἐπιθυμίαις (1.14); ἐλυτρώθητε ἐκ τῆς ματαίας ὑμῶν ἀναστροφῆς πατροπαραδότου (1.18); οἳ ποτε οὐ λαὸς νῦν δὲ λαὸς θεοῦ (2.10); and ὁ παρεληλυθὼς χρόνος τὸ βούλημα τῶν ἐθνῶν κατειργάσθαι... (4.3-4)] to suggest that the author would not have directed this kind of language to a Jewish audience.[123] However, Witherington has recently demonstrated how this language could relate to a Jewish audience as well.[124] For example, the language of 2.10 is taken from Hosea which, in its original context, refers to Israel. In addition, the language of 1.14-16 is taken from Lev. 11.44-45 which is part of the stipulations of the Holiness Code. According to Witherington, the author of 1 Peter compares his audience to Israel before the Holiness Code was given. I would add that there is a possible link between the Jewish members of Peter's audience and Israel in 1.18. There is general agreement that τῆς ματαίας ὑμῶν ἀναστροφῆς is a reference to idolatrous behaviour handed down from one's ancestor.[125] Whereas this is generally understood to refer to pagan ways of life, the surrounding context is filled with redemption and covenant imagery drawn from Exodus and Leviticus. It is conceivable, therefore, that the author's warning to his audience is one that might recall images of Israel's idolatrous behaviour at Sinai and at other stages of Israel's life (Exod. 32.4; cf. Lev. 17.7; Deut. 32.21; Jer. 8.19; Amos 5.25-27).[126] The reminder offered in 1 Pet. 1.18 serves as a basis for holy conduct, and a person of Jewish or Gentile background would have been able to relate to it.

It appears that the issue of audience should not be based solely on the recipients' ethnicity but on their ability to read and understand the message of the letter and to identify with the realities evoked therein. Chevalier notes, 'For our author, the eschatological people of God has an important distinction when compared to the people of Israel; it no longer has an ethnic or national base'.[127] Therefore, one can say that 1 Peter's audience was made of people whose geographical location, on the Anatolian peninsula, implied that they were versed in the Greco-Roman culture and mores in which they lived.[128]

---

122. E.g., Calvin, *Catholic Epistles*, p. 25; Witherington, *1 Peter*, pp. 27–8. See Michaels, *1 Peter*, pp. xlix–lv for an opposing view. For a brief assessment of Michaels, see, Davids, *1 Peter*, pp. 8–9.

123. E.g., Bechtler, *Following in His Steps*, p. 64; Davids, *1 Peter*, pp. 8–9; Richard, 'Functional Christology', p. 123; Schutter, *Hermeneutic and Composition*, pp. 9–10.

124. Witherington, *1 Peter*, pp. 28–31. See also, Jobes, *1 Peter*, pp. 23–4.

125. E.g., Elliott, *1 Peter*, p. 370; Goppelt, *1 Peter*, p.117.

126. See also, Boismard, 'Une Liturgie Baptismale', p. 194; Elliott, *Home*, p. 34.

127. Chevalier, 'Vocation des Chrétiens en Diaspora', p. 391; (author's translation).

128. On the assimilation of Jews into Hellenistic culture, see, e.g., *Jews in a Graeco-Roman World* (ed. Martin Goodman; Oxford: Oxford University Press, 2006); and Martin Hengel, *Judaism and Hellenism* (2 vols; Minneapolis: Fortress, 1998).

In addition, the author's extensive use of the Old Testament suggests that these people were so immersed in the Scriptures of Israel, which were also the Scriptures of the Early Church, that they were able to make sense of the concepts and imageries drawn from the Old Testament. More importantly, the author's focus seems to be not on the ethnicity of the audience, but on the theological realities of who they became after conversion, ἐκλεκτοῖς παρεπιδήμοις, and what they experienced as a result.

Therefore, the audience's status as 'marginal' trumps the importance of their being Gentile or Jewish. The way the author addresses the audience throughout the letter highlights their marginality in relation to their suffering. They suffer primarily because their conversion has placed them on the fringes of their sphere(s) of influence, and on the fringes of society at large. For example, in 1.3-9 the audience's new birth is mentioned in tandem with the rewards associated with it – living hope, inheritance, future salvation – and the suffering that they face in the meantime. Further, the language of 4.3-4 shows that the new birth the audience experienced and the change of behaviour that ensued are at the root of the verbal abuse directed toward them (cf. 2.11-12; 3.13-16). The author's language in 2.11-12 posits 'παροίκους καὶ παρεπιδήμους' over against 'ἐν τοῖς ἔθνεσιν', thereby using the audience's marginal status as an identity marker. This in itself is evidence that the author of 1 Peter views 'Gentile' as 'other' and that this designation is not one he is concerned with vis-à-vis his identification of the audience.

In addition, the status-oriented nature of Greco-Roman culture would allow marginality to overshadow ethnicity as an identity marker. David deSilva proposes that, 'in the ancient world, people are not just "taken on their own merits". Instead, their merits begin with the merits (or debits) of their lineage, the reputation of their ancestral house'.[129] A person's status/ honour was decided by ascription and/or by performance.[130] New birth and the change of behaviour associated with it called into question issues of kinship and issues of honour and shame that guide the way people relate to one another. This is a case in which a person's performance – the choice to follow Christ – jeopardizes the honour or status previously ascribed by the world based on one's origin. By choosing to follow the way of Christ, Jews or/and Gentiles are now members of a new household and face pressure from the group(s) they formerly belonged to.[131] Their marginality in the eyes of the world, together with (and, as a result of) their election in God's sight, thus becomes a way by which they are identified by the author. The use of familial language in 1 Peter, then, constitutes a way of establishing group solidarity among his audience (e.g., 1.17; 2.17; 4.17; 5.9). Similarly, by identifying God

---

129. David deSilva, *Honor, Patronage, Kinship, and Purity: Unlocking New Testament Culture* (Downers Grove, IL: InterVarsity, 2000), p. 158.

130. E.g., Gerhard Lenski, *Power and Privilege: A Theory of Social Stratification* (Chapel Hill: University of North Carolina, 2nd edn, 1984); deSilva, *Honor, Patronage, Kinship, and Purity*, p. 28.

131. deSilva, *Honor, Patronage, Kinship, and Purity*, pp. 43–50.

as the arbiter of honour (e.g., 2.19-20), the author eliminates the need for his audience to worry about their status in the eyes of the world.

1.3.2. *Defining 'theological hermeneutics'*

The understanding of who God is is achieved through reading about his acts on behalf of and interaction with humanity. 'Theological hermeneutics' is concerned with engaging Scripture in order to come to the knowledge of God. Kevin Vanhoozer rightly notes, 'To know God is to love and obey him, for the knowledge of God is both restorative and transformative'.[132] Therefore, the person who is engaged in the task of 'theological hermeneutics' approaches Scripture with an openness to be formed and transformed by the text. This implies that the person who approaches Scriptures assumes that they can speak to his/her present reality. It also implies that as the person becomes aware of God and of his work in the lives of others, s/he is able to order his/her life in such a way that allows God to act for him/her in a way similar to how he has acted on behalf of others in the past. 'Theological hermeneutics' can be defined as an approach in which one's understanding of God and his work in the past, as recorded in the Scriptures, forms the ways in which a person or interpretive community makes sense of (interprets) the past, present, and future. First Peter's theological hermeneutic of the Old Testament, thus, has to do with the author's understanding of the theological role the Old Testament plays in shaping the identity and behaviour of his audience, and in the formation and transformation of his audience, more specifically, as it relates to their response to suffering. In other words, the author's use of the Scriptures assumes that these Scriptures, when understood properly – i.e., when read christologically and with an eye to their simultaneity (namely, their capacity to speak to the present and past, by way of ontological association) – constitute the perspective from which to make sense of the harsh realities the audience is facing and to guide their responses to those realities.

1.4. *Proposal*

I have engaged several representatives from the three periods of the development of Petrine scholarship. I have highlighted their major contributions and some of the shortcomings of these approaches and their understanding of the christology of the epistle. Most scholars agree that the Old Testament plays a major role in the way the author of 1 Peter crafts his message; however, there are diverging opinions vis-à-vis the nature of the primary background of the letter. My purpose is to show the significance of 1 Peter's christological understanding of God's actions on behalf of Israel for its suffering audience. I

---

132. Kevin Vanhoozer, 'What is Theological Interpretation of the Bible', in *DTIB* (Grand Rapids: Baker Academic, 2005), p. 24.

want to argue that the author's understanding of Israel's Scripture has played a key role in the way he crafted his message and shaped the kind of response he encouraged his audience to display in the face of trials.

I propose that a narrative analysis of 1 Peter demonstrates that the author has identified a common, four-part fabula by which he narrates the stories of Israel, Christ, and his audience on the Anatolian peninsula, and by means of this fabula he gives theological significance to the suffering of his audience and sketches for them the nature of faithful response. In addition, the author of 1 Peter is engaged in theological hermeneutics. In appropriating the stories of the Old Testament and other Jewish literature and applying them to the life of his audience, he is working primarily with theological realities that are analogous to both groups. At the core of this theological hermeneutics is God's work in, through, and on behalf of Jesus Christ. This leads the author of 1 Peter to read the Old Testament christologically, and to place Christ as the paradigm for his audience. The purpose of his exemplary suffering is that his followers will relate to God as he did, so that they can benefit from God's favour as he did, and be vindicated by God as he was. In this way the christology of the epistle constitutes a means to at least two ends; one, to present Jesus as the perfect example of obedience to and dependence on God and of his steadfastness in suffering; and two, to celebrate God's actions and ability to save.

Further, the author's engagement with the Scriptures of Israel is done in such a way that his description of, and exhortation to his audience transcends the temporal gap that separates them from these Scriptures. He treats the word of God addressed to Israel as addressed directly to his audience. Therefore, one way of engaging in theological hermeneutics is to read 1 Peter narratively. The author 'theologizes' by rehearsing the stories of Jesus and Israel while crafting his message to his audience. He presents Jesus not only as the model of innocent suffering but as the model of the ideal servant of Yahweh who trusts Yahweh for deliverance. In addition, the author of 1 Peter locates his message in the Old Testament and uses the experience of Israel as a case in point to help the suffering communities that constituted his audience make sense of their own situation. Although the readers were living in a Greco-Roman context, their understanding of the message would have been shaped by their knowledge and understanding of the Old Testament and the stories that the author of 1 Peter drew from. The epistle was written at a time when most people were illiterate; therefore, orality and narrativity must have played an important part in their lives.[133] In the course of this study, I will apply a narratological approach that takes seriously into account the

---

133. The degree to which early Christians and the Greco-Roman world at large were literate is debated, so is the notion of how 'literacy' is to be understood. For a discussion, see, e.g., Harry Y. Gamble, *Books and Readers in the Early Church: A History of Early Christian Texts* (London: Yale University Press, 1995), pp. 1–41; William V. Harris, *Ancient Literacy* (Cambridge, MA: Harvard University Press, 1989); and William D. Shiell, *Reading Acts: The Lector and the Early Christian Audience* (BIS, 70; Leiden: Brill, 2004), pp. 1–33.

author's theological hermeneutics of the Old Testament in order to show the significant role the stories rehearsed or alluded to in the letter play in helping the audience understand their trying situation and shape the appropriate response.

In order to achieve this, in Chapter 2, I will lay out the methodology that will guide this study. I will explain why a narratological approach to the study of 1 Peter is useful, and will define the terminologies that are crucial to our endeavour. I will demonstrate that 1 Peter has a narrative substructure – a fabula that forms the lens through which the author encourages his audience to interpret their own experience of sufferings. The fabula that is operating in the narrative substructure of the epistle comprises four elements: election, suffering, steadfastness, and vindication. Further, I will discuss the author's theological hermeneutic of the Old Testament. Finally, I will highlight some of the contributions of social-scientific criticism to Petrine studies and its relationship to the present study. In the remaining chapters, I will use the elements of the fabula to demonstrate how the narrative substructure is at work in the epistle, how the author's theological hermeneutics of the Old Testament shapes his message to the audience, and the significance of his theological hermeneutics for the way the author expects the audience to respond to trials. The narrative substructure is made up of the 'fabula' and the 'story'. The 'text' is the surface level structure available to the reader. Therefore, I will devote the major part of the study, chapters 3–6, to show how the fabula is at work in 1 Peter. In Chapter 7, I will demonstrate the ways in which the different elements interact in the 'story'. I will deal with the 'text' throughout as it is what allows us access to the narrative substructure.

In Chapter 3, I will examine the first element of the fabula: election. For the author of 1 Peter, the nature and purpose of God's election of the audience are in many ways analogous to what God worked out in the life of Israel as a nation, and for Jesus. I will discuss briefly the concept of election in the Old Testament, and then I will focus on the election language and imagery in 1 Peter. I will demonstrate that a narrative substructure is at work in the concept of election in that the author appropriates the concept of election in terms that are reminiscent of the Old Testament language of God's choice of Israel, and the language of the 'Elect One' from *1 Enoch* and applies that language and its reality to Jesus and the audience.

In Chapter 4, I will focus on the second element of the fabula: suffering. There, I will demonstrate how Israel's own sufferings are part of the overall background of 1 Peter's message. I will discuss how the author's description of his audience comprises a paradox which in itself affects the way the audience views the difficult circumstances they face. Further, I will show the significance of the author's rhetoric as it relates to the ways in which he urges the audience to understand their trials in light of Christ's own sufferings.

In Chapter 5, I will treat the third element of the fabula: faithful response, which consists of steadfastness, doing good, and subordination. I will examine the text of 1 Peter to show the author's understanding of 'faithful response'. I will then demonstrate how the narrative substructure is at work in the epistle by highlighting the analogy between the author's language of faithful response to suffering in the Old Testament and other Jewish literature's treatment of this concept. It is also reminiscent of Jesus' steadfastness in suffering which the author of 1 Peter sets up as the paradigm for the audience's response to hardships.

In Chapter 6, I will attend to the fourth and final element of the fabula: vindication. I will look at how the concept is treated in the Old Testament and examine the text of 1 Peter in order to show the affinities between the two. I will demonstrate the connection between steadfastness and vindication, and show how the author's language regarding God's vindication of his audience is expressed in ways that are analogous to God's vindication of the righteous as recorded in the Scriptures of Israel, and reminiscent of God's vindication of Jesus.

In Chapter 7, I will discuss the other level of the narrative substructure: story. It is at this level that the different elements of the fabula are arranged by the author as an expression of his theological hermeneutic. I will highlight and offer a brief critique of Green's and Boring's contributions/approaches vis-à-vis how the author of 1 Peter manipulates events at the story level. Then, I will turn to some examples which demonstrate the author's use of these elements to narrate the story of the audience. Finally, I will provide an overview of the entire discussion, highlight the main contributions of this book to scholarship on 1 Peter, and offer some avenues for further research and discussion on the subject.

Chapter 2

METHODOLOGY

2.1. Introduction

The survey conducted in the previous chapter revealed that, whereas 1 Peter is no longer in obscurity, scholarship on 1 Peter has much ground to cover, and views on how the content and form of the epistle are to be understood continue to evolve. There are at least two things that most, if not all, scholars agree on: (1) the author of 1 Peter makes extensive use of Scripture and (2) the epistle has a strong christological undercurrent. The methodology that I propose for the present study is one that takes these two aspects into serious consideration. I propose that a narratological method can contribute much to our understanding of 1 Peter's message by offering fresh ways to approach the study of the epistle. A narratological approach pays close attention to the author's theological hermeneutic of the Old Testament which is at the core of the christological appropriation of the story of Israel attested in the epistle.

In this chapter, I will first deal with what a narratological approach to 1 Peter entails. I will explain why a narratological approach to 1 Peter is warranted, and define the terms pertinent to this enterprise. Then, I will explain my understanding of 'theological hermeneutics' and discuss the significance of the author's own theological hermeneutic of the Old Testament for the present study. Finally, I will highlight some of the contributions of social-scientific criticism to the present study and potential constraints a narrow social-scientific reading of 1 Peter poses for theological hermeneutics.

2.2. A narratological approach to 1 Peter

Several methodological approaches have been applied to the study of 1 Peter in recent years, including Schutter's literary, Pearson's tradition-historical, and Bechtler's social-scientific analyses. Although these approaches have contributed to our understanding of the message of 1 Peter, I will demonstrate that scholarship on 1 Peter has much to gain from narrative analysis as well.

Narrative studies of 1 Peter are still in what we might call an infancy state. Eugene Boring uses some of the work done in the Pauline epistles as a springboard to draft the narrative world of 1 Peter.[1] In 2004, J. Ramsey Michaels acknowledged the presence of narrative within 1 Peter. He suggests, 'While not a narrative in the strict sense, 1 Peter could be thought of as Peter's passion narrative in the sense that it purports to give the author's testimony to the "sufferings of Christ"'.[2] More recently, J. de Waal Dryden, in his monograph *Theology and Ethics in 1 Peter*, draws on the notions of symbolic universe, developed by Peter Berger, and narrative substructure, proposed by Richard Hays, to argue for the presence of a narrative world and narrative substructure in 1 Peter.[3] Similarly, Joel Green has offered a scheme of the narrative of 1 Peter and demonstrated how the author's instruction is set within and determined by a temporal map.[4] While making a case for narrative theology in an epistle, Green suggests, '1 and 2 Peter are self-evidently epistolary; they do not tell a story. Nevertheless, even these books participate in a narrative – or better, they manipulate the grand story of God's engagement with the world and his people for theological purposes'.[5] Although it is true that letters are primarily non-narrative texts, it is also true that letters may and often do contain a narrative substructure wherein events and materials that are essentially narrative in nature are alluded to and become pertinent to understanding the message conveyed in the letter.[6] This is true of 1 Peter in that the text contains many allusions, quotations, and references to events and experiences from the Old Testament and the life of Jesus that, the author urges, are similar to those of 1 Peter's audience. These events that the author draws from constitute the narrative substructure of the epistle, which serves, then, as a lens through which the audience reads and understands the epistle's message. It could also be said that 1 Peter's message is the lens through which the narrative is constructed. In a sense, there is a mutual influence exerted by Scripture on 1 Peter's message because God's actions on behalf of his people as narrated in Scripture is formative to the author and his message. Similarly, the message of 1 Peter, once constructed, exerts some influence on Scripture as it invites a kind of reading/understanding of the narrative which the audience is being invited to participate in.[7] The main contribution of this chapter will be to

---

1.   Boring, *1 Peter*, pp. 183–207. Boring claims to be the first person to embark on such an endeavour in Petrine scholarship.

2.   Michaels, 'St. Peter's Passion'.

3.   Dryden, *Theology and Ethics in 1 Peter*, pp. 64–89.

4.   Green, 'Narrating the Gospel'.

5.   Green, 'Narrating the Gospel', p. 266.

6.   Richard Hays makes a similar argument in relation to the Pauline epistles (*The Faith of Jesus Christ: An Investigation of the Narrative Substructure of Galatians 3:1-4:11* [Chico, CA: Scholars Press, 1983]). Though the language may be similar, the method I propose for the study of 1 Peter is different from what Hays advanced for the Pauline epistles.

7.   See, Fitzmyer, 'The Use of Explicit OT Quotations', p. 22. In discussing the way the Old Testament was appropriated at Qumran and by New Testament writers Joseph A. Fitzmyer explains, 'usually it is a new situation which determines the use of the Old Testament text; a situation is found in the Old Testament which is analogous to the new one and the two are linked together by the common element in such way that the old one sheds light and meaning on the new and invests it with a deeper significance'.

provide a methodology that allows one to see how a narrative substructure operates within the primarily non-narrative text of 1 Peter to generate meaning.

Most of the methods and approaches to the study of biblical narrative relate to portions of the Bible that are essentially narrative in character. Accordingly, the application of narratological methods to non-narrative texts may seem counterintuitive.[8] Why use a narratological approach in the study of an epistle like 1 Peter? In what follows, I will demonstrate that a narratological approach is warranted on two counts: (1) its potential to contribute to the development of biblical scholarship in general, and Petrine studies in particular; and (2) the centrality of narrative to human experience.

There have appeared several narratological studies of the Pauline epistles which have gone a long way toward making a case for the narratological study of epistles, and to provide an *entrée* into the narrative aspects or functions of epistles.[9] For example, in 1983, Richard Hays published *The Faith of Jesus Christ*, in which he investigates the narrative substructure of Gal. 3.1–4.1 and proposes that a sacred story, a narrative structure, is central to Paul's theology. He argues that Paul does not simply retell the story, but alludes to it constantly in order to draw out implications for shaping the beliefs and practices of his infant churches. Hays is convinced that it is possible to 'identify Paul's allusions to his story of Jesus Christ, to discern some features of its narrative "shape", and to examine the way in which this story operates as a constraint governing the logic of Paul's argumentation'.[10] This story 'provides the foundational substructure upon which Paul's argumentation is constructed'.[11] Hays explains that some interpreters of Paul before him have acknowledged the presence of allusions to a gospel story of some sort in Paul's letters, though only a few used the term 'story' to describe what they have recognized.[12] Although Hays does not seek to deny or minimize the importance of a non-narrative element in Paul, he suggests that a gospel story is foundational to Paul's theological discourse. In this way, he has paved the way for the discussion of the presence of and relationship between narrative elements in non-narrative texts in Pauline scholarship.

---

8.   For the sake of clarity and consistency, this study will use the term 'narratology' to refer to the method(s) applied in the study of narrative. See the section on Definitions, below.

9.   E.g., Stephen Fowl, *The Story of Christ in the Ethics of Paul* (Sheffield: JSOT Press, 1990); Katherine Grieb, *The Story of Romans: A Narrative Defense of God's Righteousness* (Louisville: Westminster, 2002); Hays, *The Faith of Jesus Christ*; Petersen, *Rediscovering Paul*; Witherington, *Paul's Narrative Thought World*; N. T. Wright, *The New Testament and the People of God* (Minneapolis: Fortress, 1992). For a critical assessment, see Bruce W. Longenecker, (ed.), *Narrative Dynamics in Paul: A Critical Assessment* (Louisville: Westminster, 2002).

10.   Hays, *The Faith of Jesus Christ*, p. 6.

11.   Hays, *The Faith of Jesus Christ*, p. 7.

12.   Hays, *The Faith of Jesus Christ*, pp. 37–83.

In 1985, Norman Petersen, in an early endeavour to unite literary criticism and sociology, brought the literary notion of 'narrative world' to bear on notions of interpretation and understanding of Paul's writings, particularly Philemon. He explains the difference between a *contextual history* generally associated with the time of writing and a *referential history* that has to do with the narrative world of the text.[13] He suggests that, whereas in letters contextual history and referential history are one and the same, for the historian contextual history is a primary source while the narrative world is secondary.[14] Petersen starts with the premise that letters have stories and argues that it is from these stories that the narrative worlds of both the letters and their stories are constructed.[15]

Ben Witherington's *Paul's Narrative Thought World* appeared in 1994. There, he argues that in reading Paul, one discovers narratives about Christ, about Paul himself, about Israel, about the origins of the Christian community, and about the world outside the community of faith.[16] Witherington goes so far as to argue that all of Paul's ideas and arguments are ultimately grounded in a story that finds its source, in part, in the Hebrew Scriptures, and in oral traditions that derive from reflections on the latter.

More recently, in *Narrative Dynamics in Paul*, Bruce Longenecker spearheads a project in which a group of Pauline scholars seeks to assess the merits and demerits of the narratological approach to Paul.[17] The project uses the five narrative components that James Dunn has identified in Paul's discourse as the structure for the study, namely, God and creation, Israel, Jesus, Paul, and Christian communities.[18] The scholars focused on Romans and Galatians in an attempt to answer the following questions:

1. Do Galatians and Romans share a basic, identifiable, coherent story of 'X'? If so, how does this story impact on other stories in those texts? Which stories does it affect most prominently? Does it do so in a similar fashion in both texts?
2. If both Galatians and Romans do not share an identifiable story of 'X', are there distinct stories of 'X' in Galatians and Romans? If so, to what is the difference attributable? How do those stories impact on other stories in each text? Do they show similar characteristics in this regard?
3. What is the potential of the narrative approach to Paul?[19]

---

13.   Petersen, *Rediscovering Paul*, p. 7.
14.   Petersen, *Rediscovering Paul*, p. 17.
15.   Petersen, *Rediscovering Paul*, p. 43.
16.   Witherington, *Paul's Narrative Thought World*, p. 2.
17.   See Longenecker, 'Narrative Interest in the Study of Paul', in Longenecker (ed.), *Narrative Dynamics*, pp. 11–16.
18.   James D. G. Dunn, *The Theology of Paul the Apostle* (Edinburgh: T&T Clark, 1998), pp. 17–18.
19.   Longenecker, 'Narrative Interest in the Study of Paul', p. 14.

This last question is the most important for this book since a similar question can be asked of this present endeavour; namely, 'What is the potential of the narratological approach to 1 Peter?' As a whole both the proponents of the narrative approach and their respondents seem to acknowledge the benefits of a narratological approach to the study of the Pauline epistles.[20] However, many questions are raised and suggestions put forward regarding the methodological challenges of such an endeavour. Much of the discussion revolves around (1) whether one can find a coherent grand story or stories within Paul;[21] (2) the need for methodological clarification and for a refined narratological approach;[22] and (3) the suitability of a narratological approach to Paul, and to epistolary studies in general.[23] Though our focus is on 1 Peter, this present study hopes to contribute in laying out the kind of methodological clarification and refined narratological approach that would alleviate the concerns of some of these scholars.

As to the suitability of a narratological approach to Paul, most of the scholars involved in this project would agree with Campbell that 'the correct answer to such concerns is "right use" and not "abandonment"'.[24] The most dismissive of a narratological approach is Francis Watson. He claims that Paul is not a storyteller and that the notion of story is absent from Paul's gospel.[25] Watson argues further that even the insertion of Paul's gospel into a scriptural metanarrative would not cause it to become part of a story.[26] Watson does admit that there is a narrative substructure to Pauline theology, namely, 'the scriptural narratives relating to Israel's history with God';[27] however, Paul only reinterprets those narratives, he does not retell the scriptural stories. Watson is of the opinion that a narratological approach has very little to add to the understanding already gained by other approaches to Paul's theology.

Watson's claim about the inadequacy of a narratological approach to benefit Pauline studies is valid only to the extent that some of the participants of this project could have pushed further some of the methodological issues

20. One exception to this is Francis Watson, on whom see below.

21. See Edward Adams, 'Paul's Story of God and Creation', in Longenecker (ed.), *Narrative Dynamics*, pp. 19–43; James D. G. Dunn, 'The Narrative Approach to Paul: Whose Story', in Longenecker (ed.), *Narrative Dynamics*, pp. 217–30; Morna D. Hooker, '"Heirs of Abraham": The Gentiles' Role in Israel's Story', in Longenecker (ed.), *Narrative Dynamics*, pp. 85–96.

22. See R. Barry Matlock, 'The Arrow and the Web', in Longenecker (ed.), *Narrative Dynamics*, pp. 44–57.

23. Douglas A. Campbell, 'The Story of Jesus in Romans and Galatians', in Longenecker (ed.), *Narrative Dynamics*, pp. 97–124.

24. Campbell, 'The Story of Jesus in Romans and Galatians', p. 98.

25. Francis Watson, 'Is There a Story in These Texts?' in Longenecker (ed.), *Narrative Dynamics*, pp. 231–9. However, Watson argues elsewhere that Paul's own theology is oriented toward narrative (*Paul and the Hermeneutics of Faith* [New York: T&T Clark, 2004]).

26. Watson, 'Is There a Story in These Texts?', p. 239.

27. Watson, 'Is There a Story in These Texts?', p. 232.

they were dealing with in order to bring out interpretive fruit. For example, more could have been done in this project to define terms so that there were a certain level of understanding of and consensus about how a given term related to narrative study was being used. Paradoxically, Campbell champions 'right use' while, in the same breath, resolving to 'sit loosely on any notion of definition'.[28] In fact, attending to matters of definition is crucial to 'right use'. This is all the more important as the lack of clarity and consistency regarding what is meant by 'story' and 'narrative' and how these terms are used are perhaps at the root of much misunderstanding in the appropriation of narratology to the study of the Pauline letters, as well as the basis of most opposition against this enterprise. For this reason, Watson overstates his case. For fear that Paul would be transformed without remainder into a 'storyteller', Watson takes the other extreme in claiming that the term 'storyteller' should not be attributed to Paul, and that his gospel is non-narratable. However, in his article, 'Is Paul's Gospel Narratable?' Richard Hays rightly shows that one cannot affirm that Paul's theology is grounded in narrative while at the same time denying the intertexual character of Paul's discourse.[29] Hays recognizes that the lack of definitional clarity is at the root of the disagreement on how to assess 'narrative' in Paul.[30] He expresses his agreement with Watson that Paul is not a 'storyteller'. Hays himself prefers to think of Paul as an 'interpreter of stories' because Paul normally alludes, summarizes, or reflects upon the stories of Israel and Jesus. Paul rarely retells Old Testament stories explicitly, but his references to these stories seek to place salvation history at the heart of Israel's Scripture.[31]

Hays' agreement with Watson on this point is potentially confusing, based on the argument that Hays puts forward in his article. Although it is clear that Paul's letters differ from the four Gospels, as Watson suggests,[32] the claim that Paul is simply not a 'storyteller' is too broad and simply unwarranted. For example, it is evident that Paul is retelling the story of his life to his audience in Gal. 1.11–2.21; to that extent one can argue that Paul does tell and rehearse stories and, then, that he is a 'storyteller'. Hays could have pushed his argument further as Watson's argument is based on a narrow understanding of 'storyteller', as Hays himself has shown. However, Hays aptly shows the inadequacies of Watson's claims and puts forward some of the benefits of a narrative reading of Paul by showing that Watson's claim is beside the point.[33] In addition, Hays shows that one cannot affirm that Paul draws on scriptural narratives and, at the same time, deny the

28.   Campbell, 'The Story of Jesus in Romans and Galatians', p. 99. Andrew T. Lincoln also speaks of employing the category of 'story' loosely ('The Stories of Predecessors and Inheritors in Galatians and Romans', in Longenecker (ed.), *Narrative Dynamics*, p. 197).
29.   Richard B. Hays, 'Is Paul's Gospel Narratable?', *JSNT* 27 (2004), pp. 217–39.
30.   Hays, 'Is Paul's Gospel Narratable?', p. 221.
31.   Hays, 'Is Paul's Gospel Narratable?', p. 334.
32.   Watson, 'Is There a Story in These Texts?', p. 232.
33.   Hays, 'Is Paul's Gospel Narratable?', p. 236.

interconnectedness between those narratives and Paul's gospel.[34] Finally, Hays shows that Watson's claim arises from an erroneous understanding of 'narrative' and a dichotomy that seeks to build a divide between human events that are 'narratable' and divine events that are beyond the scope of human storytelling.[35]

In sum, although there are legitimate concerns raised regarding what a narratological approach to the study of epistles should look like, this call for methodological clarification has itself left much to be desired. The essayists gathered together by Longenecker and Hays' own critical response encourage the view that biblical scholarship can benefit from studying epistles from a narratological perspective.

Further, a narratological approach to the study of 1 Peter is warranted because of the centrality of narrative to human experience.[36] Narrative plays an important role in identity formation.[37] Stephen Cornell explains the extent to which narrative plays a significant part in creating ethnic identity.[38] In situations of breakdown, people tend to turn to narrative in order to create a sense of order, a sense that things make sense after all.[39] Members of the group intentionally or unintentionally claim a certain narrative as their story. This process involves:

- selection – choosing events from unlimited amounts of past, anticipated or imagined experience a limited number of happenings that constitute the episodic components of the narrative;
- plotting – linking these events together in causal, sequential, associational, or other ways, and linking the group in question to those events, and assigning roles; and
- interpretation – making claims about what the events and plot signify, and the degree to which that particular plot and its constituent events define the group as subjects.[40]

This process is at work in the way the author of 1 Peter crafts his message, and among his audience as they interpret their experience in light of the

34. Hays, 'Is Paul's Gospel Narratable?', p. 237.

35. Hays, 'Is Paul's Gospel Narratable?', pp. 237–8.

36. Michael Cook, *Christology as a Narrative Quest* (Collegeville, MN: Liturgical, 1997), p. 19.

37. See Peter Brooks, 'The Law as Narrative and Rhetoric', in Peter Brooks and Paul Gewirtz (eds), *Law's Stories: Narrative and Rhetoric in the Law* (New Haven: Yale University Press, 1996), pp. 14–23; see also Kay Young and Jeffrey Shaver, 'The Neurology of Narrative', *Substance* 30 (2001), pp. 72–84.

38. Stephen Cornell, 'That's the Story of Our Life', in Paul Spickard and Jeffrey Burroughs (eds), *We Are a People: Narrative and Multiplicity in Constructing Ethnic Identity* (Philadelphia: Temple University Press, 2000), pp. 41–53.

39. Cornell, 'That's the Story of Our Life', p. 45. See also, Jerome Bruner, *Acts of Meaning* (Cambridge, MA: Harvard University Press, 1990), pp. 39–43.

40. Cornell, 'That's the Story of Our Life', p. 43.

author's exhortations. First Peter is interwoven with stories of God's actions on behalf of Israel and Jesus. The audience lived in a hostile environment, and faced challenges that affected their daily existence. The exhortation, 'Beloved, do not be surprised at the fiery ordeal that is taking place among you to test you, as though something strange were happening to you' (4.12), fits this context and, therefore, highlights the importance of exploring the narrative substructure of this letter which calls for a narrative method of inquiry.

2.3. Definitions

Several narrative theories and methods are championed today, so it is not surprising that we find in biblical studies several approaches to narrative criticism.[41] Wallace Martin observes, 'There is no single theory of the subject acceptable to a majority of those who have addressed it, and the unresolved differences among the critics cannot be either easily adjudicated or cavalierly dismissed'. [42]

The scope of this study does not allow me to account for all of these different approaches. Though there is something to be gained in variety, this book will not be concerned with insights that can be gained from an array of approaches championed in the field of narratology.[43] Instead, I will use Mieke Bal's three-layered distinction of narrative laid out in her book *Narratology* as the springboard to formulate an approach I want to propose for the study of 1 Peter. I will not appropriate Bal's approach in its entirety, nor will I attempt a thoroughgoing evaluation of it. I will refer to other scholars' works only insofar as they are able to contribute to the development of the method by way of interaction with Bal's treatment.

41.   James Resseguie, *Narrative Criticism of the New Testament: An Introduction* (Grand Rapids: Baker, 2005), pp. 17–40.

42.   Wallace Martin, *Recent Theories of Narrative* (London: Cornell University Press, 1986), p. 30. He explains further 'Modern theories of narrative fall into three groups, depending on whether they treat narrative as a sequence of events, a discourse produced by a narrator, or a verbal artifact that is organized and endowed with meaning by its readers' (pp. 81–129 [82]).

43.   I use the term narratology to refer to the narrative theories used by narrative critics, and narrative criticism to refer to that form of narratology that has been applied more specifically to biblical narratives. The phrase 'narrative criticism' is not used outside the field of biblical criticism. See Resseguie, *Narrative Criticism of the New Testament*, p. 18. David Rhoads used the term 'narrative criticism' in 'Narrative Criticism and the Gospel of Mark', *JAAR* 50 (1982), pp. 411–34; and Mark A. Powell laid the groundwork of what constitutes 'narrative criticism' in his book, *What Is Narrative Criticism?* (Minneapolis: Fortress, 1990). Mieke Bal defines narratology as the theory of narratives, narrative texts, images, spectacles, and events, that tell a story, yet warns against defining the narrative corpus as consisting 'of all narrative texts and only those texts which are narrative' (*Narratology: Introduction to the Theory of Narrative* [2nd edn; Toronto: University of Toronto Press, 1997], p. 3).

Bal rightly points out that narratology need not be privileged as an approach to texts that are traditionally classified as narrative.[44] Because theories of narrative take into account several media – film, drama, music, and painting, as well as the printed page – elements of narratology cannot be appropriated wholesale into the domain of narrative criticism. Therefore, my discussion will focus primarily on the elements that are relevant to this study. In the process these elements will be appropriated in a way that will help me establish a method that will allow us to read 1 Peter as a non-narrative text that within which operates a narrative substructure.

Why have I chosen to work with Bal? Although many approaches to narratology employ a twofold distinction reminiscent of Seymour Chatman's work on 'story' and 'discourse',[45] Bal's theory of narrative rests on the three-layered distinction of text, story, and fabula in which (1) the *narrative text* is a text in which an agent relates ('tells') a story in a particular medium, such as language, imagery, sound, buildings, or a combination thereof; (2) *story* is a fabula that is presented in a certain manner; and (3) *fabula* is a series of logically and chronologically related events that are caused or experienced by actors.[46]

Bal is not the only person to promote a three-layered distinction, nor is she the first person to use the term *fabula*. The early Russian formalists used the terms *fabula/sjuzhet*, where *fabula* referred to the pre-literary materials, and *sjuzhet* referred to the narrative as told or written. Those terms, rendered in French as *fable* and *sujet*, respectively, have affinities with *histoire* and *discours* as used by French structuralists, or 'story' and 'discourse' as used by Chatman.[47] Bal's use of the term *fabula* is different both in regard to the structure wherein the term is used and with respect to its definition.

Bal's three-layered distinction presents an essential difference from other scholars who understand narrative by means of a twofold division. For Chatman, for example, the narrative has two main elements: 'story', which is the content of the narrative expression; and 'discourse', which is the form of that expression.[48] H. Porter Abbott makes a similar distinction, identifying story as the event or sequence of events *per se*, and narrative as the way the story is told, the narrative discourse.[49] He suggests that the difference between story and narrative discourse rests primarily on the difference between two kinds of time, and two kinds of order. The reading of a non-narrative text involves only one kind of time – the time it takes to read the

44. Mieke Bal, *On Meaning-Making: Essays in Semiotics* (Sonoma, CA: Polebridge, 1994), p. 25.

45. Seymour Chatman, *Story and Discourse: Narrative Structure in Fiction and Film* (Ithaca, NY: Cornell University Press, 1989).

46. Bal, *Narratology*, p. 5.

47. Martin, *Recent Theories*, p. 108; Michael Toolan, *Narrative: A Critical Linguistic Introduction* (London: Routledge, 1988), p. 9.

48. Chatman, *Story and Discourse*, p. 23.

49. H. Porter Abbott, *The Cambridge Introduction to Narrative* (Cambridge: Cambridge University Press, 2002), p. 13.

text. When reading a narrative text, however, one is aware of two kinds of time: (1) the time of reading and the order in which things are read, and (2) the time the events in the story are supposed to take and the order in which they are supposed to occur.[50] This is a helpful observation, yet those who work with a twofold distinction tend to deploy the term 'narrative' loosely and interchangeably with 'story' or 'discourse'. Abbott seems to be aware of this difficulty but chooses to use the terms 'story' and 'narrative discourse' and claims that 'the distinction of "story" and "narrative discourse" is now widely used enough in the discussion of narrative to serve us well'.[51]

A three-layered understanding allows one to take into account the narrative substructure of certain non-narrative texts and attest to their complexity. As such, *contra* Abbott, the reading of those non-narrative texts does involve more than one kind of time. There is the time it takes to read the (non-narrative) text, as Abbott suggested, but in the reading process, one is aware of the time(s) of the story or stories that constitute the narrative substructure of the text in question. For example, when one reads,

> Blessed be God, the Father of our Lord and Savior Jesus Christ, who according to his great loving kindness has caused us to be born again for a living hope through the resurrection of Jesus Christ from the dead ...' (1 Pet. 1.3)[52]

one is not only aware of the few seconds it takes to read the phrase, but also (1) of the time involved in the regeneration process alluded to, (2) of the time when the regeneration in question takes place (becomes effective) in the life of a given individual, and (3) of the time that relates to the resurrection event.[53] Therefore, a three-layered approach allows the reader to attest for the complexity of the text in a way that is not readily available in a two-layered approach.[54]

Gérard Genette recognizes the confusion that a twofold distinction can create. Although he once held to a twofold distinction in his theory of narrative, he subsequently observed that story and discourse, or narrative and discourse, are not relevant unless one adds a third term, 'narrating', to create the triad: story, narrative, and narrating.[55] Genette's proposition is a much-needed improvement in discussion about and definitions of narrative. He rightly understands the benefit of discussing 'narrative' in terms of a

50.   Abbott, *Introduction to Narrative*, pp. 14–15.
51.   Abbott, *Introduction to Narrative*, p. 15.
52.   Unless otherwise noted, biblical citations in English, except for 1 Peter, are from NRSV. Where the MT and/or the LXX numbering differ from the NRSV, the MT and/or the LXX text numbering will be bracketed and noted accordingly. English citations from 1 Peter are author's translation. Citations from the Greek text of 1 Peter are from the UBS 4th edn.
53.   Even if 1–3 were to be merged into one kind of time, namely, story-time, the point still stands. Because each of these elements (1–3) can be a story in itself one can argue for the presence of multiple kinds of time in that single phrase.
54.   Bal, *Narratology*, pp. 78–114.
55.   Gérard Genette, *Nouveau Discours du Récit* (Paris: Seuil, 1983), pp. 10–11.

triad, even though the terms he uses are already loaded with meaning, and can potentially create confusion for students of narrative.

Another essential difference between Bal's three-layered definition and a twofold definition is that the former allows one to pay closer attention to the content of a given text. In the twofold distinction, discussion of the form tends to take precedence over the substance of the narrative.[56] Narrative critics tend to focus on recreating the narrative world of the author and his or her audience. This consists of identifying the main events in the narrative and placing them on a timeline.[57] However, there are instances when the ordering of events in a story and their sequence in the narrative world is so complex that it is not possible or relevant to reconstruct the chronological sequence of the narrative world.[58] As I will explain below, there are several ways events can be arranged. In making a distinction between 'fabula', 'story', and 'text', Bal's method allows one to take a closer look at 'events' and attest for the complexity of their ordering, their arrangement into, and/ or their relationship within a story. This approach allows one to gain insight in a way that is not readily accessible from a twofold approach where 'events' are treated primarily in terms of how they are arranged chronologically in the 'story'.[59]

Finally, Bal's terminological distinctives allow an entrée into the narratological study of texts that are not essentially narrative in nature. The categories 'fabula', 'story', and 'text' are such that in cases where the surface layer is not primarily narrative in nature, as in the case of 1 Peter, it is possible to acknowledge the 'non-narrative text' and inquire how the sub-layers (the narrative substructure) operate as meaning-making tools in the text.

One of the concerns raised by scholars who question the use of a narrative approach in an epistle is its ability to yield new insight.[60] I will demonstrate that this approach does in fact help to broaden our understanding of 1 Peter's message. In what follows, I will provide definitions of the terms that are important to this endeavour for the sake of clarity and to establish a common vocabulary for this study. Definitions are needed that will allow us to keep in mind that letters are primarily non-narrative texts that may contain a narrative substructure, based on events and stories that are rehearsed therein. Because the definition of text depends on that of story, which in turns depends on that of fabula, it may prove helpful to provide

56. See Chatman, *Story and Discourse*, p. 25.

57. See Boring, *1 Peter*, pp. 183–207; Green, 'Narrating the Gospel', pp. 262–77.

58. Bal, *Narratology*, p. 81.

59. Chatman, *Story and Discourse*, pp. 41–95. See also, Toolan, *Narrative*, pp. 10–11; Shlomith Rimmon-Kenan, *Narrative Fiction: Contemporary Poetics* (London: Routledge, 1983). Chatman does recognize the fact that the way 'events' are arranged in a 'story' does not necessarily have to be chronological. The point here is not that the twofold approach is not aware of these issues, but that Bal's treatment is more effective as a way of addressing them.

60. E.g., Watson, 'Is There a Story in These Texts?', p. 231.

the definitions starting from the most basic unit of the narrative, the fabula. In addition, this three-layered distinction is primarily theoretical in nature since the text layer is the only layer that is directly accessible to the reader.[61] Finally, though these layers do not necessarily 'exist' independently of each other, it is possible to study them separately.[62]

2.3.1. *Fabula*

Bal describes *fabula* as 'a series of logically and chronologically related events that are caused or experienced by actors'.[63] It consists of the material or content – events, actors, time, and location – that is worked into a story according to certain rules; namely, the 'logic of events', which Bal defines as 'a course of events that is experienced by the reader as natural and in accordance with some form of understanding of the world'.[64] The 'fabula' allows the reader to experience the world described in the narrative. Fabula serves as the basic structure of the narrative. In this present study the notion of fabula will be closely connected with the concept of 'intertextuality'.[65] Consequently, when reference is made to 'fabula' in 1 Peter, I refer to those events and experiences that the author draws from the Old Testament, the Jesus-story, and perhaps other canonical and non-canonical sources, arranges in a certain way to create meaning, and uses as the basis for his exhortations.[66] Similarly, 1 Peter's audience will make sense of their life experiences based on their understanding of the world that the fabula projects or creates.

One cannot fully understand 'fabula' without an adequate understanding of 'events' and how they operate. An 'event' is 'the transition from one state to another state, caused or experienced by actors'.[67] An event comprises a process that carries with it the idea of development, succession, alteration, and interrelation among the elements. Bal discusses three criteria that must be met for an element to be considered an event:

- change – there must be change from one state to another, from one location to another, or from one time to another;

61. Bal, *Narratology*, pp. 5–7.
62. Bal, *Narratology*, p. 6.
63. Bal, *Narratology*, p. 5.
64. Bal, *Narratology*, p. 177.
65. Joel B. Green also embraces the notion of 'fabula' but describes it differently. For Green the 'fabula' is the story behind the story. It is what guides the narrating of a story. Green approaches narrative as a two-level structure, 'story' and 'narrative', with the 'fabula' serving as an underlying thread and overall theme that links biblical stories together (*Seized by Truth* [Nashville: Abingdon, 2007], p. 62). In essence, Green is operating with a three-level structure – fabula, story, and narrative – without acknowledging this fact.
66. See Schutter, *Hermeneutic and Composition*, pp. 19–84 for a discussion on the possible sources that Peter may have drawn from in crafting his letter.
67. Bal, *Narratology*, pp. 182–9.

- choice – an event should open a choice between two possibilities, realize the choice, or reveal the result of the choice; and
- confrontation – at least two actors or groups of actors are confronted by each other.[68]

Whether one takes these criteria together or individually, deciding what constitutes an event can be a confusing, and daunting task. Ideally, no event should stand alone. It is only in a series that events become meaningful for the further development of the fabula. As a specific grouping of a series of events, the fabula as a whole also constitutes a process.[69] Within a given fabula, there are several ways events can be grouped in order to convey meaning:

- events can be placed against a time lapse;
- events can be grouped on the basis of the identity of the actors involved;
- events can be classified on the basis of the nature of the confrontation; and
- events can be grouped based on the locations at which the events occur.[70]

Given this complexity, one can find several fabulae that function as meaning-making tools at that basic level of the narrative substructure of the letter based on how the author selects and arranges events.

2.3.2. Story

The next level of the narrative substructure of the letter consists of the 'story'. Bal describes 'story' as the manner in which a fabula is presented. She suggests that the material that constitutes the story is not different from what is presented in the fabula and the text, but that material is approached from a different angle.[71] Bal's description is helpful in so far as it shows the interrelatedness between 'fabula' and 'story'. The ways the elements of 'fabula' and that of the 'story' relate to each other are of utmost importance. It is an everyday occurrence that two people who witness a similar set of events tell their own version of these events, thereby telling two different stories. Two people of identical background may face the same situations in life but interpret and react to them differently – thereby, living different lives, having different stories. Further, two people of different background who witness a similar set of events, interpret, and react to them in a similar manner may speak of 'the story of our lives'. Therefore, 'the point of

68. Bal, *Narratology*, pp. 182–5.
69. Bal, *Narratology*, pp. 182–8. See also Toolan, *Narrative*, p. 6.
70. Bal, *Narratology*, p. 194.
71. Bal, *Narratology*, p. 78.

view from which the elements of the fabula are being presented is often of decisive importance for the meaning the reader will assign to the fabula'.[72] The way in which the elements of the 'fabula' are ordered becomes a 'story' which may or may not resemble the experiences of the reader. To the extent that narrative plays a role in identity and character formation, this is also important because the meaning the reader assigns to the 'fabula' will affect the meaning she assigns to the story of her life. 'Story' as an ordering of events can, then, be understood as relating to the way events are ordered in the 'fabula', and the way events occur in the life of an individual, events that an actor experiences.

Since 'story' and 'fabula', as the constitutive elements of the narrative substructure of the epistle, contribute to meaning making, then a narratological approach, which allows us to take into account the way these two concepts relate to each other, is warranted in order to understand adequately the message of the letter, the message of the 'text'.

2.3.3. Text

According to Bal, a 'text' is where a narrative agent tells a story.[73] The 'text' is the finished product. If at the 'story' level the focus was on the actors and the characters, at the level of the 'text' the focus is on the narrator. Although at the 'story' level the focus was on the way the events were arranged, at the level of the 'text' the focus is on the actual telling of these events; this is the level where the story is narrated. The 'text' is the surface level; this is what is readily available to the reader. Though the text of 1 Peter is primarily non-narrative, it is nonetheless permeated with narrative texts; thus it comprises a narrative substructure. Old Testament quotations, allusions, and references abound in the midst of the exhortations which the author offers to his audience. He is a narrator for his mentioning of a particular 'event' or 'events', in the process of his writing, evokes the corresponding 'story' in its entirety.[74] In this instance, 'intertextuality' takes the form of, or gives place to 'embeddedness'. Bal explains the several relationships that exist between texts and the notion of embeddedness.[75] Embedded texts can be both narrative and non-narrative: confidences, descriptions, reflections, self-reflection.[76] As such one can view 1 Peter both as a non-narrative text with

---

72. Bal, *Narratology*, p. 79.
73. Bal, *Narratology*, p. 16.
74. Similarly, in discussing the narrative world of 1 Peter, Dryden explains, 'The author only refers to key elements of the story of salvation to evoke an entire narrative worldview that is familiar to both author and readers. This sort of shorthand description of key elements is typical of paraenesis where only a few key points need to be reviewed and emphasized ... The author's goal is to be relevant not comprehensive' (*Theology and Ethics in 1 Peter*, p. 66).
75. Bal, *Narratology*, pp. 53–75.
76. Bal, *Narratology*, p. 60.

a narrative substructure, and a non-narrative text embedded in the larger narrative of God's action on behalf of his people that spans from creation to re-creation. Our approach to gaining more insight into the meaning of the message of 1 Peter involves keeping both of these perspectives in mind as we take a close look at those narratives that the author is rehearsing, analysing and comparing, and assessing how they relate to each other and contribute in shaping the message of 1 Peter.

The 'text' of 1 Peter is structured to help the readers know that their experience is not unique. The pattern of events that the audience experienced was similar, though not identical, to a pattern of events that occurred in the lives of Israel and Jesus. Through the use of the Old Testament and the life of Jesus, the author is able to demonstrate to his audience that not only do God's people face similar circumstances, but God's way of dealing with his people has not changed. The author's exhortations and the elements he uses as bases for giving them help his audience interpret the events in their lives through the same lens – a christological understanding of God's actions on behalf of Israel. Consequently, they would assign a common meaning to their experience which would in turn urge them to behave in a manner that is characteristic of the people of God. Ultimately, to the extent that the author of 1 Peter understands (and encourages the audience to do the same) the events that are happening in the life of the audience to follow a similar pattern to the life of Israel, Jesus, and other Old Testament figures, we can claim that the author is dealing with one main story: the story of God's action on behalf of his children. Understanding 1 Peter's message then involves the readers' allowing themselves to be drawn into the world to which the author is inviting them, and to write their own story into another story that is already unfolding in which God is the main actor.[77]

Having defined the terms that are most pertinent to this enterprise, I will now endeavour to identify elements of the narrative substructure in 1 Peter, and demonstrate how it operates. Because of the importance of the opening section of an epistle, it is the primary place to look for the presence of these elements.

2.4. *The letter opening as a summary statement*

There is general agreement that 1.1-2 comprises the letter's prescript, where the sender and recipients are identified, and a wish or prayer is offered on behalf of the recipients.[78] First Peter 1.3-12 opens with a eulogy directed

77. Dryden makes a similar argument regarding the function of the author's construction of a narrative worldview of God's action in the world in 1.3-12. For Dryden, the greater story within which the audience needs to understand how their lives fit is 'the story of God's "plan of salvation"' (*Theology and Ethics in 1 Peter*), pp. 39, 55–89 (66).

78. E.g., Troy W. Martin, *Metaphor and Composition in 1 Peter* (SBLDS, 131; Atlanta: Scholars Press, 1992), pp. 47–8; Schutter, *Hermeneutic and Composition*, p. 24; Thurén,

towards God and ends with the author's description of the angels' attitude toward the content of the things which form the content of the gospel.[79] That this pericope ends at v. 12 is also supported by the fact that an independent clause is introduced in v. 13, which is governed by the aorist imperative 'ἐλπίσατε'. Whereas the inferential conjunction 'διό' in v. 13 links the two sections syntactically – what the author is about to tell his audience is on the basis of how he describes them in 1.1-12 – there is evidence that διό also serves as a transitional marker.[80] This is the case even if one treats ἀναζωσάμενοι and νήφοντες as imperatival participles.[81] In addition, there is a noticeable change from the indicative mood (is) in 1.3-12 to the imperative mood (ought) from 1.13 onward as evidence for the boundaries of this pericope.[82] Some scholars treat 1.3-12 as part of the letter body;[83] others argue that vv. 3-12 together with vv. 1-2 form the opening section of the letter or the *exordium*.[84] Syntactically, 1 Pet. 1.3-12 constitutes one sentence-thought where the author addresses the situation of the audience.[85]

Most scholars agree that 1 Pet. 1.3-12 contains in a nutshell the essence of the author's entire message to his audience. Generally, the *exordium* serves to introduce the main goals of a discourse.[86] It follows that one should find in this pericope (1) the main elements that constitute the fabula that serves as skeleton for 1 Peter's narrative substructure, which provides a picture of

---

Rhetorical Strategy, pp. 84–8. For a discussion on epistolary structure see, John L. White, 'New Testament Epistolary Literature in the Framework of Ancient Epistolography', *ANRW* II, 25.2 (1984), pp. 1730–56 (1738–9); idem, *Light from Ancient Letters* (Philadelphia: Fortress, 1986), p. 186.

79.   Norbert Brox, (*Der erste Petrusbrief*, EKK, 21; Zürich, Benziger, 1993) e.g., claims that 1.3-9 and 1.10-12 are two independent units, (p. 68).

80.   E.g., Eph. 2.11. See Jack T. Sanders, 'The Transition from Opening Epistolary Thanksgiving to Body in the Letters of the Pauline Corpus', *JBL* 81 (1962), pp. 348–62.

81.   It can be argued that ἀναζωσάμενοι and νήφοντες are not true participial imperatives because they do not fit the exact pattern of such participles. A participial imperative normally stands in an independent clause, plays the role of a finite verb, is generally in the nominative case, and cannot be found in a periphrastic construction. Both ἀναζωσάμενοι and νήφοντες stand in an attendant circumstance position and are dependent on the main verb ἐλπίσατε. See Scot Snyder, 'Participles and Imperatives in 1 Peter: A Re-Examination in the Light of Recent Scholarly Trends', *FilNT* 8 (1995), pp. 187–98.

82.   Joel B. Green, *1 Peter* (THNTC; Grand Rapids: Eerdmans, 2007), p. 33.

83.   E.g., Brox, *Der erste Petrusbrief*, pp. 55–72; Jobes, *1 Peter*, pp. 56–7; Senior, *1 Peter*, p. 11.

84.   E.g., Thurén, *Rhetorical Strategy*, p. 90; idem; *Argument and Theology in 1 Peter: The Origin of Christian Paraenesis* (JSNTSup, 114; Sheffield: Sheffield Academic Press, 1995), pp. 88–105; Tite, *Compositional Transitions*, p. 92.

85.   So Goppelt, *1 Peter*, p. 79; Green, *1 Peter*, p. 22.

86.   Thurén, *Argument and Theology*, p. 91. Similarly, Kendall argues that 1.3-12 constitutes the first main division of the letter. There, 'the author's declarations concerning the nature of Christian existence serve as the foundation for the exhortations that comprise the bulk of the epistle (1.13 – 5.11)'. See, David W. Kendall, 'The Literary and Theological Function of 1 Pet 1:3-12', in Charles H. Talbert (ed.), *Perspectives on First Peter* (NABPRSS, 9; Macon, GA: Mercer University Press, 1986), pp. 104–6.

the author's understanding of the situation of his audience (vv. 3-9); and (2) the author's theological hermeneutic of the Old Testament, which provides us with an entrée into his theological thought (vv. 10-12).[87]

This twofold subdivision is a conceptual one. Green rightly shows that the concept of salvation permeates this pericope, and can serve both as an attestation to its unity and as a guide to how it can be subdivided.[88] The pericope is also held together thematically since (1) God is the main character whose lovingkindness is being celebrated in this pericope;[89] (2) everything that is done is for the benefit of the audience.[90] However, there seems to be a significant shift from the author's relating the life situations of the audience in vv. 3-9 (including, but not limited to, the audience's salvation) to his retelling of the prophets' attempt to understand the nature and outworking of that salvation (vv. 10-12). From a narratological perspective, the main subject of the sentence is understood as the main character of the event(s) in question.[91] Therefore, any character who participates directly with the main character in making the event(s) possible 'takes centre stage' with the

87. Schutter, *Hermeneutic and Composition*, pp. 100–9. I am indebted in part to Joel B. Green (e.g., 'Scripture and Theology: Uniting the Two So Long Divided', in Joel B. Green and Max Turner (eds), *Between Two Horizons: Spanning New Testament Studies & Systematic Theology* [Grand Rapids: Eerdmans, 2000], pp. 23–43; idem, *Seized by Truth*, pp. 27–102; idem, 'Living as Exiles: The Church in the Diaspora in 1 Peter', in Kent E. Brower and Andy Johnson (eds), *Holiness and Ecclesiology in the New Testament* [Grand Rapids: Eerdmans, 2007], pp. 311–25) for the terminologies and some of the ideas contained in the discussion about Peter's theological hermeneutic of the Old Testament which follows below.

88. Green, *1 Peter*, p. 22. Green addresses the importance of the 'salvation' theme and subdivides this pericope in three units.

89. 'ὁ θεὸς καὶ πατήρ' (1.3) functions as the main (not, the only) subject of the entire sentence (Martin, *Metaphor and Composition*, p. 52). The rest of the sentence is crafted with subordinate clauses that depend on the main clause 'Blessed be the God and Father of our Lord Jesus Christ …'. Further, in vv. 10-12, the author first presents the Spirit of Christ as working through the prophets, then goes on to talk about the work of the Holy Spirit in the proclamation of the gospel in the same context. The language suggests that the author of 1 Peter is identifying the Holy Spirit with Christ. In sum, both the work of the Spirit of Christ through the prophets, and the work of the Holy Spirit in the proclamation of the gospel are put in the context of what God himself has done on behalf of the audience. The passive, 'πνεύματι ἁγίῳ ἀποσταλέντι ἀπ' οὐρανοῦ' (1.12), is a divine passive that implies God as the agent, and the Holy Spirit as the instrument or means through which the proclamation was done. It should also be noted that although trinitarian theology postdates 1 Peter, there is evidence of the genesis (or anticipation) of the understanding of the triune God in the author's rhetoric (1.1-2).

90. The author of 1 Peter shows that even the trials ultimately may have a positive outcome (1.7).

91. Although 1 Peter was not acted out as a play, it is clear that as the letter was read (and re-read!) to the congregation, people would 'picture' things in their minds so as to 'see' what the author was talking about. That the letter contains so many metaphors attests to the fact that Peter was depending on his audience to use their minds to make sense of his message. See Bonnie Howe, *Because You Bear This Name: Conceptual Metaphor and The Moral Meaning of 1 Peter* (Leiden: Brill, 2000).

main character, although other characters are present. In 1 Pet. 1.3-9 the characters on the scene (at different junctures) are God, Jesus Christ, the author, and the audience. There, the focus is on life as a child of God that spans from new birth which is brought about by Jesus' resurrection (1.3) to the eschatological hope that is being realized in the now, and will be fully realized at the appearing of Jesus Christ (1.8-9). In 1 Pet. 1.10-12 new actors are introduced: the prophets. For a brief moment they become the focus, as the author describes not only the prophets' actions, but also the work of the Spirit of Christ through them on behalf of the readers.[92]

2.4.1. Identifying the fabula of 1 Peter

Identifying the fabula of 1 Peter has to do with finding the elements (events, experiences, actions) that are common to the stories that the author rehearses throughout the letter. The 'fabula' is the lens through which the audience is to read and understand its own situation. Whereas there may have been an aspect (or aspects) of the ordeal that the audience was experiencing that was peculiar to each member, each household, each congregation, or even each geographical region, as I will demonstrate, there was something that was fundamentally common to all – something with which everyone could identify.

An inquiry into the text of 1 Peter shall reveal four elements that constitute the 'fabula' of 1 Peter: (1) election/new birth, (2) sufferings/trials, (3) faithful response, and (4) vindication. These elements are events or concepts that the stories rehearsed in 1 Peter share to a greater or lesser extent, and experiences that the actors in these stories have witnessed (or hope to witness). Taken together, these events create the narrative substructure of the letter, through which the audience is able to make sense of the message the author tries to convey to them. I suggest that the author of 1 Peter forejoined these four elements in order to show that the stories of Israel, Jesus, and the audience share a common fabula. In this sense, the stories of Israel and Jesus are able to function effectively and normatively as bases for the admonitions, or examples with which the author substantiates his claims.

Scholars have put forward several proposals regarding what constitutes 1 Peter's controlling metaphor, theme, or concept. For example, Elliott proposes that 'the household of God' serves as the root metaphor and organizing ecclesial image in 1 Peter.[93] Feldmeier has argued that the controlling

---

92.   God serves as the agent (sometimes implied) in many instances where Peter uses the passive voice – 'τετηρημένην ἐν οὐρανοῖς εἰς ὑμᾶς' (1.4); 'τοὺς ἐν δυνάμει θεοῦ φρουρουμένους' (1.5); 'οἷς ἀπεκαλύφθη' (1.12); 'πνεύματι ἁγίῳ ἀποσταλέντι ἀπ' οὐρανοῦ' (1.12). Since the prepositional and dependant phrases in 1.10-12 are governed by the passive 'ἀπεκαλύφθη', it follows that the prophets, their search and activity, come into focus in the author's mind at that particular moment.

93.   Elliott, *Home*, pp. 165–266; idem, *1 Peter*, p. 113.

metaphor of the epistle is that of 'strangerhood'.[94] Troy Martin has claimed that the controlling metaphor of 1 Peter is that of 'diaspora'.[95] Richard proposes that the themes suffering/death and glory/right hand form the basic framework the author is working with.[96] Schutter argues that the author of 1 Peter uses the 'sufferings/glories' pattern as an organizing principle in the way he has read the Scriptures.[97] Bechtler follows Schutter and argues that the suffering-and-glory pattern function as part of the letter's response to the audience's suffering as the letter superimposes Christ's experience onto that of his followers.[98] Similarly, Pearson argues that the sufferings/glories pattern, which is dependent on the humiliation/vindication pattern found in Isa. 53, comprises the method and message of 1 Peter.[99] Whereas these are helpful categories, they fail to take into account the overall tenor of the author's theological/christological thought by focusing only on the suffering and glorification of Christ and their implications. The language the author of 1 Peter employs in rehearsing Jesus' experience suggests that he has in view not just the suffering and glory of Jesus Christ but a wider scheme or pattern. That pattern includes the concepts of election, suffering, faithful response, and vindication.

Achtemeier proposes that Israel is the controlling metaphor that the author uses to express his theology. He argues that the author identifies his audience with the reality of Israel as the chosen people of God in such a way that the audience assumes the role that Israel once played in its entirety.[100] On that basis, the inquiry into the author's identification of the audience with Israel should encompass the extent to which Israel's election and experience of strangeness in exile, Israel's suffering and subsequent vindication, and Israel's role in and mission to the world as designed by God bear upon the audience's understanding of their own situation and their interpretation of 1 Peter's message. The story of the vindication and glory of the rejected and suffering righteous has as its starting point (explicitly or implicitly) the election of the righteous. Vindication cannot be divorced from election.

In what follows, I will demonstrate that the four elements that constitute the fabula of 1 Peter can be found in the opening section of the letter, where the author rehearses the story of his audience.[101] In reading 1 Pet. 1.3-9, it is clear that the author is recalling certain events that occurred in the life of his audience and ordering them in a certain way for rhetorical effect. The themes

---

94.   Feldmeier, *Die Christen als Fremde*; idem, *The First Letter of Peter* (trans. Peter H. Davids; Waco, TX: Baylor University Press, 2008), pp. 13–17.

95.   Martin, *Metaphor and Composition*, p. 274.

96.   Richard, 'Functional Christology', pp. 121–39 (134).

97.   Schutter, *Hermeneutic and Compostion*, pp. 100–9.

98.   Bechtler, *Following in His Steps*, pp. 1, 182.

99.   Pearson, *Christological and Rhetorical Properties*, pp. 11, 43, 147–9.

100.   Achtemeier, 'Christology', pp. 140–54; idem, 'Newborn Babes', pp. 207–36; idem, 'Suffering Servant', pp. 176–88.

101.   Some of the themes (e.g., election) are already introduced in 1.1-2. See my discussion in subsequent chapters.

that are evidenced there are developed further in the rest of the epistle as the author exhorts his audience and writes their story into that of Israel and Jesus. Some of the events recalled are:[102]

- God gives new birth (to audience members) through the resurrection of Jesus Christ from the dead.
- New birth (wrought by God) provides audience members the right to an inheritance.
- Inheritance is being kept in heaven (by God) for the audience members.
- Audience is expecting Jesus' return.
- Jesus' return will bring the audience's hope and salvation to full realization.
- Audience is suffering while awaiting Jesus' return.
- Audience is rejoicing in the midst of suffering.

Further analysis will prove that these 'events' both include or imply change, choice, and/or confrontation. For example, there is a change brought about by the new birth in that it allows the person to take hold of 'a living hope', 'an inheritance' – something they did not have before, or a state they have not experienced before. The audience chooses to rejoice in the midst of suffering. Similarly, they choose to live in expectation of Jesus' future revelation. These events do relate to each other chronologically. However, as suggested above, the author's ordering is not so much chronologically determined as it is conceptually guided with salvation as the primary focus. In this pericope, the author of 1 Peter rehearses events that, taken together, constitute the story of God's act of regeneration carried out for the members of his audience with some of its implications for their lives. It is a story that focuses on the present and future realities that the audience faces. The past is only assumed.[103]

Whereas the ordering and telling of the events shape the story that the author rehearses, the events in themselves constitute the fabula, the basic structure of the story. At this level, one can identify four basic elements that constitute the fabula of the story of God's action on behalf of the audience. Because of the rhetorical and hermeneutical properties of this pericope, I will

102. It is not my intention to identify a comprehensive list of all the possible events that can be found in this pericope. The list provided is just a sample that serves as evidence for the claim that in 1.3-9 the author of 1 Peter is rehearsing certain aspects of the story of the audience's life.

103. Important here is the notion of kinds of time. For example, the resurrection of Jesus is both a past and present experience. On one level, it is past because the resurrection occurred at a time that precedes the redaction of 1 Peter, and because the new birth that it makes possible must have already taken place in the lives of those addressed. On another level, it is a present reality because of its effect which is experienced and actualized in the process of the new birth. On yet another level it transcends (human) time because the author of 1 Peter speaks of Christ as being chosen before the foundation of the world (1.18-21). As I will demonstrate later, Christ's election and the purpose for which he was elected are two related concepts.

demonstrate below that the elements of this fabula are similar to and can be found in the other stories that the author of 1 Peter rehearses in the letter. The elements of this fabula can be described as:

- *Election* (vv. 3-5), where God is the actor causing the event, which the author expresses in terms of 'new birth'. Jesus Christ's resurrection is the means by which the event is made possible; and the inheritance that will be bestowed and the salvation that will be revealed are the purpose or end result of the new birth. The author introduced this element earlier in vv. 1-2 when he addressed the audience as 'ἐκλεκτοῖς παρεπιδήμοις διασπορᾶς'.
- *Suffering/trials* (vv. 6-7), which is a present, short, and passing reality the audience is experiencing.
- *Faithful response* (vv. 6-7) which is summed up by the 'genuineness of your faith' and expressed through the metaphor of the gold being refined. The author of 1 Peter implies here what will be developed later in terms of faithful response. This metaphor mirrors the audience's experience of suffering and conveys the attitude that the audience has and should have in order to benefit reward and vindication. For the author, 'faithful response' entails steadfastness, doing good, and subordination, and constitutes the proper response to suffering (see further below, Chapter 5).
- *Vindication* (vv. 7-9) – i.e., praise, glory, and honour is the outcome of faithful response. The author describes this – praise, glory, and honour – both as something that the audience will get to experience and as something that is ultimately ascribed to God. While in 1.7 it is not clear who is/are the recipient(s) of the praise, glory, and honour that will be ascribed when Jesus Christ is revealed, in 2.12 it is clear that one of the possible outcomes of the Christian's good conduct is that those who malign them may glorify God one day. At this time also, the salvation hoped for will be realized; joy will be restored, and the inheritance will be received.

The relationships between these elements are evident. The *election* that brings about inclusion into God's family is at the root of the *suffering and trials* that have come upon the believers who are now encouraged to *respond faithfully* to the difficult situations they have faced. Their choice will bring glory to God, who rewards and *vindicates* those who live such lives.

The relationships between these elements are also complex. Whereas they can be put on a timeline, they cannot be strictly time-bound, since there is evidence of a certain overlap in the way they relate to each other. For example, for the author of 1 Peter, *election* is something that happens in the past, but has a lasting effect in the present and future. Further, one would be hard pressed to know exactly where on a timeline it should be placed.[104]

---

104. For example, even the biblical witness gives different accounts of the time when the election of Israel took place (see below, Chapter 3).

In addition, *faithful response* permeates the entire existence of the child of God; therefore, it would occupy the entire span of – or, at least, the majority of – the timeline.

These elements not only shape the story about the audience's situation rehearsed by the author in 1.3-9 but, as I will demonstrate in the remainder of the study, they are also common to the story of Israel and that of Jesus that the author rehearses in the epistle. These elements constitute the fabula of 1 Peter and form the lens through which the author encourages the audience to interpret its situation. Because God is the main actor in that story, I have named it, 'The fabula of God's actions on behalf of his people'.[105] That this fabula is located in the opening section implies, rhetorically, that it permeates the rest of the epistle and the narrative substructure thereof; that it does so and why this is theologically significant, sets the agenda for the chapters that follow.

Having established the presence of the elements of the fabula that shapes the stories which create the narrative substructure of the letter, I will now turn to the discussion of the author's theological hermeneutics of the Old Testament.

2.4.2. *1 Peter's theological hermeneutic of the Old Testament*

First Peter's theological hermeneutic of the Old Testament has to do with the author's understanding of the theological role the Old Testament plays in shaping the identity and behaviour of the audience, and in the formation and transformation of his audience, more specifically, as it relates to their response to suffering. It has been rightly argued that the author's understanding of and approach to the Old Testament is expressed in 1.10-12.[106] Schutter has termed this passage a 'hermeneutical key' to

105. There can be as many fabulae as there are elements that an author may draw from and ways in which the author chooses to relate these elements to each other. To inquire about all the possible fabulae that are present in the text, though fruitful, can become a daunting task, which takes one away from the main message or messages that the text conveys. See Daniel Patte, 'One Text: Several Structures', *Semeia* 18 (1980), pp. 3–22.

106. Much has been written regarding this passage and its importance for understanding 1 Peter. For a survey of the discussion, see, e.g., Schlosser, 'A.T. et Christologie', pp. 65–7; idem, 'La Résurrection de Jésus', pp. 441–56 (448); Achtemeier, 'Christology', pp. 140–57; idem, 'Suffering Servant', pp. 176–88; Samuel Bénétreau, 'Évangile et Prophétie: Un Texte Original (1 P 1,10-12) Peut-il Éclairer un Texte Difficile (2 P 1,16-21)?' *Bib* 8 (2005), pp. 174–91; Schutter, *Hermeneutic and Composition*, pp. 100–9; Thurén, *Argument and Theology*, pp. 101–4; Elliott, *1 Peter*, pp. 345–53; Jobes, *1 Peter*, pp. 97–106; Davids, *1 Peter*, pp. 60–5; Michaels, *1 Peter*, pp. 38–50. It is beyond the scope of this study to do an extensive critical engagement of every aspect of the discussion. My focus is on how the author's theological hermeneutics of the Old Testament is borne out in the passage and in light of the present study. As I have argued above, its strategic location in the opening section of the letter implies that the understanding conveyed therein permeates the entire epistle.

the epistle because it 'allows for convenient access to his use of the OT elsewhere in the letter'.[107] Further, Schutter has helpfully highlighted the ways in which the author's hermeneutic has affinities to the hermeneutical methods of '*pesher*-like exegesis' carried out at Qumran.[108] I propose that the author's theological hermeneutic of the Old Testament can be gathered, in addition, from the greeting section of the epistle (1.1-2) where an exodus motif is attested. As such, I will demonstrate that the author's theological hermeneutic of the Old Testament is also dependent on his understanding of God's actions on behalf of his people narrated in Scripture. In what follows, I will discuss the author's theological hermeneutic of the Old Testament by focusing (1) on the affinities between 1 Peter's hermeneutic and the *pesher* hermeneutic practised at Qumran and (2) on the narrative dynamics at work in the author's theological hermeneutic.

2.4.3. 1 Peter and 'pesher' hermeneutic

Schutter's work helpfully highlights the way in which 1.10-12 provides an entrée into how the author uses the Old Testament.[109] Several scholars have recognized and discussed the affinities between the hermeneutic present in 1 Peter and that which was at work at Qumran.[110] For example, Barnabas Lindars proposed that 'Qumran pesher exegesis, in which texts and textual traditions were chosen and even modified to fit the theological needs and historical situation of the community, provides a fruitful model for understanding the development of Old Testament exegesis within the primitive church'.[111] Further, Richard Longenecker affirmed that the author of 1 Peter expresses a distinctly pesher approach to Scripture.[112]

The author's approach to the Old Testament is characterized by a christological/theological reading of God's actions in and through the life of Israel.[113] The extent to which the author of 1 Peter uses the Old Testament in crafting his message attests to the way both he and his audience were immersed in Scripture. Further, the author's identification of his audience

---

107. Schutter, *Hermeneutic and Composition*, p. 109.

108. Schutter, *Hermeneutic and Composition*, pp. 109–23.

109. It should be noted that Schutter is not the first person to speak of the importance of the Old Testament as a background to 1 Peter, or to point out the central role of 1.10-12 in understanding the message of the epistle (cf., e.g., Schlosser, 'A.T. et Christologie', pp. 65–7). However, Schutter's work brings this section of the letter into particular focus.

110. E.g., Best, 'I Peter II: 4-10'; Elliott, *The Elect and the Holy*; Osborne, 'l'Utilisation de l'AT'; Goppelt, *1 Peter*; Richard Longenecker, *Biblical Exegesis in the Apostolic Period* (Grand Rapids: Eerdmans, 1975), pp. 200–4.

111. Barnabas Lindars, *New Testament Apologetic: The Doctrinal Significance of the Old Testament Quotations* (Philadelphia: Westminster, 1961), p. 169.

112. Longenecker, *Biblical Exegesis*, p. 200.

113. So also Bénétreau, 'Évangile et Prophétie', p. 178. Bénétreau agrees that 1.10-12 anticipates the author's use of the Old Testament in the epistle, and proposes that the author's reading of the Old Testament is 'strictly christological'.

with Israel is an indication of his concern that his audience embody the Old Testament. For the author of 1 Peter, the best way to shape the behaviour of his audience, the best way to form and transform them, is to encourage them to read their experiences through the lens of what God has done in Jesus and Israel.

Whereas 1 Peter's theological hermeneutics of the Old Testament is clearly stated in 1.10-12, that hermeneutic permeates the entire epistle. For example, we see a similar principle at work in 1.18-21. In both passages, the author has in view the salvation of the audience, Jesus' suffering and glories (following his resurrection, in v. 21), the reality of the past, and that of the present. In both cases, we find a seamless movement from the past to the present and vice versa. For the author of 1 Peter, Christ's life and work constitute a reality that transcends time. It is a reality that was present in the mind of God even before the world came into being. This is why the prophets had access to it and were able to get a glimpse of it.

The language of 1.10-12 implies both continuity and unity in the outworking of God's purpose for his children. The relative clause 'περὶ ἧς σωτηρίας' in v. 10 connects the two units (1.3-9 and 1.10-12), and serves to reaffirm the author's focus on the salvation of the audience, and consequently, the celebration of what God has accomplished on their behalf. The author goes on to speak of the activity of the prophets on behalf of the audience.[114] The past and the present are held together by the activity of God in and through the lives of his people, specifically, by the activities of the Holy Spirit through the prophets of old and the evangelists of now.[115]

A similar approach to Scripture was taken by the commentators at Qumran. Maurya P. Morgan explains,

> The Qumran commentators believed (1) that the words of the books that they were interpreting were full of mysteries revealed by God [1QpHab 7.4]; (2) that the mysteries hidden in the biblical books referred to history, specifically to the history of their community [1QpHab 2.9-10]; (3) that the interpretation of these mysteries was revealed to the Teacher of Righteousness and to selected interpreters who followed him [1QpHab 7.4-5].[116]

114. Some scholars argue that 'prophets' here refers to Christian prophets (e.g., Michaels, *1 Peter*, p. 41; Selwyn, *First Epistle of St. Peter*, pp. 134, 259–68; Duane Warden, 'The Prophets of 1 Peter 1:10-12', *ResQ* 31 [1989], pp. 1–12). Others propose that the prophets refer to Old Testament prophets (e.g., Elliott, *1 Peter*, p. 345; Bo Reicke, *The Epistles of James, Peter, and Jude* [AB, 37; New York: Doubleday, 1980], p. 80; Senior, *1 Peter*, p. 33). For an assessment, see Schutter, *Hermeneutic and Composition*, pp. 103–4. The author's language seems to refer to Old Testament prophets although he did not find it necessary to specify. His focus lies elsewhere, namely, in the prophets' activity and the Spirit of Christ's work through them.

115. See, Green, *1 Peter*, p. 31. Bénétreau lists the elements of continuity that the author's language implies: one divine plan, one God who speaks, one Spirit who works, the same Word ('Évangile et Prophétie', p. 176).

116. Maurya P. Morgan, *Pesharim: Qumran Interpretations of Biblical Books* (CBQMS, 8; Washington: The Catholic Biblical Association of America, 1979), p. 229. See further, William H. Brownlee, 'Biblical Interpretation among the Sectaries of the Dead

The commentators at Qumran approached the biblical text as if it were written to them as if it were speaking to their situation. In other words, their community was the embodiment of the true Israel. Timothy H. Lim suggests, 'They saw themselves as participants in the unfolding revelation of God, even when the end-time had been delayed. They adapted biblical laws, and supplemented them where there were perceived gaps, and found correspondences between events and figures of biblical prophecies'.[117] Joseph A. Fitzmyer inquired about the way in which the commentators at Qumran made use of the Old Testament and proposed that there were four classes of Old Testament quotations in Qumran literature:

- The Literal or Historical class, in which the Old Testament text is quoted in the same sense in which it was intended by the original authors;
- The class of Modernization, in which the Old Testament text, which originally had a reference to some event in the contemporary scene at the time it was written, was applied to some new event in the history of the Qumran sect;
- The class of Accommodation, in which the Old Testament text was wrested from its original context, modified or deliberately changed by the new writer in order to adapt it to a new situation or purpose; and
- The Eschatological class, in which the Old Testament quotation expressed a promise or threat about something to be accomplished in the *eschaton* and which the Qumran writer cited as something still to be accomplished in the new *eschaton* of which he wrote.[118]

Fitzmyer surveys the New Testament and the literature produced at Qumran and offers evidence for the categories described. He argues that the *pesharim* provide the best example for the case of modernization of the Old Testament text and uses 1QpHab 7.1-5 and 7.7-8 as cases in point. He goes on and discusses how the 'modernization' of the Old Testament text is evidenced in the New Testament.[119]

More recently, George J. Brooke has offered an outline of the principal aspects of biblical interpretation at Qumran. There, he focuses on 'the types of biblical interpretation found in the compositions most clearly to be associated with the Qumran community or the wider movement of which it was a part, and the theological issues that lie behind discerning the variety

Sea Scrolls', *BA* 14 (1951), pp. 54–76; Frederick F. Bruce, *Biblical Exegesis in the Qumran Texts* (Grand Rapids: Eerdmans, 1959); Longenecker, *Biblical Exegesis*, pp. 39–45; Daniel Patte, *Early Jewish Hermeneutic in Palestine* (SBLDS, 22; Missoula: Scholars, 1975), pp. 303–8. George J. Brooke, 'Biblical Interpretation at Qumran', in James H. Charlesworth (ed.), *The Bible and the Dead Sea Scrolls* (Vol. 1; Waco, TX: Baylor University Press, 2006), pp. 287–319.

117. Timothy H. Lim, *Holy Scriptures in the Qumran Commentaries and Pauline Letters* (Oxford: Clarendon, 1997), p. 120.

118. Fitzmyer, 'The Use of Explicit OT Quotations', pp. 16–17.

119. Fitzmyer, 'The Use of Explicit OT Quotations', pp. 23–33.

of types of interpretation taking place in the Qumran texts'.[120] He surveys previous research on the subject and notes the advances that have taken place in the field, then discusses five types of biblical interpretation that can be found in the Qumran texts: legal, exhortatory, narrative, poetic, and prophetic.[121] In discussing the prophetic type of interpretation, Brooke explains that one should no longer restrict prophetic interpretation to the commentaries that contain continuous or thematic interpretation of the texts of some of the prophetic books and the Psalms.[122] Pesherite exegesis is also at work in unfulfilled promises, blessings and curses as well.[123]

There is a sense in which the prophetic exegesis at Qumran contained a narrative component because the prophecies, promises and blessings were uttered within the larger context of the community's experiences with God and with each other. In fact, one finds traces of *pesher* exegesis at work within the *Commentary on Genesis A*, which is primarily concerned with narrative interpretation (4Q252 4.3-7).[124] It is possible that the narrative process inherent to the identity formation of a community was at work at Qumran as they appropriated and interpreted Scripture in order to make sense of their own situation.[125] Through the appropriation of Scripture they sought to locate themselves in the unfolding story of God's revelation, a story that finds its eschatological realization within their community.

The understanding of the nature and function of *pesher* within the tradition of the use and interpretation of the Old Testament at Qumran is evolving. Yet the points of contact between the hermeneutic of 1 Peter and the *pesher* hermeneutic practised at Qumran remain. In a sense, an improved understanding of the types of interpretations carried out at Qumran provides impetus for further comparative study of the relationship between 1 Peter and the Qumran texts. The intersection of *pesher* and narrative modes of interpretation present at Qumran can also be seen in 1 Peter due to the author's theological hermeneutic of the Old Testament which contains some narrative dynamics in addition to its *pesher*-like characteristic. One of the characteristic features of *pesher* exegesis is the conviction there exists a unity and continuity in the way God deals with his children. In 1 Peter, that unity and continuity is evident in the author's articulation of his understanding of the story of salvation which includes the elements of Christ's election,

120. Brooke, 'Biblical Interpretation at Qumran', p. 287.

121. Brooke, 'Biblical Interpretation at Qumran', pp. 304–13.

122. Brooke explains that one of the advances made in scholarship has to do with a better understanding of *pesher* as a genre and the fact that there exists a spectrum of pesherite exegesis as opposed to just the two forms: continuous and thematic exegesis (pp. 291–2). See also, Jean Carmignac, 'Le Document de Qumran sur Melkisédeq', *RevQ* 7 (1969–71), pp. 360–1; Geza Vermès, 'Bible Interpretation at Qumran', *ErIsr* 20 (1989), pp. 184–91.

123. Brooke, 'Biblical Interpretation at Qumran', p. 312.

124. Brooke, 'Biblical Interpretation at Qumran', pp. 307–8, 312–13.

125. Cornell, 'That's the Story of Our Life', p. 43. See above, 'A narratological approach to 1 Peter'.

sufferings, faithful response, and vindication by God.[126] In so doing, Christ's life becomes the lens through which Israel's own salvation is interpreted.[127] Therefore, understanding the message of 1 Peter requires one to take into account Israel's election, their suffering, faithful response, and vindication by God. Further, this also opens the way for us to talk about the narrative dynamics of 1 Peter's theological hermeneutic.

2.4.4. *Narrative dynamics in 1 Peter's theological hermeneutic*

I propose that the theological hermeneutic of the Old Testament in 1 Peter contains some narrative dynamics evidenced by the presence of exodus motifs in the epistle's prescript (1.1-2). There one finds some of the same characteristics of the author's hermeneutic as evidenced in 1.10-12. The language of the author conveys a unity and continuity between the experiences of the audience and that of Israel by applying to the audience images and concepts that are reminiscent of the Exodus. The rehearsal of exodus motifs at this crucial juncture in the epistle implies that the author has in mind the events surrounding God's deliverance of Israel from Egyptian bondage as he reflects on the experience and identity of the audience. Therefore, the theological hermeneutic of the Old Testament warrants a narratological approach to the study of the epistle because at the core of this hermeneutic is the author's appropriation of stories from the life of Israel, interpreted through the life of Jesus, for the sake of his audience.

The epistle opens with an exodus motif located in the author's description of the audience as 'ἐκλεκτοῖς παρεπιδήμοις διασπορᾶς...' (1.1). This is a compounded image that recalls, in one breath, Israel's own experience of election, wilderness wanderings, and exile to Babylon, and the suffering attached to them.[128] The author of 1 Peter, thus, identifies his audience with Israel so that they can make sense of their own suffering, put it in perspective, and fill it with new meaning.[129] Goppelt has pointed out the similarities between the author's identification of the audience with Israel in the exodus motifs present in the prescript (1.1-2) and the self-understanding of the Essene community expressed in the *Damascus Document*.[130]

> As God ordained for them by the hand of the Prophet Ezekiel, saying, *The Priests, the Levites, and the sons of Zadok who kept the charge of my sanctuary when the children of Israel strayed from me, they shall offer me fat and blood* (Ezek. Xliv, 15).

126. Bénétreau ('Évangile et Prophétie', p. 176) and Achtemeier ('Christology', pp. 144–7) make a similar argument using the 'sufferings/glories' pattern. I have demonstrated that the author of 1 Peter is working with a wider scheme.
127. See, Green, 'Living as Exiles', p. 316.
128. See also, Deterding, 'Exodus Motifs'; Feldmeier, *The First Letter of Peter*, p. 24.
129. Green, 'Living as Exiles', p. 321.
130. Goppelt, *1 Peter*, pp. 68–72.

> The *Priests* are the converts of Israel who departed from the land of Judah, and the (the *Levites* are) those who joined them. The *sons of Zadok* are the elect of Israel, the men called by name who shall stand at the end of days. Behold the exact list of their names according to their generations, and the time they lived, and the number of their trials, and the years of their sojourn, and the exact list of their deeds … (CD 3.21 – 4.6).[131]

In this text one finds the concepts of election, residence in a foreign land, and the trials associated with exilic existence.[132] One finds an analogous principle at work in 1 Peter in regard to the language used to identify those who belong to the community and the household of God respectively.

Another exodus motif is signalled by the phrase, 'because of the obedience and the sprinkling of the blood of Jesus Christ' (1.2),[133] which contains an allusion to the establishment of the covenant between God and the children of Israel in Exod. 24.7-8. It refers to the obedience Israel pledged to God and to the blood that was poured out on the congregation of Israel as a ratification of the covenant between them and YHWH. To this motif, the author of 1 Peter joins the notions of Christ's obedience and sufferings and locates the audience's relationship with God on the basis of Jesus' obedience and suffering. This creates a rapprochement between the obedience that Israel once pledged to God, the obedience that Jesus has displayed to God,

---

131. Translation taken from Geza Vermes, *The Complete Dead Sea Scrolls in English* (rev. edn; London: Penguin, 2004), pp. 131–2. Emphasis original.

132. So also, Goppelt, *1 Peter*, p. 69.

133. In the clause 'εἰς ὑπακοὴν καὶ ῥαντισμὸν αἵματος Ἰησοῦ Χριστοῦ' (the preposition εἰς can denote, e.g., cause ('because of') or purpose ('for', 'in order that'). Achtemeier, e.g., treats εἰς as introducing a purpose clause (*1 Peter*, pp. 79, 86–9). Consequently, 'ὑπακοήν' is taken as referring to the audience, with 'Ἰησοῦ Χριστοῦ' understood as an objective genitive on the one hand; and a subjective genitive, on the other hand, vis-à-vis its relationship with 'ῥαντισμὸν αἵματος'. Achtemeier avoids the double usage of the genitive by suggesting that 'ὑπακοήν' has no relationship to the genitive. The LSG treats 'ὑπακοήν' as referring to the audience exclusively ('*afin qu'ils deviennent obeissants, et qu'ils participent à l'aspersion du sang de Jesus-Christ*' – 'that they may become obedient, and participate (share) in the sprinkling of the blood of Jesus Christ' [author's translation]). Peter uses εἰς to indicate purpose elsewhere (e.g., 1.3, 5; 2.5, 21; 3.7; 4.2, 7). However, the context of the sentence seems to favour a causal understanding of εἰς with both accusatives used in parallel to the preposition, and Ἰησοῦ Χριστοῦ having a single usage, a subjective genitive that complements both accusatives. This treatment of εἰς makes more sense syntactically and theologically, as demonstrated by Francis H. Agnew ('1 Pet 1:2 An Alternate Translation', *CBQ* 45 [1983], pp. 68–73). Understood this way, the clause highlights Jesus' role in the audience's election, sets up the author's treatment of Jesus' obedience to God and his sufferings as an example for the audience to follow, and prepares for his treatment of the obedience of the audience (e.g., 1.14, 22). This rendering implies a narrative understanding and highlights the author's theological hermeneutic and the audience's identification with Israel and with Jesus. On causal εἰς see further, e.g., J. R. Mantey, 'Unusual Meanings for Prepositions in the Greek New Testament', *Expositor* 25 (1923), pp. 453–60; idem, 'The Causal Use of *eis* in the New Testament', *JBL* 70 (1951), pp. 45–8; idem, 'On Causal *eis* Again', *JBL* 70 (1951), pp. 309–11. For a discussion see R. Marcus, 'The Elusive Causal *eis*', *JBL* 71 (1952), pp. 43–4. See also, Feldmeier, *The First Letter of Peter*, pp. 57–60.

and the obedience that the author encourages the audience to display (1.14, 22). As such, the narrative dynamics at work in the author's appropriation of events in the life of Israel are integral to his theological hermeneutic of the Old Testament. In a sense, the author's theological hermeneutic, explicitly stated in 1.10-12, is already at work in the letter's prescript (1.1-2). In light of this, a narratological approach is useful because it contributes to our understanding of the author's theological hermeneutic.

Two more things need to be noted in favour of a narratological approach to 1 Peter. First, a narratological approach is warranted by virtue of the nature of the Old Testament, which is overwhelmingly narrative, and the author's dependence on the Old Testament. The text of 1 Peter falls in the epistolary genre. However, the author's overwhelming use of the text of the Old Testament creates a narrative substructure in the epistle, which generates the need for a narratological approach in order to extricate the relationship between the message of the letter and the Old Testament texts that are found therein. This is true also of the prophetic and poetic texts that the author draws from because, in their original contexts, these texts participate in the larger narrative of God's unfolding revelation to and his continued dealings with Israel.

Second, the theological realities that the author is dealing with are embedded in the stories and events narrated in the Old Testament. By paying attention to the narrative dynamics that are at work within the epistle's substructure, on the one hand, and between the epistle and the Old Testament stories that are rehearsed in the letter, on the other hand, one is able to gain a greater awareness of the theological affirmations with which the author operates. We come to know God through the stories that are told recounting his deeds through and on behalf of humanity. Gerard Loughlin rightly notes: '[Christian] faith is sustained through and as commitment to a story ... The story is simply told, and faith is a certain way of telling it, a way of living and embodying it, a habit of the heart'.[134] This is analogous to what one finds taking place in the life of the patriarchs according to Genesis. Their faith in God was expressed in the way they told God's story to their descendants (e.g., Gen. 48.15-16, 21; 50.24-25). Further, subsequent generations appropriated that story in order to make sense of their situation. For example, according to Deuteronomy, the children of Israel were to identify themselves with the patriarchs' pilgrimage (Deut. 26.5-6). The people in exile in Babylon appropriated the story of the Exodus in order to convey their trust in God's ability to deliver them. Even the message of God's deliverance heralded through the prophet Isaiah is given in the language that is reminiscent of the Exodus (Isa. 43.1-21). In the case of 1 Peter, the author's theological hermeneutic of the Old Testament is a continuation of the practice of rehearsing and embodying God's story and is in and of itself an expression of faith and trust in God, and an invitation to

134. Gerard Loughlin, *Telling God's Story: Bible, Church and Narrative Theology* (Cambridge: Cambridge University Press, 1996), p. 33.

his audience to do the same. Given that 'story' is used to convey knowledge of God, a narrative methodology can be put at the service of the theological hermeneutic enterprise.

2.5. 1 Peter and social-scientific criticism

Thus far, I have offered and discussed several reasons why a narratological approach to the study of 1 Peter is warranted: (1) because of its potential to contribute to the development of biblical scholarship in general and Petrine studies in particular and (2) because of the centrality of narrative to human experience. I have also argued that, (3) although the other methodological approaches applied to 1 Peter have contributed to our understanding of the author's message, much can be gained from other methodological considerations not yet fully explored. More specifically, I have proposed that, (4) because the author of 1 Peter is engaged in theological hermeneutics, reading 1 Peter invites our interest to theological hermeneutics. And, one way of engaging in theological hermeneutics is to read 1 Peter narratively. In what follows I will discuss briefly the relationship between the approach I am proposing and social-scientific criticism by highlighting some of the contributions of social-scientific criticism to the advancement of Petrine scholarship and to this present study in particular.

David Horrell rightly points out, 'The social sciences surely offer tools for exploring the social context within which the "theology" of the New Testament was forged, and resources for investigating the ways in which early Christian writings formed and shaped patterns of interaction within congregations'.[135] Social-scientific criticism of 1 Peter contributes to the present conversation because it offers helpful insights into the nature of the social-political realities 1 Peter's audience was facing and their relationships to and implications for understanding the message of 1 Peter. It helps us to understand the particulars of what is at stake in the situation faced by the audience and, therefore, how the author might address those particulars. One major contribution of the social-scientific approach to 1 Peter that is helpful to this study is the discussion on the Petrine *Haustafel*. [136]

---

135. David G. Horrell, 'Social-Scientific Interpretation of the New Testament: Retrospect and Prospect', in David G. Horrell (ed.), *Social-Scientific Approaches to New Testament Interpretation* (London: T&T Clark, 1999), pp. 3–27 (12).

136. The uniqueness of 1 Peter's household code is noted in David L. Balch, 'Household Codes', in David E. Aune (ed.), *Greco-Roman Literature and the New Testament* (SBLRBS, 21; Atlanta: Scholars, 1988), pp. 25–50; idem, *Let Wives Be Submissive: The Domestic Code in 1 Peter* (SBLMS, 26; Chico, CA: Scholars Press, 1981); idem, 'Hellenization/ Acculturation in 1 Peter', in Charles H. Talbert (ed.), *Perspectives on First Peter* (NABPRSS, 9; Macon, GA: Mercer University Press, 1986), p. 81; Betsy J. Bauman-Martin, 'Women on the Edge: New Perspectives on Women in the Petrine *Haustafel*', *JBL* 123 (2004), pp. 253–79 (259–69); James E. Crouch, *The Origin and Intention of the Colossian Haustafel* (FRLANT, 109; Göttingen: Vandenhoeck & Ruprecht, 1972), p. 12; deSilva, *Honor,*

The conversation about the source, nature, and function of the *Haustafel* in 1 Peter has been ongoing for several decades. The debate between Balch and Elliott has set the tone for the discussion.[137] Balch and Elliott shared similar views regarding the origin and nature of the Petrine *Haustafel* but reached opposing conclusions about the relationship of 1 Peter's audience regarding the world that surrounded them. Both authors locate the origin of the Petrine *Haustafel* in discussions of household management in Aristotle and other Greek philosophers, and Roman figures like Cicero, Seneca and Augustus Cesar.[138] However, Elliott argues that the author's purpose in writing is to encourage his audience to resist the pressures of the surrounding culture, while Balch concludes that the author was urging his audience to assimilate.[139] 'Resistance' and 'assimilation' constitute two major positions scholars have had to choose from in this conversation.[140] Several variations and alternatives to these positions have been offered, with Talbert proposing that the solution is not 'either-or', but 'both-and';[141] and Lauri Thurén agreeing with Talbert, but suggesting there were two types of audiences – one urged to assimilate, and the other asked to resist the surrounding culture.[142] In 1992, Reinhard Feldmeier argued that the answer was neither resistance nor assimilation, but a call to live 'in the middle' while holding the two in tension.[143] The primary issue is the 'proper relationship with and behavior toward a hostile outside world and along with this the Christian commission in this world, that of "doing good"'.[144] Following Feldmeier, Miroslav Volf

Patronage, Kinship, and Purity, pp. 199–239; Marie-Louise Lamau, *Des Chrétiens dans le Monde: Communautés Pétriniennes au 1er Siècle* (LD, 134; Paris: Cerf, 1988), pp. 198–99; Clarice J. Martin, 'The *Haustafeln* (Household Codes) in African American Biblical Interpretation: "Free Slaves" and "Subordinate Women"', in Cain Hope Felder (ed.), *Stony the Road We Trod: African American Biblical Interpretation* (Minneapolis: Fortress, 1991), pp. 206–31; Martin, *Metaphor and Composition*, pp. 124–34.

137. Elliott, *Home*; Balch, *Wives*.

138. Balch, 'Hellenization/Acculturation', in Talbert (ed.), *Perspectives on First Peter*, p. 81.

139. John H. Elliott, '1 Peter, Its Situation and Strategy: A Discussion with David Balch', in Charles H. Talbert (ed.), *Perspectives on First Peter* (NABPRSS, 9; Macon, GA: Mercer University Press, 1986), pp. 61–78; Balch, 'Hellenization/Acculturation', in Talbert (ed.), *Perspectives on First Peter*, pp. 79–101.

140. For example, Elliott, '1 Peter, Its Situation and Strategy'; Bauman-Martin, 'Women on the Edge'; and Achtemeier, 'Newborn Babes', pp. 207–36, have argued for resistance; while Balch, 'Hellenization/Acculturation', and Eduard Schweizer, 'Traditional Ethical Patterns in the Pauline and Post-Pauline Letters and their Development Lists of Vices and House-Tables', in *Text and Interpretation: Studies in New Testament Presented to Matthew Black* (eds E. Best and R. Wilson; Cambridge: Cambridge University Press, 1979), pp. 195–209, have argued for assimilation.

141. Talbert, 'Once Again: The Plan of 1 Peter', in Talbert (ed.), *Perspectives on First Peter*, pp. 146–8.

142. Thurén, *Rhetorical Strategy*.

143. Feldmeier, *Die Christen als Fremde*; idem, *The First Letter of Peter*, pp. 150–92.

144. Feldmeier, *The First Letter of Peter*, p. 156.

rightly suggests that 1 Peter transcends 'these unhelpful alternatives'.[145] Since there is evidence of both difference and acculturation in 1 Peter, the question one needs to be asking is 'how were the processes combined?'.[146] He suggests that the addressees are not necessarily outsiders who need to figure out how to become insiders or maintain their status and identity as outsiders. They are 'insiders who have diverted from their culture by being born again. They are by definition those who are not what they used to be, those who do not live like they used to live'.[147] The focus on a combination of difference and acculturation reveals that a member of the Petrine community would be 'free from the pressure either simply to reject or simply affirm the surrounding culture'.[148] Volf thinks that 1 Peter's audience had to decide in a piecemeal fashion when it was appropriate to reject or affirm the surrounding culture. For Volf the decision to either affirm or reject the surrounding culture is not dictated from the outside, by the surrounding culture, but from the inside.

In his 1998 monograph, Bechtler proposes that the author of 1 Peter was urging his audience to embrace a liminal existence. Subsequent to their conversion to Christianity, 'they occupy a place that is neither fully within society nor completely removed from it'.[149] Most recently, Torrey Seland echoes Volf's argument and states that 'acculturation and assimilation have not been used in a way that is helpful for understanding the social strategies in 1 Peter'.[150] Seland discusses the inadequacies of Balch's and Elliott's approaches and argues that since Christianity was the primary culture for the author of 1 Peter, his intention was to promote acculturation into Christianity and not assimilation to the Greco-Roman society.[151] For Seland, 1 Peter's audience was largely made up of first-generation Christians of primarily Greco-Roman origin who were 'in dire need of further acculturation/assimilation into the Christian social world, i.e., its ideology and symbols'.[152]

In sum the discussion on the Petrine *Haustafel* has highlighted the importance of the religious, social, and political dynamics at work within the community of believers the epistle is addressed to, on the one hand, and between the community and the outside world, on the other hand. Yet, one weakness is inherent to that approach. Throughout the letter the author uses imagery that is rooted in the Old Testament to identify his audience, to describe the situation in which they live, and to express the course of action they should take (e.g., elect sojourners [1.1, cf. Gen. 23.4; Deut. 26.5]; a

145. Miroslav Volf, 'Soft Difference: Theological Reflections on the Relation between Church and Culture in 1 Peter', *ExAud* 10 (1994), pp. 15–30.

146. Volf, 'Soft Difference', p. 22.

147. Volf, 'Soft Difference', pp. 18–19. Feldmeier, *The First Letter of Peter*, pp. 124–30.

148. Volf, 'Soft Difference', p. 22.

149. Bechtler, *Following in His Steps*, p. 118.

150. Torrey Seland, *Strangers in the Light: Philonic Perspectives on Christian Identity in 1 Peter* (BIS, 76; Leiden: Brill, 2005), p. 148.

151. Seland, *Strangers in the Light*, pp. 148–70.

152. Seland, *Strangers in the Light*, p. 168.

cluster of images are found in 2.9, namely, elect race [Isa. 43.20]; royal priesthood, holy nation [Exod. 19.6]; a people acquired by God [Exod. 19.5; Isa. 43.21]).[153] Scholars recognize the prominence of the Old Testament in the author's thought,[154] but the premise that the Petrine *Haustafel* originates from Greco-Roman culture has caused much of the discussion to focus almost exclusively on the implications of 1 Peter's message in terms of Greco-Roman realities without adequate consideration to how the author's use of Old Testament imagery might be brought to bear upon our understanding of the exhortation to the audience.[155]

Given the author's understanding of his audience as members primarily of the household of God,[156] and the prominence of the Old Testament in 1 Peter, I propose that the discussion on the Petrine *Haustafel* can be informed by a narratological approach that takes seriously into account 1 Peter's theological hermeneutic of the Old Testament. In other words, our understanding of the message of 1 Peter can be further informed by considering the implications of locating the characteristic features of the household of God in the Old Testament, into which the author is drawing his audience, while at the same time keeping sight of the Greco-Roman socio-political realities that the audience face. The overall scheme of the letter is not so much to call for conformity, adaptation, or disassociation with the surrounding culture, as it is to shape the expectation, behaviour, and lifestyle of its audience in regard to what it means to be among the elect children of God living in a hostile environment. The first function of the *Haustafel* in 1 Peter is to raise the audience's awareness of their membership in God's household and its consequences. [157]

Another important contribution of social-scientific criticism to Petrine scholarship that is crucial to this study is the treatment of the concepts of honour and shame. Bruce Malina has argued for the centrality of the concept of honour in the Mediterranean society, and developed the concept of challenge-and-repost.[158] Barth L. Campbell has applied social-scientific

153. Schutter, *Hermeneutic and Composition*, discusses the way Peter might have used the Old Testament and other sources. See also Achtemeier, *1 Peter*, pp. 12–13; Elliot, *Home*, pp. 21–58.

154. For example, Bauman-Martin, 'Women on the Edge', p. 268; Elliott, *Home*, p. 64; idem, *1 Peter*, pp. 95–6, 101; Balch, 'Hellenization/Acculturation', in Talbert (ed.), *Perspectives on First Peter*, pp. 80–1; idem, *Wives*, pp. 74–5; Stephen Ayodeji A. Fagbemi, *Who Are the Elect in 1 Peter?: A Study in Biblical Exegesis and Its Application to the Anglican Church of Nigeria* (SBL, 104; New York: Peter Lang, 2007), pp. 27–49.

155. Notable exceptions are Bechtler, *Following in His Steps*; Feldmeier, *Die Christen als Fremde*; Aìda B. Spencer, 'Peter's Pedagogical Method in 1 Peter 3:6', *BBR* 10 (2000), pp. 107–19; Dryden, *Theology and Ethics*.

156. From the beginning of the letter, Peter seeks to locate the audience's identity in God. He is God the Father who has given the audience new birth (1.3). See my discussion on the fatherhood of God as election imagery in Chapter 3.

157. Feldmeier, *The First Letter of Peter*, pp. 150–1.

158. Bruce Malina, *New Testament World: Insights from Cultural Anthropology* (Louisville: John Knox, 1981).

criticism with classical-rhetorical criticism to the study of 1 Peter.[159] In his 1998 publication, *Honor, Shame, and the Rhetoric of 1 Peter* he adopts Malina's proposal, focuses on the language of honour and shame employed by the author of 1 Peter, studies the semantic fields of these two terms and concludes: 'The cultural value of honor seems to govern 1 Peter's language and strategy as a theoretical perspective. Derived from that perspective is the model of the honor contest which features challenge and repost'. He adds, 'According to the author's argument, the harassed household of God stands in a divinely honored position and can look forward to a reversal in the honor contest occurring'.[160] Stephen R. Bechtler puts forward a similar argument and proposes that (1) the main problem 1 Peter's audience faced was the pervasive threat to their honour inherent in their social interaction with society at large, and (2) the purpose of the letter is to help the addressees respond to the threats to their honour that arise from outside the community by providing a means for them to retain their honour in spite of society's disapproval.[161] Bechtler is, therefore, convinced that 'the key to understanding the problem of suffering in 1 Peter lies in the letter's use of the language of honor and dishonor'.[162] Bechtler has also helpfully pointed out that in 1 Peter, God is both the arbiter of claims to honour and the source of honour for his people. The honour denied by society at large is granted by God to those who follow Christ's example.[163] From this perspective, it is clear that the author of 1 Peter holds in tension the societal norms that lay certain claims on the lives of the audience and the theological realities that now dictate how they should live in society. The honour and shame language in 1 Peter is an integral part of the author's treatment of the vindication of the audience (see my discussion in Chapter 6).

A close reading of 1 Peter reveals that the author of 1 Peter understands and acknowledges the cultural realities of his audience, yet he encourages the audience to look at those realities in fresh ways. For example, on the one hand, the author seems to follow concepts of social inequality, and structures of ruler versus ruled that is characteristic of Greco-Roman culture;[164] on the other hand, he presents Sarah and not Abraham as an example for the audience to follow (3.1-7).[165] On the one hand, the author acknowledges the socio-political authority and structure of the world in which his audience live; on the other hand, he subtly undermines it. He encourages his audience to 'be subject to every human institution' (2.13); but in the same breath the emperor is listed last on the honour list that is provided (2.17). The author of 1 Peter calls his audience to challenge the status quo not by reversing

159. Campbell, *Honor, Shame, and the Rhetoric of 1 Peter*.
160. Campbell, *Honor, Shame, and the Rhetoric of 1 Peter*, pp. 236–7.
161. Bechtler, *Following in His Steps*, p. 20.
162. Bechtler, *Following in His Steps*, p. 94.
163. Bechtler, *Following in His Steps*, pp. 202–4.
164. See, e.g., Elliott, *1 Peter*, pp. 571–99; Balch, *Wives*, pp. 97–109.
165. See discussion below, 'Daughters of Sarah, not sons of Abraham?' in Chapter 5.

the social order, but by embodying the characteristic qualities of those who belong to God's household.[166] In a culture in which several factors determine how and to whom honour is to be ascribed, the admonition to 'honour everyone' is countercultural.[167] Volf rightly suggests, 'If the injunction to be subject appears at first to function as a religious legitimation of oppression, it turns out, in fact, to be a call to struggle against the politics of violence in the name of the politics of the crucified Messiah'.[168]

In sum, social-scientific analysis has contributed much to the advancement of Petrine studies. Yet, scholarship on 1 Peter has much to gain from an analysis that focuses on the ways in which our understanding of the author's theological hermeneutic can help us make sense of the message of the letter. Because of 1 Peter's christological appropriation of the story of Israel, which is a product of the author's theological hermeneutic, a narratological approach will help us investigate the substructure of the letter in order to better understand 1 Peter's message and the claims that it exerts on the life of his audience.

2.6. Conclusion

In this chapter, my concern has been to lay out the methodology that will guide this study. In the first instance I addressed and demonstrated why a narratological approach is warranted for the study of 1 Peter which is a non-narrative text. I offered a brief survey of previous attempts to apply narratological methods to the study of epistles. Then, I made the case for the need for a three-layered understanding of narrative: fabula, story, and text; and defined the terms that are pertinent to this study. I demonstrated that 1 Peter contains a narrative substructure that is generated by the author's extensive use of the Old Testament. This narrative substructure contains the fabula of 1 Peter, whose four elements – election, suffering, faithful response, and vindication – constitute the lens through which the author desires his audience to interpret their situation. I also discussed the matter of theological hermeneutics and showed how the author's engagement in theological hermeneutics invites our own interest in the same and warrants a narratological approach to the study of the epistle. Finally, I highlighted some of the contributions of social-scientific criticism that are crucial to this present study.

Having formulated my methodology, I will now turn to the task of examining the text of 1 Peter, using a narratological perspective. I will use the four elements of the fabula as points of reference because 1 Peter's

166. See Green, 'Faithful Witness', pp. 288–9. Feldmeier, *The First Letter of Peter*, p. 155.

167. See Campbell, *Honor, Shame, and the Rhetoric of 1 Peter*; deSilva, *Honor, Patronage, Kingship, and Purity*, pp. 43–93.

168. Volf, 'Soft Difference', p. 22.

message is dependent on what goes on in the narrative substructure of the epistle. Therefore, Chapter 3 will focus on election in 1 Peter, Chapter 4 will deal with suffering in 1 Peter, Chapter 5 will consist of faithful response in 1 Peter, and in Chapter 6 I will discuss vindication in 1 Peter. In Chapter 7, I will offer some examples of how these four elements are brought together (narrated) by the author to show the ways in which the 'story' level operates in the essentially non-narrative text of 1 Peter. Then I will conclude the book by proposing some avenues for further research.

Chapter 3

ELECTION IN 1 PETER

3.1. Introduction

In the previous chapter I argued that 1 Peter exhibits a narrative substructure that provides an entrée for applying a narratological approach to the study of this epistle. I also discussed the centrality of the Old Testament as the primary background for this letter. The author of 1 Peter appropriates the Old Testament by using a theological hermeneutic through which he reads the Old Testament christologically. For the author, the life of Christ interprets the Old Testament and is interpreted by the Old Testament. Finally, I highlighted some of the contributions of social-scientific criticism of Petrine scholarship. Whereas the issues raised and proposals advanced by social-scientific exegesis contribute to our understanding of the letter and its cultural environment, additional insights can be gained from fresh ways of approaching the study of 1 Peter.

The author's 'theologizing' is evident, in part, in the manner in which he uses and interprets stories from the Old Testament and the life of Jesus while crafting his message.[1] The stories of exilic existence, suffering, resistance, and vindication of the righteous rehearsed in the letter form a narrative substructure that comprises the lens through which events in the life of 1 Peter's audience are to be understood. Our inquiry into the narrative substructure of the letter revealed four main elements that constitute the fabula of the letter:

1. Election
2. Suffering

---

1.   The author's language regarding Jesus suggests that he has knowledge of events that occurred in Jesus' life as well as elements of Jesus' teachings and draws from them throughout the letter while crafting his message. For example, it is evident that the author is aware of Jesus' suffering, death, and resurrection (1.2-3, 19-20; 2.21-25; 3.18; 4.1), his ascension (3.22), and his future coming (1.7, 13). The author's admonition to non-retaliation (3.8-9) shares some affinities with Jesus' teaching as recorded in Mt. 5.38-48. It is worth noting that in that pericope in Matthew Jesus is appealing to the father-son/children relationship (or the possibility thereof) between God, the heavenly father, and the audience as a basis for his admonition. A similar rhetoric is present in 1 Peter (see below).

3. Faithful Response
4. Vindication

This fabula is the common thread that binds together the stories that the author rehearses in the letter. It is also the lens through which 1 Peter's audience is encouraged to read their own story as they seek to make sense of their situation. The purpose of this chapter is to examine the text of 1 Peter closely in order to bring to light the way in which this fabula is at work in the epistle – particularly the way the concept of election, the first element of the fabula, is employed in the author's use of events in the lives of Israel, Jesus Christ, and the audience. I will attend to the other elements in the subsequent chapters.

The author of 1 Peter does not retell the story of the life of Jesus in its entirety. Rather, some aspects of that story are rehearsed by the author, others are alluded to, and yet others are not mentioned but implied. The same is true of his appropriation of the story of Israel and of God's dealings with the audience. The author applies a similar language to Jesus, Israel, and the audience in discussing their relationship with God, what God does on their behalf, and how they are to face suffering. It is a story in which the main elements are experienced in similar fashion by different actors, and in which God is the main actor.

In this chapter, I will examine the author's understanding of election. I propose that (1) the author of 1 Peter appropriates the concept of election in terms that are reminiscent of the Old Testament language of God's choice of Israel and applies that language and its reality to Jesus and the audience. Therefore, (2) the nature and purpose of God's election of the audience is in many ways analogous to what God worked out in the life of and intended for Israel as a nation, and for Jesus. In what follows, I will discuss briefly the concept of election in the Old Testament, and then I will focus on the election language and imagery in 1 Peter. I will attend to the fatherhood language the author uses, its relationship to the concept of election, and the implications of using the term 'Father' for God. I will then focus on some of the implications of election present in the epistle: election and holiness, election and fellowship, and election and witness. The last two concepts are embedded in the stone metaphor which also contributes to the election imagery present in the letter.

3.2. *The election of Israel in the Old Testament*

That the author of 1 Peter has an interest in Israel's election is supported by the fact that the language that he draws from the Old Testament to discuss the audience's election originates from instances in Israel's life when there was and/or needed to be an awareness of their election. The author's allusions to events that evoke the Exodus attest to this fact. For example, the language of 'obedience and sprinkling of the blood' (1.2), 'inheritance'

(1.4), 'gird up the loins' (1.13), 'redemption ... by blood' (1.18-19), and the call to holiness (1.17), 'royal priesthood, and a holy nation', 'a people acquired by God' (2.9) has points of contact with the Exodus event. The concepts of 'obedience' and 'sprinkling' are reminiscent of the ratification of the covenant when the blood was poured out on the people and they pledged obedience to God (Exod. 24.6-8).[2] The language of inheritance, which is closely connected to new birth in 1 Peter, is similar to the language used to describe God's gift of the land of Canaan to Israel subsequent to their birth as a nation (Lev. 20.24). The concepts 'gird up the loins' and 'redemption ... by blood' evoke memories of Israel's departure from Egypt (Exod. 12.5-11). Finally, the call to holiness in 1.17 and the description of the audience in 2.9 use terms that, in their original context, referred to Israel (Lev. 19.2; Exod. 19.6). In addition, the author's discussion of the 'living stone' and 'living stones' is an appropriation of election language originally referred to Israel, which he now uses to describe Jesus' election and the election of the audience.

The discussion of the election of the audience also shows that the author of 1 Peter is aware of and rehearsing some themes that are connected to Israel's election. For example, the author's use of 'ἐκλεκτοῖς παρεπιδήμοις διασπορᾶς' evokes Israel's election, wandering, deportation, and exile, and the suffering connected to these realities (Deut. 26.5-6). This language also highlights Abraham's (and Sarah's) own election, experience of wandering, and the dangers associated with that (Gen. 23.4; cf. Gen. 12.10-20). He will later draw from Abraham and Sarah's story in the context of his exhortation to the wives in the audience (see my discussion in Chapter 5). In addition, one finds other themes like the means of election (1.2, 19; cf. Exod. 24.8); election and holiness (1.15-17; cf. Lev. 19.2); election and obedience (1.21; cf. Exod. 19.6; 24.3); election and fellowship (2.4-8; cf. Isa. 43.21); election and vindication (2.6-8; cf. Ps. 118.22 [117.22, LXX]; Isa. 8.14); and election and witness (2.9; cf. Isa 43.21).

The concept of election is expressed in the Old Testament mainly through the Hebrew word 'בחר', which conveys the idea of deliberately choosing someone or something from among others after carefully considering the alternatives. It includes the idea of separation from a group for the purpose

2.   In 1 Peter, this image is applied to Jesus (his obedience and the sprinkling of his blood) as the means through which the audience's election is made possible. The author's identification of Jesus with the 'ἀμνοῦ ἀμώμου καὶ ἀσπίλου' is made more explicit in 1.19. Feldmeier argues that the author of 1 Peter never speaks of Jesus' obedience and that it is preferable to interpret 'obedience' as pertaining to the audience (*The First Letter of Peter*, p. 60). However, the author applies to Jesus terms such as 'righteous' (3.18) and 'elect' (2.4), for example, which imply and necessitate obedience to God. Further, since Jesus' experience is presented as an example to the audience, this attests to the points of contact that exist between the stories of Israel, Jesus, and the audience and the way in which Peter brings them together. One can, therefore, speak of Jesus' obedience in 1 Peter. See, Jobes, *1 Peter*, pp. 46-8 (47).

of serving the whole.[3] The word is used to describe both divine actions (Deut. 7.6-7; 12.5) and human decisions and actions (Exod. 17.9; Deut. 30.19; Josh. 24.15, 22; 1 Sam. 17.40).[4] It is used mainly to describe God's choice of Israel from among the nations to become his own people (Deut. 7.6). The LXX uses mainly the verb ἐκλέγομαι (Deut. 14.2; 1 Sam. 16.10), to translate 'בחר', and the adjective ἐκλεκτός (Deut. 12.11), to translate the corresponding Hebrew adjective.[5] The New Testament also uses ἐκλέγομαι (e.g., Mk 13.20; Acts 13.17; 1 Cor. 1.27) and ἐκλεκτός (Lk. 18.7; Col. 3.12) to convey the idea of making a choice, or the fact of being chosen, respectively. In addition, the noun ἐκλογή occurs seven times in the New Testament (Acts 9.15; Rom. 9.11; 11.5, 7; 1 Thess. 1.4).[6] However, this concept is in no way limited to these terms exclusively. For example, 'בחר' is translated with προαιρέομαι in Deut. 7.6 (αἱρέομαι is attested in 2 Thess. 2.13), and by ἐπιλέγω in Deut. 21.5. In addition, the call or election of Abraham is expressed in terms of God's knowledge of Abraham. The idea of 'knowing' (ידע) shows up repeatedly in the Old Testament in the context of God's choosing or calling an individual for a special purpose, and in the context of God's election of Israel.[7] It is attested in Gen. 18.19 in the story of God's call of Abraham, in which the LXX renders 'ידע' as οἶδα.[8] The same term is used in the account of God's call of Jeremiah (Jer. 1.5), which the LXX renders as ἐπίσταμαι. Further, in Amos 3.2 the language of 'knowing' is used to refer to God's choice of Israel.[9] In sum, the concept of election in the Old Testament relates to both divine choices of individuals for service and of Israel as his treasured possession, and of human choices that involve daily mundane decisions.

---

3.   See Horst Seebass, 'בחר', in *TDOT* (Vol. 2; Grand Rapids: Eerdmans, 1977), pp. 73–87; Emile Nicole, 'בחר', in *NIDOTE* (Vol. 1; Grand Rapids: Zondervan, 1997), pp. 638–42. The scope of this study does not permit me to engage in length the discussion of the (historical) development of the concept of election in the Old Testament, and the source-critical issues that surround it. For an assessment, see Byron E. Shafer, 'The Root *bhr* and Pre-Exilic Concepts of Chosenness in the Hebrew Bible', *ZAW* 89 (1977), pp. 20–42; George E. Mendenhall, 'Election', in *IDB* (Vol. 2; Nashville: Abingdon, 1962), pp. 76–82; Joel Kaminsky, 'Chosen', in *NIDB* (Vol. 1; Nashville: Abingdon, 2006), pp. 594–600.
4.   Dale Patrick, 'Election', in *ABD* (Vol. 2; New York: Doubleday, 1992), pp. 435–41. See Mendenhall, 'Election', 2.76–82; J. O. F. Murray, 'Election', in *DB* (Vol. 1; Paris: Letouzey et Ané, 1895), pp. 678–81; Walther Zimmerli, *Old Testament Theology in Outline* (Atlanta: John Knox, 1978), pp. 43–8.
5.   Seebass, 'בחר', 2.73–87.
6.   See J. Eckert, 'ἐκλεκτός', in *EDNT* (Vol. 1; Grand Rapids: Eerdmans, 1990), pp. 417–19.
7.   So also Brevard Childs, *Biblical Theology of the Old and New Testament: Theological Reflection on the Christian Bible* (Minneapolis: Fortress, 1992), p. 426; Seock-Tae Sohn, *The Divine Election of Israel* (Grand Rapids: Eerdmans, 1991), pp. 24–5.
8.   See further, Uppsala Bergman and Bonn Botterweck, 'ידע', in *TDOT* (Vol. 5; Grand Rapids: Eerdmans, 1977), pp. 448–81 (468–9).
9.   There, 'γινώσκω' is used to convey the corresponding meaning of 'ידע'.

I will focus on the concept of election mainly as it relates to God's choice of Israel as his treasured possession and its implications. God's election of Israel, its nature and purpose, is summed up in Deut. 7.6-8.[10]

> For you are a people holy to the LORD your God; the LORD your God has chosen you out of all the peoples on earth to be his people, his treasured possession. It was not because you were more numerous than any other people that the LORD set his heart on you and chose you – for you were the fewest of all peoples. It was because the LORD loved you and kept the oath that he swore to your ancestors, that the LORD has brought you out with a mighty hand, and redeemed you from the house of slavery, from the hand of Pharaoh king of Egypt.

From this text one can gather several things: (1) the election of Israel is the work of God, done purely out of love, and is set within the context of God's promise to Abraham, Isaac, and Jacob; (2) the election of Israel is worked out and/or expressed in the Exodus event; and (3) the election of Israel sets Israel apart as God's special treasure from among the surrounding nations.

In Deut. 7 Israel is reminded above all of God's faithfulness and love toward them. Their election is the work of God alone. They have done nothing to deserve God's love. The larger context of this passage shows that God's expression of love toward Israel is to be matched by Israel's obedience toward God (7.9-11). That obedience will insure that Israel receives God's blessing (7.12-26). The reception of blessing is reminiscent of God's call of Abraham, where God not only promises to bless Abraham, but also to bless the nations of the earth through him and his children (Gen. 12.1-3; 18.18-19). As Israel's election is cast in the context of God's faithfulness to his promise to Abraham, so Israel is bound to live up to and carry out the stipulations of that promise. In fact, later in Deuteronomy, the children of Israel are encouraged to narrate their story in the context of God's promise to Abraham, and see Abraham's experience as the starting point of their own story (Deut. 26.1-11). Verse 11 assumes the presence of outsiders in the midst of Israel's worship of God and the celebration of what God has done on their behalf.

In addition, Israel's election is squarely located in the Exodus event (Deut. 7.8; cf. Exod. 19.4-6). Consequently, the idea of Israel's chosen status cannot be divorced from the memory of the wilderness wanderings, nor the sufferings of Egypt.[11] The Exodus is God's act of redemption and vindication of his chosen people from oppression, from the house of servitude.[12] Israel

---

10. Patrick D. Miller proposes that Deut. 7 is one of the primary Old Testament texts for understanding the meaning of Israel's election (*Deuteronomy* [Interpretation; Louisville: John Knox, 1990], p. 110). See also Mark E. Dibble, *Deuteronomy* (SHBC; Macon, GA: Smyth & Helwys, 2003), p. 137.

11. For more on Israel's sufferings as part of the background of this letter, see below, Chapter 4.

12. That YHWH is regarded as the God of Israel even before the Exodus is undeniable (Hos. 13.4). Yet Scriptures at different junctures place different emphasis on where God's relationship with Israel began (cf. Ezek. 20; 23; Isa. 51.9-10; Deut. 32.10; Hos. 9.10). So Zimmerli, *OT Theology in Outline*, pp. 21-3.

was not to pride themselves on their chosen status but to hold in tandem the reality of their special position in God's economy and their humble beginnings. Even after Israel would have settled in the land, Israel's worship would serve as a reminder of this very fact. The liturgy that accompanies the offering of the first fruits rehearses Israel's story:

> A wandering Aramean was my ancestor; he went down into Egypt and lived there as an alien, few in number, and there he became a great nation, mighty and populous. When the Egyptians treated us harshly and afflicted us, by imposing hard labor on us, we cried to the LORD, the God of our ancestors; the LORD heard our voice and saw our affliction, our toil, and our oppression. The LORD brought us out of Egypt with a mighty hand and an outstretched arm, with a terrifying display of power, and with signs and wonders; and he brought us into this place and gave us this land, a land flowing with milk and honey. (Deut. 26.7-9)

At the core of Israel's identity as a nation is the memory of their alienness. That memory highlights God's faithfulness toward them, and reminds them of the need to live in obedience to God and be merciful to the strangers in their midst.

Finally, Deut. 7.6 shows a close connection between the concepts of Israel's election and that of Israel's holiness. The idea of the 'holy' in the Old Testament is generally conveyed by the Hebrew root 'קדשׁ', and its derivatives. The meaning(s) conveyed by the terms vary based on the context in which a given word is used.[13] For example, when used in relation to God, the ideas express God's uniqueness (Exod. 15.11) and moral perfection (Ps. 89.35 [36]). When used in relation to Israel, the concept is mainly one of consecration, belonging to YHWH, being set apart as God's 'treasured possession' (Deut. 7.6). However, this is often accompanied with a warning against idolatry (Deut. 7.1-5), and/or association with what is ceremonially impure (Exod. 22.31[30]).[14]

Israel's holiness means that they are set apart from other peoples and from pagan religious practices,[15] to be God's own and to worship him alone (Exod. 19.5-6; Deut. 14.2). Their holiness is expressed in their keeping the covenant.[16] Therefore, Israel as a holy people must abide by the moral and ethical obligations of the covenant which are an expression of God's character (Lev. 19). Israel's chosen status does not set them above the nations, but rather causes them 'to exist in a sacral relationship to the God of all the nations, serving the Lord, dedicating themselves totally as a people to God, setting themselves apart from other loyalties, and manifesting the Lord's just and righteous way in the world'.[17]

---

13.   Walter Kornfeld and Helmer Ringgren, 'קדשׁ', *TDOT*, 12.521–45. See also, David P. Wright, 'Holiness', in *ABD* (Vol. 3; New York: Doubleday, 1992), pp. 237–49.

14.   Kornfeld and Ringgren, 'קדשׁ', 12.531.

15.   So Duane L. Christensen, *Deuteronomy 1-11* (WBC, 6a; Dallas, Texas: Word, 1991), pp. 158–9.

16.   Diddle, *Deuteronomy*, p. 138; Zimmerli, *OT Theology in Outline*, pp. 45–7.

17.   Miller, *Deuteronomy*, pp. 111–12.

In the *Similitudes of Enoch* one finds several occurrences of the terms 'Elect One' or 'Chosen One' (e.g., *1 En.* 39.6; 40.5; 49.2), and 'elect ones' (e.g., *1 En.* 39.6; 48.2, 9). On the one hand, the term 'Elect One' is used to refer to one who is in the presence of the Lord of the Spirits. It is used interchangeably with other designations like 'Son of Man', 'Righteous One', and 'Anointed One' to refer to an eschatological hero who shares authority with the Lord of the Spirits.[18] The writer seems to draw from the descriptions of the 'Son of Man' in Dan. 7, and the servant of Yahweh in Second Isaiah for his portrayal of this eschatological figure.[19] On the other hand, some of the language used to describe the 'Elect One' shares close affinities with 1 Peter's descriptions of Jesus (e.g., cf. *1 En.* 45.3; 46.3-5, and 1 Pet. 3.18-22). In the *Similitudes*, the term 'elect ones' is used once (*1 En.* 39.1) to refer to angels, but seems to refer generally to the community of the faithful, the people of God. It is often complemented with 'righteous ones' and 'holy ones' (e.g., 47.4; 48.2; 50.1). The epithet 'righteousness' is also used to describe the 'Elect One' (e.g., 39.5; 46.3). This principle of identification at work in *1 Enoch* is similar to what is attested in 1 Peter; e.g., Jesus is the 'living stone' and the audience is identified as 'living stones'. Further, the author of 1 Peter also uses the epithets and concepts of 'elect' (cf. 2.6 and 1.1), 'righteous' (cf. 3.18 and 4.18), and 'holy' (cf. 1.19; 2.22 and 1.15; 2.9) in relation to both Jesus and the audience.

The language that the author of 1 Peter employs to describe the reality of his audience is in many ways analogous to the Old Testament understanding of Israel's election by God and shares some affinities to the description of the elect in *1 Enoch*.

3.3. *Election language and imagery in 1 Peter*

The concept of election is prominent in the author's thought and evidenced in the manner in which he addresses the audience at the beginning of the letter (1.1). The term 'ἐκλεκτοῖς παρεπιδήμοις'[20] creates an obvious paradox

18. James C. Vanderkam, 'Righteous One, Messiah, Chosen One, and Son of Man in 1 Enoch 35-71', in *From Revelation to Canon: Studies in the Hebrew Bible and Second Temple Literature* (JSJSup, 62; Boston: Brill, 2002), pp. 413–38. See also, Darrell L. Bock, *Blasphemy and Exaltation in Judaism and the Final Examination of Jesus* (WUNT, 2.106; Tübingen: Mohr Siebeck, 1998), pp. 113–83; Johannes Theisohn, *Der auserwählte Richter* (SUNT, 12; Göttingen: Vandenhoeck & Ruprecht, 1975).

19. See Vanderkam, '1 Enoch 35-71', pp. 432–8; Joseph Coppens and Luc Dequeker, *Le Fils de l'Homme et les Saints de Très-Haut en Daniel VII, dans les Apocryphes, et dans le Nouveau Testament* (ALBO, 3.23; Paris: Université de Louvain, 2nd edn, 1961); John J. Collins, 'The Heavenly Representative: The "Son of Man" in The Similitudes of Enoch', in George W. E. Nickelsburg and John J. Collins (eds), *Ideal Figures in Ancient Judaism* (SCS, 12; Ann Arbor: Scholars, 1980), pp. 111–34.

20. Some mss (ℵ*, sy) add καί between the two adjectives possibly to prevent one from treating ἐκλεκτοῖς as modifying παρεπιδήμοις. Both words describe in complementary fashion the identity of the audience.

that permeates the epistle. The author introduces another phrase in 2.11, 'παροίκους καὶ παρεπιδήμους', to convey the same idea and describe the same reality: they are chosen in the sight of God while experiencing life as sojourners and facing hostility and rejection from those among whom they live as sojourners.[21]

In his book, *A Home for the Homeless*, Elliott argues extensively that 'πάροικος' and 'παρεπίδημος' are to be understood literally as the social, legal, and political designations of 1 Peter's audience.[22] The former designates the 'resident alien who dwelled permanently in a foreign locale', while the latter denotes the 'transient stranger visiting temporarily in a given foreign locale'.[23] Consequently, 1 Peter's audience was composed of people of lower class status 'whose legal, economic, and social rights were limited because they were foreigners'.[24] He arrives at this understanding through his reading of 1 Peter done in light of the social, political, and economic world of first-century Asia Minor. He calls into question the way these terms have been rendered and suggests that their meaning is frequently obscured in modern translations.[25] He uses the story of Abraham and the experience of the children of Israel as cases in point to show how the terms have been used in a literal sense to describe their situation. Elliott has helpfully highlighted the importance of the social realities that the audience had to deal with. He is right in challenging interpretations that treat these terms exclusively as theological terms or spiritual designations of the audience's situation and arguing against a merely metaphorical understanding of these terms. Yet, he commits the same mistake by arguing that the terms should be understood exclusively as sociological designations of 1 Peter's audience.[26] These terms carry both theological and sociological connotations, and, therefore, lend themselves to be understood from both perspectives.

In his monograph, *Following in His Steps*, also using a social-scientific approach, Bechtler challenges Elliott's interpretation and argues that Elliott's claim that 1 Peter's audience were literal resident aliens and visiting strangers in Asia Minor is unwarranted.[27] Bechtler contends that both words are used figuratively and offer several reasons for understanding 1 Peter's designation of the audience as 'aliens' and 'sojourners' in a metaphorical sense.[28] First,

21. Feldmeier, *The First Letter of Peter*, pp. 53–5; Green, 'Living as Exiles', pp. 311–25, (317); Jobes, *1 Peter*, pp. 44–5, 61–2.

22. Elliott, *Home*, pp. 23, 48–9, 231–2; idem, *Conflict, Community, and Honor*, pp. 14–30. So also, Armand P. Tàrrech, 'Le Milieu de la Première Épître de Pierre', *RCT* 5 (1980), pp. 95–129. For an assessment, see Achtemeier, *1 Peter*, pp. 82, 173; idem, 'Newborn Babes', pp. 222–8; Bechtler, *Following in His Steps*, pp. 64–83; Michaels, *1 Peter*, pp. 7–8.

23. Elliott, *1 Peter*, p. 312; idem, *Home*, pp. 24–37.

24. Elliott, *Conflict, Community, and Honor*, p. 20; idem, *1 Peter*, pp. 477–8.

25. Elliott, *1 Peter*, pp. 457–8.

26. Elliott, *1 Peter*, p. 313.

27. Bechtler, *Following in His Steps*, pp. 74–83.

28. Bechtler, *Following in His Steps*, pp. 75–81.

Bechtler points out the weaknesses in Elliott's linguistic argument and goes on to show how the terms that the author of 1 Peter uses in 1.1 and 2.11 are drawn from the reality of Israel's life as opposed to a Greco-Roman context (e.g., Deut. 28.25; 30.4; 2 Esd. 11.9; Isa. 49.6; Dan. 12.2; *Pss. Sol.* 8.28; 9.2; *T. Ash.* 7.3).[29] Elliott's argument fails because, on the one hand, he acknowledges that 'πάροικος' and 'παρεπίδημος' are not synonymous terms, on the other hand, he advances that the author of 1 Peter addresses his entire audience as 'παρεπίδημοι', thereby, implying that his use of these terms is somewhat loose. Second, Bechtler proposes that one must take seriously 1 Peter's description of the audience in 1.1 as 'ἐκλεκτοῖς παρεπιδήμοις διασπορᾶς' in order to understand fully the nature of the addressees. He argues that the use of the word 'διασπορά', found only once outside of Jewish and Christian literature (i.e., in Plutarch), suggests that one is dealing in the realm of early-Jewish terminology rather than the Greco-Roman legal language about citizenship.[30] As such even the word 'διασπορά' carries some metaphorical understanding. Third, Bechtler infers that since 'διασπορά' can be understood metaphorically, so can 'ἐκλεκτός'. Fourth, Bechtler argues that the author of 1 Peter is appropriating the language of Gen. 23.4 and Ps. 38.13, which describes Abraham as the 'resident alien' *par excellence* and applying it figuratively to the socioreligious situation of his audience.

In addition, Torrey Seland surveys the Old Testament background of these two terms, highlights the several ways in which they have been understood in the Old Testament, and suggests that these words as used by the author of 1 Peter are part of 'proselyte terminology'.[31] Further, he inquires into the usage of 'πάροικος' in Philo before concluding that the passage in 1 Peter where these words occur 'should be read against the background of Diaspora-Jewish descriptions of proselytes'.[32] He argues that members of 1 Peter's audience became 'παρεπίδημοι' at conversion and understand their conversion as being a central part (cause) of their suffering.[33]

By forcing a choice between a metaphorical and a literal reading, Elliott fails to recognize that *any* reading of 'alien' life in 1 Peter is metaphorical. Elliott seems to equate 'metaphorical' with 'allegorical' or 'not real'.[34] Green has rightly pointed out that the 'metaphorical versus literal' discussion is wrongheaded because the primary issue is not sociological but theological. Following Lakoff and Johnson, he suggests, 'Metaphors pervade the whole of everyday life, and our day-to-day conceptual systems operate in terms that are fundamentally metaphorical. In other words, "metaphor" has to do with how we conceive of the world and not simply with how we represent the

29. Bechtler, *Following in His Steps*, pp. 75–6. See Elliott, *Home*, p. 36.
30. Bechtler, *Following in His Steps*, pp. 75–6. So also, Feldmeier, *The First Letter of Peter*, pp. 53–5.
31. Seland, *Strangers in the Light*, p. 56.
32. Seland, *Strangers in the Light*, p. 61.
33. Seland, *Strangers in the Light*, p. 72.
34. Elliott, *1 Peter*, p. 479.

world linguistically'.[35] Further, even in Elliott's reading, for example, these terms do have metaphorical value.[36] Finally, Elliott's definition of alien life in economic terms is anachronistic, reflecting more the categories of social stratification at work in a post-industrial age than in Roman antiquity.[37]

The use of 'πάροικος' and 'παρεπίδημος' evokes Abraham's experience (Gen. 23.4; Deut. 26.5), Israel's situation in Egypt and in the wilderness, their exile in Babylon, and even their situation under Roman occupation.[38] The events that brought about Israel's wilderness wanderings or their exile to Babylon differ from what caused 1 Peter's audience to experience life as sojourners. Israel's suffering in the wilderness and in exile came as a result of their disobedience. For 1 Peter's audience, suffering comes about as a result of their choice to live in obedience to God's call and forsake their former ways of life. First Peter's use of the phrases 'ἐκλεκτοῖς παρεπιδήμοις' and 'παροίκους καὶ παρεπιδήμους' invites us to hold the terms in tension. The collocation of these terms describes, on the one hand, the reality of the audience's situation: God's elect face the world's hostility and live in a situation of alienness; on the other hand, the author is driving home to his audience the truth that alienness is not a contradiction of election.[39] This collocation is also attested in *1 Enoch*. There, reference is made to the 'blood of the righteous' (47.1, 4), which implies that the 'elect ones' also suffer. This concept is attested in Wis. 2.12-20 as well. So, in using language that is reminiscent of the Old Testament and other Jewish literature and encouraging his audience to identify with Israel, the author is working with a similar principle which was at work in Deuteronomy. As the Israelites were encouraged to see the patriarch's story as their own (Deut. 26.5), so the author of 1 Peter is inviting the audience to see Israel's story as their own (1 Pet. 1.1).

The concept of election is evident not only in the author's utilization of the word ἐκλεκτός (1.1; 2.4, 6, 9), but also in his use of terms drawn from a vast semantic field that includes, ἐλεέω (2.10), ἔλεος (1.3), χάρις (1.2, 10, 13; 2.19-20; 3.7; 5.10), ἀναγεννάω (1.3, 23), κληρονομία (1.4), πρόγνωσις (1.2), προγινώσκω (1.20), and καλέω (1.15; 2.9, 21; 3.9; 5.10). The *rapprochement* between the stories of Israel, Jesus, and 1 Peter's audience can be seen here in that some of the terms used apply to Jesus and/or the audience. The fact that they are drawn from the Old Testament

35.   Green, *1 Peter*, p. 16. George Lakoff and Mark Johnson, *Metaphors We Live By* (Chicago: University of Chicago Press, 1980). See also George Lakoff. 'How the Body Shapes Thought: Thinking with an All-Too-Human Brain', in Anthony J. Sanford (ed.), *The Nature and Limits of Human Understanding* (The 2001 Gifford Lectures London: Clark, 2003), pp. 49–73; idem, 'How to Live with an Embodied Mind: When Causation, Mathematics, Morality, the Soul, and God Are Essentially Metaphorical Ideas', in Sanford (ed.), *The Nature and Limits of Human Understanding*, pp. 75–108.

36.   Elliott, *Home*, p. 42.

37.   See further, Jobes, *1 Peter*, pp. 61–6.

38.   So Craig A. Evans, 'Jesus and the Continuing Exile of Israel', in Carey C. Newman (ed.), *Jesus and the Restoration of Israel: A Critical Assessment of N. T. Wright's 'Jesus and the Victory of God'* (Downers Grove, IL: InterVarsity, 1999), pp. 77–100.

implies their connection to the story of Israel. For example, 'ἐκλεκτός' is employed in reference to Jesus' chosen status in 2.4 and 2.6 with a quotation that shows the use of the term in reference to Israel. It refers to the audience in 1.1. In addition, the idea of God's foreknowledge is present in both cases. In 1 Pet. 1.2, 'πρόγνωσις' complements the description of the audience's election; while 'προγινώσκω' functions in the same manner to describe Jesus' election in 1.20. The image of the sacrificial lamb connects the thought to Israel's own election, because it recalls the Exodus when the blood of the lamb served as the means by which God's protection and deliverance of Israel were carried out. Further, The notion of inheritance (κληρονομία) refers to the reward bestowed to the audience as a result of their new birth/ election (1.4); this concept is inherent in Israel's election. It refers to the land of Canaan which was given to the children of Israel subsequent to their birth as a nation (Exod. 23.30; Lev. 20.24; Num. 14.31).[40]

As the author of 1 Peter reads the Old Testament christologically, his understanding of Jesus' election and its implications for the audience also permeate the epistle. Jesus' election in 1 Peter serves as a means to help the audience identify with Jesus whose life of holiness, obedience, and dependence on God is presented as the norm they need to live by. Our discussion on the election language and imagery in 1 Peter will focus on 1.3-5, in which one finds the themes of fatherhood of God, inheritance, protection, and obedience; on 1.13–2.3, which contains that author's call to holiness; and on 2.4-10 that comprise the stone metaphor.[41]

3.3.1. *The fatherhood of God as election imagery (1.3-5)*

The author of 1 Peter speaks of God in terms that highlight the familial relationship that exists between God and Jesus, between God and the audience, and by implication, between Jesus and the audience. The opening eulogy attests to the christological tenor of the letter as well as its theocentric focus: 'Blessed be God, the father of our Lord Jesus Christ, who in accordance with his great lovingkindness has caused us to be born again into a living hope through the resurrection of Jesus from the dead' (1.3). Jesus is addressed in terms that underline his relationship with the audience: '*our* Lord Jesus Christ'. But the focus is on what God does on behalf of the audience through him. Christ's own election comes more sharply into focus in the stone metaphor in 2.4-10 (see below). Here, the father–son

39. See Feldmeier, *The First Letter of Peter*, pp. 13–17 (14).
40. Feldmeier, *The First Letter of Peter*, pp. 70–8 (71).
41. In his 1966 monograph, John H. Elliott argues for the presence of the theme of election (as opposed to just a word) in 1 Peter. Although important, his treatment of that theme is only limited to 2.4-10 (*The Elect and the Holy*, pp. 141–5). The same can be said of Jo Bailey Wells, whose study of the themes of holiness and election in 1 Peter is primarily concerned with 2.4-10 (*God's Holy People: A Theme in Biblical Theology* [JSOTSup, 305; Sheffield: Sheffield Academic Press, 2000], pp. 208–40).

relationship between God and Jesus is evident in the author's language, as God is described as the 'father of our Lord Jesus Christ'. In the same breath, the author introduces the audience into that familial relationship because the same God has caused the audience to experience new birth.[42] The author has already hinted in the introduction that the audience's election is 'in accordance with the foreknowledge of God the father' (1.2). Here he expands on the idea and brings the audience to the point not only of understanding God as father but of identifying themselves as his children. He will later use this as the basis for admonishing his audience – 'as obedient children' (1.14), 'since you call as father' (1.17), 'having been given new birth' (1.23), and 'like new born babies' (2.2). As such, his discussion of the fatherhood of God establishes the audience's familial relationship with God, thus underlining their chosen status in God's sight; the role Jesus Christ played in the process of God's outworking of the audience's election; and the obligations that befall the audience.

The fatherhood of God is a concept that can be traced in the Old Testament and other Jewish texts (e.g., Wis. 2.16; *3 Macc.* 5.7).[43] Though there are very few Old Testament references where God is addressed directly as father, the father–son relationship between God and Israel is ubiquitous in the Old Testament.[44] For example, in Exod. 4.22-23, God speaks of Israel as his 'firstborn son' whom Pharaoh needs to send away from Egypt. In Hos. 11.1, the prophet picks up that imagery and speaks of God's love for Israel as that of a father for his son: 'When Israel was a child, I loved him, and out of Egypt I called my son'.[45] In Deut. 1.31, that same image is used to speak of God's care for Israel: '... The LORD your God carried you like one carries his son'. God is identified explicitly as Israel's father in Deut 32.6;

---

42. The idea of 'new birth', 'regeneration' is not explicitly attested in the Old Testament, but is evidenced in other Jewish texts (e.g., b. Yeb. 22a; 1QH 3.19-23). The author of 1 Peter is the only New Testament writer to use the term ἀναγεννάω but the concept is attested outside of 1 Peter (e.g., John 3.5-7; 2 Cor. 5.17; Titus 3.5). Davids, *1 Peter*, p. 51; Senior, *1 Peter*, p. 36. Reinhard Feldmeier argues that there is a close relationship between the concepts of 'birth' and 'the people of God tradition' present in the Old Testament which Peter integrates in his discussion of the new birth of his audience ('Wiedergeburt im 1. Petrusbrief', in Reinhard Feldmeier (ed.), *Wiedergeburt* [Göttingen: Vandenhoeck & Ruprecht, 2005], pp. 75–99 (91–3); idem, *The First Letter of Peter*, pp. 23–5.

43. Marianne Meye Thompson, *The Promise of the Father: Jesus and God in the New Testament* (Louisville: Westminster, 2000), p. 18.

44. So Paul Niskanen, 'YHWH as Father, Redeemer, and Potter in Isaiah 63.7–64.11', *CBQ* (2006), pp. 397–407.

45. It should be noted that the LXX renders וממצרים קראתי לבני as 'ἐξ Αἰγύπτου μετεκάλεσα τὰ τέκνα αὐτοῦ' (Hos. 11.1b). It can be argued that the same principle that caused the LXX to choose τέκνα over υἱός, the Greek equivalent of the Hebrew בן, was at work in 1 Peter as he encourages his audience to read their story into that of Israel. Replacing 'my son' with 'his (Israel's) children' is a way of interpreting the story that would have helped the readers and audience of the LXX to identify more readily with the event/action being spoken of by the prophet.

Isa. 63.16; and Jer. 3.4, 19. God is also spoken of as father to David and his descendants in 2 Sam. 7.14 and Ps. 89.27 (88.26, LXX). The father–son relationship is closely tied to the concept of election. Niskanen rightly notes, 'It is in redeeming Israel from slavery in Egypt that YHWH became their father and brought forth into existence a nation. This relationship is formalized in the covenant that creates a legal bond of kinship expressed in father-son terminology'.[46] God has chosen Israel for himself, brought them out of Egypt from the house of slavery, given them the land as inheritance, and required Israel's allegiance in return. The Exodus is the chief act through which God's election of Israel is worked out (Exod. 19.4-6). Though the biblical materials locate the Exodus event also within the framework of God's promise to Abraham (e.g., Deut. 7.8; Ps. 105 [104].42-43), the psalmist and the prophets would refer back to the Exodus as the defining moment of Israel's relationship with God.

In the Gospel tradition,[47] God testifies of Jesus as his beloved son (Mk 1.11; 9.7). Jesus also speaks of God as his father (Mt. 11.25-27; Lk. 10.21-22; Jn 14–15; 17.1), and teaches his disciples to address God in the same manner (Mt. 6.11; Lk. 11.2).[48] Marianne Meye Thompson helpfully summarizes the three most prominent, characteristic descriptions of a father, particularly of God as Father, in the Old Testament as '(1) the father is the head of a clan or family, and hence the "ancestor" who gives life to and bequeaths an inheritance to his heirs. (2) The father is one who loves and cares for his children. (3) The father is a figure of authority, who is worthy of obedience and honor'.[49] She, then, proposes that in the Gospels 'Jesus' use of Father for God testifies to his convictions that as the Father of Israel, God was now carrying out his promise to give Israel its inheritance, calling Israel to obedience, and was prepared to discipline his people in preparing them to receive their inheritance'.[50] The author's appropriation of the 'father' language has some affinities with the way God as father was understood in the Old Testament and by Jesus, according to the Gospels.

First, God the Father who created Israel and gave them the land of Canaan as an inheritance (e.g., Deut. 32.6; Jer. 3.19), raised Jesus Christ and gave him glory (1.3, 21), and now by means of the resurrection of Jesus Christ from the dead, has caused the audience to be born again into a living hope and into an inheritance that is not subject to decay, that cannot be defiled, and that is unfading (1.3-4).

46. Niskanen, 'YHWH as Father', p. 403.
47. It is evident that Peter is aware of the Jesus-tradition from which the Gospel gathered materials about the life and teachings of Jesus and that this forms part of the background of 1 Peter. I am not suggesting that Peter knows that tradition in a certain form or the Gospels per se. That (some of) these events are also recorded in the four Gospels makes them a point of reference. See, Jobes, *1 Peter*, p. 51.
48. Romans 8.15 and Gal. 4.6 provide further evidence of how the Jesus-tradition is at work in the writings of the New Testament. In both passages Paul is offering a warrant for his audience to call God 'Abba, Father'.
49. Thompson, *The Promise of the Father*, p. 18.
50. Thompson, *The Promise of the Father*, p. 72.

Second, God the Father who expressed his love for Israel by freeing them
from slavery, cared for them, and protected them through the wilderness
(e.g., Isa. 63.16; Exod. 6.6) is the same who has given the audience new
birth and is now protecting and caring for them (1.5). The author's use of the
fatherhood of God as election imagery and his identification of his audience
with Israel is further evidenced here in at least two ways. (1) In Isa. 63.16,
the imagery of God as Father is coupled with that of a defending kinsman.[51]
The term 'גאל' offers a picture of God as a father who cares deeply for the
welfare of his children. It was the role of the defending kinsman to protect
and defend his kin by 'standing up for him and maintaining his rights'.[52]
It is no coincidence that the author of 1 Peter upholds before his audience
a portrait of Jesus as one who 'entrusted himself to the one who judges
justly' (2.23). The author has already introduced the image of God as Father
and Judge (1.17-18). There, he also brought together the images of father
and redeemer. This is evidenced by the proximity between 'πατέρα' and
'ἐλυτρώθητε' in the text;[53] and by the fact that ἐλυτρώθητε is in the passive
voice where God is the implied agent and the precious blood of Christ is the
means through which the redemption took place. For the author then, to call
upon God as Father implies dependence and trust in his ability to protect,
save, and deliver. This is exactly what God did in raising Jesus Christ from
the dead. Therefore, the exhortation to submission, non-retaliation, and
endurance in suffering are not a call to passively endure abuse, but an appeal
to actively wait on God the Father, the just Judge, the defending kinsman of
Israel to come and bring deliverance and vindication on the day of visitation.
(2) The author uses covenant language in his description of the process of
new birth – 'in accordance with his (God's) great lovingkindness' (1.3). The
word that the author employs here is ἔλεος, which the LXX used to translate
חסד. In the Old Testament, God's lovingkindness is the basis upon which
God's election and redemption of Israel are carried out. For the author of
1 Peter, God's action on behalf of his audience, their new birth, draws its
significance from what God has done in giving birth to Israel as a nation.

Third, the author's emphasis on obedience confirms his awareness that his
audience faced the same obligations that Israel and Jesus faced. Obedience
to the Father plays a central role in the audience's relationship with God.
Whereas their new birth is brought about 'through the resurrection of the
Jesus Christ from the dead' (1.3), their election is made possible 'because of
the obedience and the sprinkling of the blood of Jesus Christ' (1.2).[54] He is
the ultimate example because of his devotion to the Father. Jesus Christ's
sufferings, the sprinkling of his blood, were done as acts of obedience to
God. Whereas his suffering was unique in nature,[55] in his obedience to God

51.   Niskanen, 'YHWH as Father', pp. 401–4.
52.   Helmer Ringgren, 'גאל', *TDOT* (Vol. 2; Grand Rapids: Eerdmans, 1977), pp.
350–5.
53.   Syntactically, 1 Pet. 1.17-18 is part of a single sentence that ends at v. 20.
54.   See my discussion on the translation of 'εἰς ὑπακοὴν καὶ ῥαντισμὸν αἵματος
Ἰησοῦ Χριστοῦ' in Chapter 2.
55.   See my discussion in Chapter 4.

the audience finds a pattern they can follow (2.21). Obedience to the Father is what will allow the audience to conduct themselves in a way that brings honour to him (1.14, 22).

In addition, the fatherhood language the author uses to describe God's election of the audience sets God as the main actor in the different stories that are rehearsed. The language here is as much christological as it is theocentric. It is God who brought about the new birth, who raised Jesus Christ from the dead, who gave and is preserving the inheritance, and it is by God's power and faithfulness that the audience is being protected.[56] David Horrell raises the question 'Whose faithfulness is it in 1 Peter 1.5?' and discusses whether 'διὰ πίστεως' refers to God's faithfulness toward the audience or the audience's faithfulness toward God.[57] He provides evidence in support of both readings and leaves the question unanswered, although he seems to favour the idea the reference is to the audience's faith(fulness).[58] Given the overall tone of 1.3-5 and its immediate context, it can be said that 'διὰ πίστεως' refers to God's faithfulness toward the audience and the audience's faithfulness toward God. The ambiguity could be intentional on the part of the author. Horrell rightly notes that 'διὰ πίστεως' does not occur in the Old Testament, yet the concept that God's own are sustained by God's faithfulness is attested in Hab. 2.4b: 'ὁ δὲ δίκαιος ἐκ πίστεώς μου ζήσεται'. The *pesher* of this text, provided in 1QpHab 7.15–8.3, highlights God's deliverance of the righteous as a result of his (the righteous) faith in the Teacher of Righteousness: 'Interpreted, this concerns all those who observe the Law in the House of Judah, whom God will deliver from the House of Judgment because of their suffering and because of their faith in the Teacher of Righteousness' (8.1-3). It appears that 1 Peter shares some conceptual affinities with the commentary on Habakkuk; namely, (1) God provides deliverance/protection for the righteous/elect from suffering; (2) because the righteous/elect are faithful (implied) in the midst of suffering; and (3) because the righteous place their faith in God's servant. In 1QpHab, the righteous' faith is in the Teacher of Righteousness; in 1 Peter, the object of the faith is not specified. Elsewhere, the author of 1 Peter encourages his audience to set their faith and hope on God himself (1.21).

Further, the psalmist often brings together God's goodness, usually expressed by the adjectives χρηστός and ἀγαθός, and his lovingkindness (ἔλεος)[59] when singing about the mighty deeds God has accomplished on behalf of Israel (Pss. 105 [104], 118 [117], 136 [135]). The author's discussion of the fatherhood of God sets God as the primary actor in the life of Israel, Jesus, and the audience. That the readers would depend on God's faithfulness is all the more necessary since they live on the margins, and are in a precarious situation. Further, the believers had certain responsibilities

56. Feldmeier, *The First Letter of Peter*, p. 65.
57. David Horrell, 'Whose Faith(fullness) Is It in 1 Peter 1.5?' *JTS* 48 (1997), pp. 110–15.
58. Horrell, 'Whose Faith(fullness)?', pp. 114–15.
59. These three words are part of the same semantic domain.

in the way they live toward God, the brotherhood (and sisterhood) of believers, and toward outsiders (their detractors). Therefore, the author pens the epistle in order to help the audience figure out how to live in a hostile environment. He offers guidance to the believers in the first paraenetic section of the epistle (1.13–2.10), in which the themes of holiness, service as worship and witness, and suffering (rejection) are introduced to complement the theme of election.

3.3.2. *Election and holiness (1.13-21)*

The theme of holiness is prominent in 1 Peter. The author's treatment of this concept shows some affinities with the Old Testament in that a similar connection between election and holiness found in the Old Testament is evident in the letter.[60] After reminding the audience of their chosen status and its implications, the author goes on to explain to his audience that election necessitates holiness because of (1) the familial relationship that has been established between the audience and God the Father, and (2) the means by which the audience's election was carried out.

The author of 1 Peter locates his admonition to the audience within the context of Israel's experience at Sinai. The words that were spoken to Israel are appropriated and applied to the audience's experience because the holiness to which they are being called is consistent with God's character as revealed in God's dealings with the community of Israel.[61] In fact the phrase, 'ἀναζωσάμενοι τὰς ὀσφύας τῆς διανοίας ὑμῶν' (1 Pet. 1.13), is reminiscent of the instruction the Israelites received vis-à-vis how they should eat the Passover meal: αἱ ὀσφύες ὑμῶν περιεζωσμέναι (Exod. 12.11, LXX). What was spoken to the community of Israel during their preparation for the Exodus is appropriated in 1 Peter as a reminder for the audience of what they have already done (and what God has done for them), and a basis for what they are now to do (and what God will do on their behalf). They are to (1) set their hope fully on the grace that will be brought to them at the revelation of Jesus (1.13), (2) live holy in all their conduct (1.15), and (3) live in reverent fear during the time of their sojourning life (1.17).

Further, in 1.16, the author quotes Lev. 19.2 almost verbatim from the LXX. Leviticus 19.2 is part of a larger context where God lays out the guidelines of how Israel is to conduct the many aspects of community life. For the believers, these written words should resonate as fresh and binding as when they were first spoken. The author's identification of his audience with Israel had certain limitations.[62] The way the admonition should be lived out in the lives and context of 1 Peter's audience was different than the way

60. So Davids, *1 Peter*, p. 17; I. Howard Marshall, *1 Peter* (IVPNTC; Downers Grove, IL: InterVarsity, 1991), p. 27; Pheme Perkins, *First and Second Peter, James, and Jude* (Interpretation; Louisville: John Knox, 1995), p. 21; Green, 'Living as Exiles', p. 312.
61. So Jobes, *1 Peter*, p. 113.
62. So Jobes, *1 Peter*, pp. 114–15.

Israel lived it out. There were certain aspects in the daily cultural, cultic, and social life of Old Testament Israel that could not be replicated in a Greco-Roman context. Yet, the author's call to holiness to his audience reveals that (1) as Israel was set apart to be God's treasured possession, so the audience has now become God's special people by the new birth they have received through the death and resurrection of Jesus Christ; (2) as Israel was called to display God's character in every aspect of life, so the audience is required to display the kind of behaviour that is becoming to a member of God's family; and (3) as Israel was set apart to show the nations the way to God, so 1 Peter's audience is expected to witness God's grace and lovingkindness to the people around them, even their detractors.

First, election necessitates holiness, because the elect is brought into God's family. As such that person is expected to embody the character of God who is the head of the household: 'as obedient children … rather [conforming] after the image of the one who called you, you yourselves must be holy, for it is written, you will be holy for I am holy' (1.14-15). The author speaks of the recipients' obedience as a matter of fact. He assumes that they are living in obedience to God the Father and encourages them to pattern their whole life after God's character. This is further supported by the fact that the admonition to 'love one another deeply' is given on the basis that they have purified their minds 'through obedience of the truth' (1.22). As was the case for corporate Israel whose election was followed by a pledge of obedience to God (Exod. 19.8; 24.3), obedience plays a central role in the audience's response to God's act of mercy and faithfulness on their behalf. Whereas Jesus' obedience makes their election possible (1.2), their obedience ensures that the relationship that is thus established is maintained as they display the kind of behaviour that is characteristic of those who are members of God's household.

The proper response, the natural outcome of being born again is the change that distances a person from their former way of life and brings that person to the place where she can embody the holy nature of God the Father.[63] Green describes this as a change of perspective, a conversion of the imagination.[64] The language offers a not-so-subtle polemic between his audience's previous location or family membership and their current one. 1 Peter evokes several contrasting pictures that describe that change:[65]

---

63. Wells, *God's Holy People*, p. 212.
64. Green, *1 Peter*, p. 26.
65. Bechtler proposes that the author of 1 Peter is contrasting two competing realities, or perceptions of reality: the one is the truth, and the other is ignorance (*Following in His Steps*, pp. 110–11). I propose that the contrast goes beyond these two concepts. Bechtler puts side by side several elements that show the difference between life prior to new birth and life subsequent to it (e.g., the kind of inheritance, the kind of father, the kind of behaviour, the means of redemption, and the perspective on life). Some contrasts are more explicit than others; nonetheless, they are all evident in 1 Peter's rhetoric. On contrasts between the former and current state of 1 Peter's readers, see also Jobes, *1 Peter*, p. 113.

- Formerly, they lived in ignorance and held desires that arose from an empty way of life. Now they live as obedient children who are to live in reverent fear.
- Formerly, their lives were conformed to their fathers (ancestors) whose empty way of life they inherited.[66] Now they call on a Father who bestows upon them an inheritance that cannot fade, that is kept in heaven, and whose holiness beckons them to love and lead a life characterized by good behaviour.
- Formerly, they were at home (by implication). Now they lead the life of pilgrims.

Bechtler has argued that the author of 1 Peter is encouraging his audience to lead a 'liminal' existence in society.[67] He is convinced that the problem 1 Peter is addressing is primarily sociological. It consists of a threat to the honour of the audience which comes in the form of relentless verbal attacks from non-Christians.[68] Feldmeier recognizes the sociological aspect of the audience's predicament, but points out that the author parses that problem primarily in theological terms. He explains, 'The foreignness of the Christians is not in its essence derived from protests against society, but from correspondence to God and belonging to his new society'.[69] Similarly, Green warns of the danger to reduce the author's concern with honour and shame to social categories. He notes, 'What is especially crucial is how Peter manipulates those categories as he seeks to sculpt the identity of his audience theologically'.[70] Taken together, these statements provide a sense of the complexity of the challenge that the audience face: how to live for God in an unfriendly society. Whereas the audience are urged to understand themselves as pilgrims, their identity as pilgrims comes precisely because they are firmly located within God's family. 'It is precisely their "holiness", their divine separation from secular cultural values that renders them aliens in the eyes of that culture'.[71] Through their new birth they have transferred from ignorance to truth, from a futile way of life to a life of hope, from the tutelage of (idolatrous) fathers/ancestors to the tutelage of God the Father, from one family to another. The author's admonitions and his call to holy living, are primarily given to help them understand how to live as members of God's family.[72]

---

66. The phrase 'ἐκ τῆς ματαίας ὑμῶν ἀναστροφῆς πατροπαραδότου' may be referring to the audience's idolatrous past. In fact, the adjective μάταιος is often used in the Old Testament to condemn pagan idolatrous worship (Lev. 17.7; 2 Chron. 11.15; Est. 4.17; Jer. 2.5; 8.19). See, Green, *1 Peter*, p. 38; Elliott, *1 Peter*, p. 370; Michaels, *1 Peter*, pp. 64–5; Achtemeier, *1 Peter*, p. 127).
67. Bechtler, *Following in His Steps*, p. 112.
68. Bechtler, *Following in His Steps*, p. 103.
69. Feldmeier, *The First Letter of Peter*, p. 14.
70. Green, *1 Peter*, p. 56.
71. Achtemeier, *1 Peter*, p. 125.
72. So also, Feldmeier, *The First Letter of Peter*, pp. 14–17; Volf, 'Soft Difference', pp. 17–19.

Second, election necessitates holiness not only because the believers need to reflect the nature of God their Father, but also because of the holy nature of the means through which God brought about their election. In 1 Pet. 1.17-21 the author offers a christological grounding of the need for his audience to conduct a life of reverent fear during their sojourn existence: 'knowing that it is not by perishable things, like silver or gold, you were redeemed from the empty lifestyle you inherited from your forefathers, but by the precious blood of Christ, like that of a lamb without blemish and without defect' (1.18-19). First Peter 1.17-21 is a continuation of the thoughts and the themes already introduced in the letter (cf., e.g., ἀναστρέφω [1.17] with ἀναστροφή [1.15]; παροικία [1.17] with παρεπίδημος [1.1] – these two concepts are brought together in 2.11 [παροίκους καὶ παρεπιδήμους]; τιμίῳ αἵματι…Χριστοῦ [1.19] with ῥαντισμὸν αἵματος Ἰησοῦ Χριστοῦ [1.2]; προεγνωσμένου μὲν πρὸ καταβολῆς κόσμου [1.20] with κατὰ πρόγνωσιν θεοῦ πατρός [1.2]).

The author's theological hermeneutic of the Old Testament – that is, his use of the Old Testament as a theological source is evident. First, he likens the audience's existence to that of Israel in exile (1.17; cf. Ezra 8.35). In Ezra, the phrase 'υἱοὶ τῆς παροικίας' is used to describe those who have left Babylon. It should be noted that part of the background of this section of 1 Peter is Isa. 52, which talks also of freedom from Babylonian exile. The word παροικία, as a designation of Israel's experience, is attested in other Jewish writings as well (Wis. 19.10; *T. Levi* 11.2; *3 Macc.* 7.19), and in the New Testament (Acts 13.17).[73] Second, the author of 1 Peter describes the audience's salvation in terms that are reminiscent of the Exodus (1.18; cf. Exod. 6.6; 15.13; Deut. 7.8)[74] and/or freedom from Babylonian exile (Isa. 52.3).[75] In Isaiah, freedom is carried out with no payment of any kind. Here too, the focus is not so much on the price paid for the redemption as it is on

73. On 1 Peter's use of παροικία, see also Green, *1 Peter*, p. 43.
74. It is worth noting that in Exod. 15.13 there is a rapprochement between the ideas of redemption and that of holiness.
75. Some scholars (e.g., Michaels, *1 Peter*, p. 64; Jobes, *1 Peter*, pp. 116–17) have followed Adolf Deissmann's proposal regarding the presence of sacral manumission in Paul's writings (*Light from the Ancient East: The New Testament Illustrated by Recently Discovered Texts of the Graeco-Roman World* [New York: Harper & Brothers, 1927], pp. 319–30) and proposed 1 Peter's possible dependence on the same in his development of the concept of redemption in 1.18-19. However, 1 Peter's dependence seems to be more rooted in the Old Testament (Isa. 52.13–53.12), and Jesus' teaching as recorded in Mk 10.45 and Mt. 20.28. So Green, *1 Peter*, p. 41; Achtemeier, *1 Peter*, p. 127. Green calls into question the significance of the practice of sacral manumission for early Christian atonement theology (*1 Peter*, p. 41). So also Markus Barth and Helmut Blanke, *The Letter to Philemon* (ECC; Grand Rapids: Eerdmans, 2000), pp. 47–9; S. Scott Bartchy, *First-Century Slavery and 1 Corinthians 7.21* (SBLDS, 11; Atlanta: Scholars, 1973), pp. 121–5. Feldmeier points out that all three images (sacral manumission, freedom from exile, and atonement through Jesus' death) are not mutually exclusive and could be part of the background as they share in common the concept of freedom from dependence and lostness (*The First Letter of Peter*, p. 117).

the means by which the redemption was carried out.[76] Third, the description of Christ is connected to the image of the Passover lamb, which is itself connected to redemption from Egypt's bondage (Exod. 12) and Israel's sacrificial cultic practices (Exod. 29.1; Lev. 22.18-21).[77] The call to holiness is also grounded in the means of redemption. The audience is to be holy, because they call on a Father who is holy, and because of the holiness of the means through which their redemption was carried out.[78] The author will reiterate the purity/ethical aspect of the outcome of the addressees' election in 1.22-23. There his emphasis is on the audience's regeneration. He uses another contrast (corruptible seed versus incorruptible seed) to drive home to his audience the need for them to live a life that is worthy of obedient children of God. Here, the author has in mind Jesus' election as well as his holiness (1.19-20). In highlighting these two aspects, he is offering a warrant for the audience's need to have holiness be the outworking of their election. The Israelites were urged to do the same, according to Leviticus. More importantly, the rhetoric is such that one can sense already the implicit presence of the exhortation to follow in Jesus' footsteps that will be expressed in 2.21. The author's discussion of Jesus' election comes squarely into focus in 2.4-10. There one also finds the embedded concepts of election and service and election and witness.

3.3.3. The stone metaphor as election imagery (2.4-10)

Seock-Tae Sohn argues that the purpose of God's election of Israel is for fellowship and service, where service includes both worship and witness.[79] John Goldingay explains that this vocation was fulfilled more by being than by acting.[80] The author of 1 Peter draws from the Old Testament to explain to his audience the implications of Jesus' election in 2.4-10. In the process, he identifies the audience with Jesus, thereby making the point that similar

---

76.   τιμίῳ αἵματι is a dative of means or instrument which is connected to the passive ἐλυτρώθητε of which God is the implied agent. So also Achtemeier, *1 Peter*, p. 128.

77.   In 1 Pet. 2.22 the author draws from Isa. 53 to link the images of the suffering Christ, the suffering servant, and the Passover lamb. It can be argued that Peter already has the sufferings of the Christ in view here (1.18-20) and even earlier (1.1). So also Boring, *1 Peter*, p. 83; Davids, *1 Peter*, pp. 72–3. Achtemeier and Spicq agree that Isa. 53 is part of the background here, but deny that the image relates primarily to the Passover lamb (Achtemeier, *1 Peter*, pp. 128–9; Spicq, *Épîtres*, pp. 68–9).

78.   The author's focus here is not deliverance from sin, but deliverance from a certain way of life. So Achtemeier, *1 Peter*, p. 127; Jobes, *1 Peter*, p. 118).

79.   Sohn, *Divine Election*, pp. 194–9. These categories are helpful, yet it can be argued that worship is also part of fellowship as it is in the midst of worship that God fellowships with his people and vice versa. In the text of 1 Peter 'fellowship' and 'witness' appear to be the primary categories with 'worship' overlapping between the two (see below).

80.   John Goldingay, *Old Testament Theology: Israel's Faith* (Vol. 2; Downers Grove, IL: InterVarsity, 2006), p. 203.

implications are true of their own election. They have been chosen to have fellowship with God, and to serve as his witnesses.

3.3.3.1. *Election and fellowship (2.4-8)*

Consistent with his theological hermeneutic, the author of 1 Peter appropriates several passages (Isa. 28.16; 42.1; 43.20; Ps. 118.22 [117.22, LXX]; Isa. 8.14) and weaves them smoothly together in order to put forward a description of Jesus' election that is analogous to that of the servant of YHWH in the Old Testament.[81] The concepts of election and fellowship come to the fore in 2.4-5.

The author describes Christ as the living stone, rejected by people, but in God's sight chosen and precious (1 Pet. 2.4). He draws from Isa. 28.16 in which God, through the prophet, sends a warning to those in Judah who have not been faithful to the covenant. In its wider context, that warning gives way to an invitation for the people of Judah to put their trust in God, and the promise of a new community where justice will prevail.[82] The author has already made reference to Jesus' elect status both implicitly through the familial language used to describe Jesus' relationship with the God the Father (1.3), and explicitly in the discussion of the sacrificial death of Jesus Christ as the means for the audience's redemption (1.18-20) and his subsequent resurrection by God (1.21). This image is reinforced in the description of the stone as a 'living stone' which depicts Jesus as risen from the dead.[83] The author reiterates the preciousness of the 'living stone' by grounding the concept in Scripture (2.6-7). He combines Isa. 8.14 with Ps. 118.22 [117.22, LXX] to explain and reinforce to the believers the manner through which their relationship with God is established (2.4-5).[84] The audience already experience life in a covenantal relationship with God: they call God Father (1.17), are obedient children (1.14, 22), have tasted that the Lord is good (2.3), and are part of the community that is being built on Christ (2.4-5).[85] The author's aim in 2.6-7, then, is not only to reiterate the means of God's election of the audience, Christ the 'living stone', but also

---

81. In Isa. 8.14, the 'stone' actually refers to YHWH himself.

82. Childs, *Isaiah*, pp. 208–10; Green, *1 Peter*, p. 58; Elliott, *1 Peter*, p. 424.

83. So Elliott, *The Elect and the Holy*, p. 34; Davids, *1 Peter*, p. 85; Achtemeier, *1 Peter*, p. 154.

84. The author's christological/theological appropriation of Isa. 28.16 is evident in that whereas he introduces the quotation as 'περιέχει ἐν γραφῇ' he deviates both from the LXX and from the MT. Most of the changes are minor, but as Senior suggests, 'the addition of the phrase "in him" after "believe" – a change from the Hebrew but found in some LXX versions – reinforces the christological interpretation of the quotation' (*1 Peter*, p. 54). See also Achtemeier, *1 Peter*, p. 159; Elliott, *1 Peter*, p. 424.

85. The participle προσερχόμενοι is an attendant circumstance that depends on the main verb οἰκοδομεῖσθε. If one treats οἰκοδομεῖσθε as an imperative, then the text would read: 'Come to him ... and let yourselves be built ...' If one handles οἰκοδομεῖσθε as a present indicative, then the participle has a prepositional force to it, and the focus is not so much on the command/invitation but on the acknowledgement of an action that is already in process.

to offer the audience a glimpse of the fate of those who choose not to be a part of God's family.[86]

As in 1 Pet. 1.3 when Jesus' resurrection from the dead was used as the basis for the audience's regeneration and relationship with God, in 2.5, the image of the 'living stone' is used to remind the audience of their own status before God. They too are 'living stones'. Therefore, they share with Jesus a chosen status in God's sight, and rejection by humans.[87] Yet, just as the author's identification of the audience with Israel has its limitations, his identification of the believers with Jesus has its limitations.[88] Green proposes that the author's identification of his audience with Jesus here is done in terms of *imitatio Christi*.[89] As such the story of Jesus, his actions, his perspective on life, and his attitude toward God and human beings become normative for 1 Peter's audience.

The fellowship aspect of election is expressed in the author's description of his believers as a 'spiritual house'. This conveys the understanding that election is carried out in a corporate setting (2.5).[90] Jesus as 'the living stone' is 'the cornerstone' of the spiritual house that is formed with the 'living stones'. As such he is part of the building. In fact, it is he who holds it together.[91] The 'spiritual house' is reminiscent of the Temple where God dwells and fellowships with his people.[92] The fellowship is both horizontal and vertical. As they come together to Christ, they have fellowship among themselves, fellowship with Jesus Christ, and fellowship with God. The author complements the image of a 'spiritual house' with that of a 'holy priesthood'. The emphasis is still on the community, their corporate identity, and the role they play toward God and the world around them (2.5, 9).[93]

86. So Achtemeier, *1 Peter*, pp. 159–61.

87. Green, *1 Peter*, p. 60. Here as in 1.1, 3-6 Peter's treatment of the concept of election shows a close connection between chosenness and rejection (suffering). I will attend to this in the following chapter.

88. So Elliott, *The Elect and the Holy*, p. 144; Green, *1 Peter*, p. 60.

89. *Imitatio Christi* has to do with the Peter's call to the audience to follow Christ's example. They imitate Christ by following in his footsteps; in other words, their lives are to be patterned after that of Jesus Christ.

90. So Michaels, *1 Peter*, p. 99.

91. Green, *1 Peter*, p. 59. There are two possible meanings for ἀκρογωνιαῖος: 'cornerstone' or 'capstone'. But the context of 1 Peter, and the fact that the author quotes from Ps. 118.22 [117.22, LXX] from the LXX seem to suggest that the former is meant here. See further, J. Jeremias, 'λίθος', in *TDNT* (Vol. 4; Grand Rapids: Eerdmans, 1979), pp. 272–3; Elliott, *The Elect and the Holy*, pp. 23–6; Davids, *1 Peter*, pp. 89–90.

92. So also, Feldmeier, *The First Letter of Peter*, p. 135. Elliott, however, argues that οἶκος and οἶκος πνευματικός, in this pericope, refer to 'household' and not 'temple' (*The Elect and the Holy*, pp. 157–9; *1 Peter*, 414–18; *Home*, pp. 165–266). For an assessment of Elliott's view see Bechtler, *Following in His Steps*, pp. 139–45. See also, Green, *1 Peter*, pp. 60–1; Senior, *1 Peter*, p. 54; Achtemeier, *1 Peter*, pp. 158–9; Michaels, *1 Peter*, pp. 100–1.

93. So Green, *1 Peter*, p. 61; Elliott, *The Elect and the Holy*, pp. 166–9. Davids correctly proposes that 'holy priesthood' refers to the Christians' consecration and separation to God, similar to Aaron in Lev. 8-11, but diminishes the holiness aspect to a secondary role, and argues against a corporate understanding of this passage (*1 Peter*, p. 87).

Here as in 2.9 (holy nation) and in 1.15-17, 22, there exists a link between election and holiness. Together, as a 'holy priesthood', they fulfil the purpose of their election which is 'to offer spiritual sacrifices that are acceptable to God through Jesus Christ' (2.5).[94]

The concept of *imitatio Christi* is present as well. The author equates fellowship with God with a life of holiness that is lived *à l'instar de* Jesus Christ. The description of the reality of his audience may even parallel 1 Peter's picture of Christ in 1.18-20 as an example of obedience, devotion to, and dependence on God (1.2, 18-20; 2.23). [95] Whereas the audience's holy way of life cannot provide redemption, it has the power to draw people to God, who, through Jesus Christ, has the power to redeem them from their 'futile way of life' (2.11-12; 3.1-2). Jesus' election, obedience, and holiness made possible the audience's election and the ensuing relationship and fellowship with God. To maintain that relationship the believers must emulate the life of obedience and holiness that is characteristic of Jesus. Worship of God, the offering of 'spiritual sacrifices' to God, is not only to be done through Jesus Christ; it needs to be patterned after his life.

3.3.3.2. *Election and witness (2.9-10)*[96]

An additional argument can be made from the structure of the passage for the relationship that exists between the concepts of election and fellowship. In 1 Pet. 2.4 the author presents two groups of people. Then, he establishes a stark contrast between these two groups in 2.6-8. The one consists of those who have accepted the 'living stone', who is chosen and precious, and are coming to him. Because they believe, they enjoy 'preciousness'.[97] This group takes on the identity (and fate) of 'the living stone', enjoys fellowship with him, with one another, and with God. The other consists of those who are disobedient and have rejected the 'living stone'. That group is implicitly identified with their absence of fellowship with God. Their decision to

94.   The purpose of election is worked out in their being built into a holy priesthood (horizontal fellowship). The offering of sacrifices to God (vertical fellowship) is in itself a depiction of holy conduct.

95.   The language may be different, but in essence the concept is analogous. The author is not equating the audience's experience with that of Jesus Christ but wants the audience to pattern their lives after Jesus. Given that (1) the author's primary concern in 1.18-20 is not atonement for sin, (2) the themes of election and holiness play a major role in this context, and (3) the author is encouraging his audience to identify with Christ, one can safely say that the imagery of Jesus' sacrifice becomes a paradigm and sets the stage up for the parallel in 2.5. Furthermore, 1.18-20 has some affinities with the cultic life of Israel, and the fact that the author's focus here is corporate election, the concept of worship may also be present in 2.4-5. The offering of 'spiritual sacrifices' as an act of worship is attested elsewhere in the New Testament (e.g., Rom. 12.1; Eph. 5.2). In both cases as in 1 Peter, the emphasis is placed on holy living.

96.   Wells (*God's Holy People*, pp. 221–31) and Elliott (*The Elect and the Holy*) focus on 'election and holiness' in this section. One can see that the author is concerned with the holiness of the audience in 2.5, 9. I focus on witness here because the connection between election and holiness has already been introduced in 1.13-21.

97.   Wells, *God's Holy People*, pp. 215–16.

reject the 'living stone' causes them to stumble and fall.[98] The author's description of the audience in 2.9-10 is part of that contrast. In the process of highlighting the contrast and describing the nature of the audience, the author introduces another aspect of the purpose of election: witness.

Here the author describes his audience in terms that establish their identification with Israel of old: elect race (Isa. 43.20);[99] a royal priesthood, and a holy nation (Exod. 19.6); a people acquired by God (Exod. 19.5; Isa. 43.21); you who formerly were not a people, now are the people of God; who formerly had not been shown mercy, now have been shown mercy (Hos. 1.6, 9; 2.1, 23). These designations reaffirm for the audience their elect status and encourage the community to see themselves as a continuation of Israel.[100] For the author of 1 Peter, the community of Israel, and the community now gathered around (built on) Christ are one. God is at work in the present community in the same way he was at work in Israel. His work in and through the present community is a continuation of his purpose for the world.[101]

In 1 Pet. 2.9, the phrase 'ὅπως τὰς ἀρετὰς ἐξαγγείλητε τοῦ ἐκ σκότους ὑμᾶς καλέσαντος εἰς τὸ θαυμαστὸν αὐτοῦ φῶς' shares some conceptual affinities with Isa. 43.21 (LXX) – 'τὰς ἀρετάς μου διηγεῖσθαι'. The context of Isa. 43 points to the celebration of the Exodus in anticipation of the liberation from Babylonian captivity.[102] The author of 1 Peter appropriates this language and encourages his audience to do the same: declare God's excellences on the basis of God's deliverance carried out on their behalf through Jesus Christ (1.3, 18-21). Further, the imagery which speaks of conversion 'from darkness to light' is attested in the Old Testament (e.g., Ps. 18.28 [18.29, MT; 17.29, LXX]; 36.9 [36.10, MT; 35.10, LXX]; Isa. 2.5); other Jewish writings (e.g., 1QS 3.13-26; 1QH 4.5, 6, 23); and elsewhere in the New Testament (Acts 28.16; Eph. 5.8).[103]

98.　The divine passive 'ἐτέθησαν' in 2.8, which describes the fate of the unbelievers/disobedient ones, parallels God's action 'τίθημι' in 2.6, highlights God's control/sovereignty over the situation, and emphasizes the fact that he is the main actor throughout. Note, however, that as the election of the faithful to holiness and fellowship with God is dependent on their response to (acceptance of) Christ so the 'election' of the disobedient to falling is dependent on their response to (rejection of) Christ.

99.　This designation not only identifies the audience with Israel, but also with Jesus Christ (2.4, 6). The author already used it in 1.1 in his greeting.

100.　So also Wells, *God's Holy People*, pp. 221–2. Jerry Truex argues for the presence of a 'replacement motif' in 1 Peter ('God's Spiritual House: A Study of 1 Peter 2.4-5', *Direction* 33 [2004], pp. 185–93). Similarly, Achtemeier proposes that 'for 1 Peter, the Christian community has supplanted Israel as God's chosen people' ('Newborn Babes', p. 225, n. 76). Feldmeier notes that the point of this language is 'neither the differentiation from Israel nor that from society, but belongingness to God' (*The First Letter of Peter*, pp. 140–1.

101.　Green, 'Living as Exiles', p. 319.

102.　Wells, *God's Holy People*, p. 227; Childs, *Isaiah*, pp. 334–6.

103.　So, Wells, *God's Holy People*, p. 228.

The author is still concerned about corporate identity. The proclamation of God's wonderful acts implies corporate worship, praise and thanksgiving, which is done within the community;[104] but goes beyond the community to the world at large.[105] It is a proclamation that is lived out in and through holiness of life – spiritual sacrifices that are acceptable to God, good conduct that is conformed to the character of the God and the life of Christ.[106]

3.4. Conclusion

The threefold narrative structure I am using presses me to identify the fabula of 1 Peter, and I have identified its first element as 'election'. I have studied the text of 1 Peter in order to show how the fabula is at work in the epistle through the element of 'election'. First, I looked at the election language in the Old Testament in order to set up the discussion as the Old Testament plays a major role in the narrative substructure of the epistle. I then looked at the election language in 1 Peter and paid attention to how the author uses words and concepts to convey his understanding of election. In the process I discussed the language of the fatherhood of God and looked at the relationship between election and holiness. Finally, I conducted a treatment of the stone metaphor where the concepts of election and fellowship, and election and witness are present.

The author's description of his audience contains a paradox: they are elect strangers. That reality is expressed in terms of the audience as rejoicing in their new birth/election/salvation while at the same time being saddened because of diverse trials. That paradox echoes Israel's election and experience of diasporic and exilic existence. It is also evident in Christ's experience: Christ, the 'living stone' is precious in God's sight, but rejected by humans. That reality mirrors that of the audience which the author identifies with the 'living stone'. The proximity with which the author uses the two concepts of election and rejection (trials, suffering) implies that a link exists between the two. This paradox, the collocation of election and suffering is important because it is crucial in understanding the author's perception of the suffering of the audience. To that effect, I turn to the next chapter, which will focus on the subject of 'suffering in 1 Peter'.

104. Balch, *Wives*, p. 133; Michaels, *1 Peter*, p. 110.
105. Wells, *God's Holy People*, p. 229. *Contra* Balch, *Wives*, p. 134.
106. Wells, *God's Holy People*, pp. 229–30.

Chapter 4

SUFFERING IN 1 PETER

4.1. Introduction

In the preceding chapter I demonstrated how the concept of 'election' operates in 1 Peter as an element of the four-part fabula that constitutes the lens through which the author invites his audience to make sense of their situation. I showed how the concept of election was common to the stories of Israel, Jesus, and the audience. As the author reads the Old Testament christologically, he appropriates the language of election that is used in the Old Testament in relation to Israel, interprets it in light of the life of Jesus Christ and applies that language to his audience. That same principle is at work in the other elements of the fabula. In this chapter, I will focus on the second element: 'suffering'. Suffering plays a key role in the epistle because the author's concern about the suffering of the audience and how they should react to the hardships they face constitutes in part what motivated the composition of the letter.[1]

First, the language of 1 Peter suggests that suffering, both potential and actual, is something the audience faces partly because of who they became (1.3-9; 4.3-4).[2] Because of the new birth the audience has experienced and the change of behaviour that ensued, the audience has become the target of verbal abuse and other kinds of mistreatment (2.12, 20; 3.16; 4.3-4). The new birth the audience has been given has ushered in a bright future. However, for the audience to share in future glory it is important that they demonstrate good conduct; i.e., respond faithfully, in the face of their present trials. This is one reason the author repeatedly calls upon his audience to 'do good' (2.11-12, 20; 3.6, 8-17).[3] The expectation for the audience is that

1. So, e.g., Earl J. Richard, 'Honorable Conduct among the Gentiles: A Study of the Social Thought of 1 Peter', WW 24 (2004), pp. 412–20; Feldmeier, *The First Letter of Peter*, p. 2.
2. As I will argue below, David G. Horrell is right to claim that the audience's allegiance to Christ was at the root of the criticisms levelled at them by the outside world ('The Label Χριστιανός: 1 Peter 4.16 and the Formation of Christian Identity', *JBL* 126 (2004), pp. 361–81.
3. Horrell identifies this (to 'do good') as one of the themes of the epistle ('Χριστιανός', p. 368).

'doing good' should be a way of life. Yet, this call is squarely located in the context of suffering.

Second, the language of suffering permeates the letter. The author uses several words to speak of the reality the audience is dealing with, for example: πειρασμός (1.6; 4.12); κολαφίζω (2.20); πάσχω (2.19, 20; 3.14, 17; 4.15-16, 19; 5.10); καταλαλέω (2.12; 3.16); βλασφημέω (4.4); πάθημα (5.9).[4] Further, the concept of suffering is evident both in the introduction and the conclusion of the epistle thereby attesting to its prominence. By describing the recipients of the letter as 'elect sojourners living in the diaspora' (1.1-2), the author paints a reality which in itself conveys the idea that the audience is in a precarious situation. A similar idea is conveyed by the phrase 'aliens and strangers' in 2.11. Goppelt rightly suggests that this language implies that the situation of the audience was similar to that of Israel in Egypt.[5] The suffering of the audience is also manifest in the epistle's benediction (5.10). There the author reemphasizes the transient nature of the audience's testings and looks forward to the time when suffering is no more. It is worth noting that whereas suffering plays an important role in the letter, as it relates to the reality of the audience it is not the end of the story. It is only a passing reality, something they may have to experience for a while (1.7). In addition, the author encourages the believers to understand their trials in light of Christ's sufferings and in light of an apocalyptic timetable. Therefore, as in the case of Jesus, their suffering will be followed with glory. It is a means through which God displays his ability to save, rescue, and vindicate his own. This is at the core of the author's theological hermeneutic (1.11).

In what follows, I will demonstrate that the hardships Israel faced as God's chosen people are part of the overall tapestry that constitutes the background of the epistle. I will then discuss the author's understanding of the sufferings of Christ and focus on three aspects that are present in the letter: Jesus' sufferings as (1) prelude to glory, (2) as exemplary, and (3) as redemptive. The author's understanding of the sufferings of Christ is multifaceted.[6] I have chosen to focus on these three aspects because, as I demonstrate below, they are prominent in 1 Peter, occur in strategic places in the epistle, and play a crucial role in the author's rhetoric. His understanding of the audience's sufferings makes up the final section of this chapter. The author encourages the audience to think of their sufferings as sharing in Christ's own sufferings. As such there are aspects of Jesus' sufferings with which the author calls the audience to identify. Yet, Christ's sufferings also possess some unique characteristics that do not readily apply to the reality

---

4.   So also, Rebecca Skaggs, *The Pentecostal Commentary on 1 Peter, 2 Peter, Jude* (Cleveland: Pilgrim, 2004), p. 14; Green, *1 Peter*, p. 225; Elliott, *1 Peter*, pp. 104–9, 621.

5.   Goppelt, *1 Peter*, pp. 19, 68–70. On the vulnerability conveyed by the author's language, see also Elliott, *1 Peter*, pp. 314–15; Feldmeier, *The First Letter of Peter*, pp. 2–13.

6.   See, e.g., Green, *1 Peter*, pp. 225–7; Charles H. Talbert, *Learning through Suffering: The Educational Value of Suffering in the New Testament and in Its Milieu* (Collegeville, MA: Liturgical, 1991), pp. 42–57.

of the readers. My discussion of the author's understanding of the audience's sufferings will focus on three main aspects: (1) suffering as prelude to glory, (2) suffering as effective, and (3) suffering as witness. I will now turn to the discussion of Israel's suffering as a background for the author's treatment.

4.2. *Israel's suffering as background for 1 Peter*

I propose that Israel's suffering is part of the background of the epistle, and contributes to 1 Peter's theological hermeneutic of the Old Testament because (1) the collocation of election and suffering is attested in the Old Testament and (2) the same is indicated by 1 Peter.

We have already seen how the author's understanding of election is analogous to the theme of election in the Old Testament, and the election of Israel in particular. Two of the key Old Testament passages that describe Israel's election have embedded in them the notion of Israel's suffering (Exod. 19.4-6; Deut. 7.6-8). Exodus 19.4 refers to what God did to (against) the Egyptians, namely, the plagues and the destruction of Pharaoh's army at the Red Sea.[7] However, this reference can be read in light of the larger context of the Exodus which brings to the fore what God did for the Israelites: deliver them from the house of slavery. In revealing himself to Moses, God said, 'I have observed the misery of my people who are in Egypt … So come, I will send you to Pharaoh to bring my people, the Israelites, out of Egypt' (Exod. 3.7, 10). God speaks of Israel as 'my people' while they are still in Egypt, a claim for the existence of a relationship between the two parties prior to the Exodus. That relationship is undoubtedly cast in the context of the covenant established between God and Abraham as evidenced in Exod. 3.6, but it concerns YHWH and Israel nonetheless. In Exod. 13.3 the Passover is described to the Israelites as the day 'on which you came out of Egypt, out of the house of slavery'. Further, in Exod. 20.2, the prologue to the Decalogue, God introduces himself thus: 'I am the LORD your God who brought you out of Egypt, out of the house of slavery'. In the context of the Decalogue, liberation from the 'house of slavery' gives YHWH the right to set the commandments that Israel is to live by.[8] But the larger context also includes the pains, sufferings, and afflictions that are attached to their experience in Egypt. This is clearly borne out in Deut. 26.6 'But the Egyptians treated us badly, afflicted us, and submitted us to hard labor'.[9] Even if the emphasis on Israel's election were to be placed in the Exodus event (as opposed to preceding it), the claim is still warranted because God's chosen people still faced the wilderness wanderings and its dangers (Deut. 25.17-19, cf. Exod. 17) – and later, exile and its misery (Dan. 3).

---

7.   So William H. C. Propp, *Exodus 19-40: A New Translation with Introduction and Commentary* (AB, 2a; New York: Doubleday, 2006), p. 156.

8.   So also, Propp, *Exodus 19-40*, p. 167; John I. Durham, *Exodus* (WBC, 3; Waco, TX: Word, 1987), pp. 283–4.

9.   Author's translation.

The Israelites were exhorted to keep in mind the memory of their sufferings in Egypt and God's deliverance as a way to teach them to show kindness toward the stranger and the orphan (Deut. 24.14-18). As it turned out, suffering would be more than a memory but a present reality at several stages of the life of Israel as a nation because of the failure to heed God's word. Eventually, the Israelites would go into exile and long for a deliverance like the Exodus. Robert P. Carroll suggests that 'Deportation and diaspora are constitutive of the Jewish identity as it begins to emerge and evolve in the biblical narrative. The Bible is the great metanarrative of deportation, exile and potential return'.[10]

The language the Old Testament uses to describe the experience of sieges, deportation, and diasporic existence is one of graphic oppression and violence against God's chosen people (2 Kgs 6.26-29; 18.27; 25.2-3; Est. 3.12-15; Ps. 137 [136; MT, LXX]; Jer. 22.26-28; Lam. 2.12; 4.9-10; Dan. 3). The trauma associated with such experiences can be physical, social, and psychological.[11] The sufferings that Israel experienced were often brought about because of their disobedience. The understanding that exile comes as a result of Israel's disobedience is also attested in Jewish literature of the Second Temple period (*Sib. Or.* 3.265-79; *T. Mos.* 2.4–3.3). The wider context of this literature attests to a future restoration of Israel.[12] Throughout, God's presence has been manifested in the midst of the people's hardships to deliver them from their oppressors (1 Kgs 20.13; 2 Kgs 7.1-20; 19).

The prophets often speak of the exile in terms of God's correction, God's way of teaching Israel to live out the obedience and holiness that their status requires and in order to bring an end to their exilic life (Isa. 1.25-28; Jer. 31.31-34; Ezek. 37.21-28; Hos. 2.16-25).[13] However, there is a tendency in post-exilic and Second Temple Judaism literature to treat the exile as an ongoing reality (Ezra 9.8-9; 2 Macc. 1.27; 2.5-7, 18; 4Q504-506; *T. Mos.* 4.8-9; *2 Bar.* 68.5-7; 80.7; Wis. 19.10; *T. Levi* 11.2; *3 Macc.* 7.19).[14] What is

10.   Robert P. Carroll, 'Deportation and Diasporic Discourses in the Prophetic Literature', in James M. Scott (ed.), *Exile: Old Testament, Jewish, and Christian Conceptions* (New York: Brill, 1997), pp. 63–85 (64).

11.   Daniel L. Smith-Christopher, 'Reassessing the Historical and Sociological Impact of the Babylonian Exile (597/587-539 BCE)', in James M. Scott (ed.), *Exile: Old Testament, Jewish, and Christian Conceptions* (New York: Brill, 1997), pp. 7–36. See also, idem, *A Biblical Theology of Exile* (Minneapolis: Fortress, 1989), pp. 27–104.

12.   There is an essential difference here between Israel and 1 Peter's audience. The latter suffers because of its faithfulness to God.

13.   James Sanders, 'The Exile and Canon Formation', in James M. Scott (ed.), *Exile: Old Testament, Jewish, and Christian Conceptions* (New York: Brill, 1997), pp. 37–61 (48–9); Carroll, 'Deportation and Diasporic Discourse', in Scott, *Exile*, pp. 67–8.

14.   See James C. VanderKam, 'Exile in Jewish Apocalyptic Literature', in James M. Scott (ed.), *Exile: Old Testament, Jewish, and Christian Conceptions* (New York: Brill, 1997), pp. 89–109 (94–104); M. A. Knibb, 'The Exile in the Literature of the Intertestamental Period', *HeyJ* 17 (1976), pp. 253–72; E. P. Sanders, *Jesus and Judaism* (London: SCM, 1985), pp. 61–119; Craig A. Evans, 'Jesus and the Continuing Exile of Israel', in Carey C. Newman (ed.), *Jesus and the Restoration of Israel: A Critical Assessment of N. T. Wright's*

also clear is that the paradox attested in the Old Testament is also present in other Jewish writings, namely, that God's chosen people undergo suffering, and that life in diaspora can be a treacherous existence.

Whereas Israel might have suffered because of their disobedience to God, it is worth noting that both the Old Testament and other Jewish writings offer examples of righteous individuals who suffer persecution because of their willingness to live in obedience to God. For example, Joseph's display of integrity in the situation with Potiphar's wife was met with false accusations that cost him his freedom (Gen. 39); Mordecai's resolve not to conform to the king's order vis-à-vis Haman put his life and that of the Jewish population in jeopardy (Est. 3.1-15). In addition, Shadrach, Meshach, and Abednego faced death because of their decision not to worship the golden statue Nebuchadnezzar had made (Dan. 3); a similar fate befell Daniel for remaining steadfast to God in the midst of accusations and plots against him (Dan. 6). In 2 Macc. 7, the seven brothers and their mother accepted torture and death rather than defiling themselves.

George W. E. Nickelsburg has studied the similarities between these and other stories in Jewish literature that are concerned with the religious persecution of the righteous and argued that they all are part of a common *Gattung* which he identifies as 'the wisdom tale'.[15] He proposes that 'the basic similarities in theme, setting, characters, narrative technique, and structure are not likely the result of literary interdependence'.[16] Further, Nicklesburg suggests that these stories, which contain similar structural elements (conspiracy, trial, rescue, vindication, acclamation, etc.), are wisdom literature that contain some didactic function and seek to inculcate steadfastness in the face of persecution.[17]

In his book, *Der leidende Gerechtfertigte*, Karl Theodor Kleinknecht has conducted a thorough survey on the Old Testament-Jewish tradition of the 'righteous sufferer' in which he demonstrates the pervasiveness of the concept.[18] For example, this understanding is attested at Qumran where 'the children of righteousness' (בני צדק) are persecuted and deceived by the Angel

Jesus and the Victory of God (Downers Grove, IL: InterVarsity, 1999), pp. 77–100. Evans argues that some of Jesus' actions and teachings suggest that he too understood Israel to be in exile still.

15.   George W. E. Nickelsburg, Jr., *Resurrection, Immortality, and Eternal Life in Intertestamental Judaism and Early Christianity* (expanded edn; HTS, 56; Cambridge: Harvard University Press, 2006), pp. 67–118.

16.   Nicklesburg, *Resurrection*, p. 75. L. A. Rosenthal also points out the similarities between the stories of Joseph, Esther, and Daniel, but argues for literary dependence. See, 'Die Josephgeschichte, mit den Büchern Ester und Daniel verglichen', *ZAW* 15 (1895), pp. 278–84; idem, 'Nochmals der Vergleich Ester, Joseph-Daniel', *ZAW* 17 (1897), pp. 125–8;

17.   Nicklesburg, *Resurrection*, p. 75.

18.   Karl T. Kleinknecht, *Der leidende Gerechtfertigte: Die alttestamentlich-judische Tradition vom leidenden Gerechten und ihre Rezeption bei Paulus* (WUNT, 2.13; Tübingen: Mohr Siebeck, 2nd edn, 1998). See further, Lothar Rupper, *Jesus als der leidende Gerechte? Der Weg Jesus im Lichte eines alt-und zwischentesttamentlichen Motivs* (SBS, 5; Stuttgart: Katolisshes Biblelwek, 1972).

of Darkness and his allies (1QS 3.20-25). The concept is also found in the *Psalms Pesher* where the words of Ps. 37 are appropriated to the Community and interpreted to convey the suffering that befalls the righteous, those who practice the law (4Q171 2.13-16, 3.7-8).[19] These texts underscore the fact that the righteous sufferer will benefit God's protection and vindication.

The concept of the 'righteous sufferer' is present in Sir. 2.1-11. This text contains some striking similarities with 1 Peter both in terms of word usage and the concepts that are conveyed. The righteous are told to be ready to face trials as if they are a necessary occurrence in the lives of those who serve God. Compare, 'εἰ προσέρξῃ δουλεύειν κυρίῳ ἑτοίμασον τὴν ψυχήν σου εἰς πειρασμόν' (Sir. 2.1) with 'ὀλίγον ἄρτι εἰ δέον ἐστὶν λυπηθέντες ἐν ποικίλοις πειρασμοῖς' (1 Pet. 1.6); and, 'ὅτι ἐν πυρὶ δοκιμάζεται χρυσὸς καὶ ἄνθρωποι δεκτοὶ ἐν καμίνῳ ταπεινώσεως' (Sir 2.5) with 'ἵνα τὸ δοκίμιον ὑμῶν τῆς πίστεως πολυτιμότερον χρυσίου τοῦ ἀπολλυμένου διὰ πυρὸς δὲ δοκιμαζομένου' (1 Pet. 1.7). A similar idea is found in Dan. 11.33-35 in which one gathers that (1) the righteous will suffer for a time; (2) the righteous will be helped in their distress; and (3) that the suffering of the righteous has a purifying and cleansing effect. In addition, the concepts of steadfastness in suffering, deliverance from suffering and joy in the midst of suffering can be found in this pericope.

The concept of the 'righteous sufferer' is present in the *Similitudes of Enoch*.[20] In *1 En*. 47.1, 4 references are made to the 'blood of the righteous' which ascended to heaven and 'admitted before the Lord of the Spirits'. It is also evident in *1 En*. 103.9-10 which reads,

> In the days of our toil, we have surely suffered hardships and have experienced every trouble. We have faced many evil things and have become consumed. We have died and become few, (characterized) by the littleness of our spirit. We have been destroyed; and we have found none whatsoever to help us with a word otherwise. We have been tortured and destroyed, and could not even hope to see life from one day to the other.[21]

In the *Similitudes*, the suffering of the righteous is mentioned in the context of God's vengeance and punishment upon the disobedient: 'So he will deliver them to the angels for punishments in order that vengeance shall be executed on them – oppressors of his children and his elect ones' (*1 En*. 62.11).[22] A similar thought is conveyed in *1 En*. 98.13-14; namely, the affliction that befalls the unrighteous is a consequence of their treatment of the righteous: 'Woe unto you who rejoice in the suffering of the righteous ones' (13).[23]

---

19.   See also Kleinknecht, *Der leidende Gerechtfertigte*, pp. 140–53.
20.   See also Kleinknecht, *Der leidende Gerechtfertigte*, pp. 95–101.
21.   E. Isaac, '1 (Ethiopic Apocalypse of) Enoch: A New Translation and Introduction', in James H. Charlesworth (ed.), *OTP* (Vol. 1; New York: Doubleday, 1983), pp. 5–89 (84–5).
22.   Isaac, '1 Enoch', in Charlesworth (ed.), *OTP*, 1.43.
23.   Isaac, '1 Enoch', in Charlesworth (ed.), *OTP*, 1.78–9.

Such examples from the Old Testament and other Jewish writings provide evidence that experiences of sufferings are etched into the memory of Israel. It is also evident that they had a keen sense of their elect status even in the midst of their distress. They understood their sufferings partly as (1) God's punishment for their disobedience, (2) God's way to teach them the way back to him and (3) an outworking of their decision to remain steadfast within a culture that does not seem to know God or that operates by standards that are different from what God sets for his children. The fact that different stories in the Old Testament and other Jewish writings contain similar structural elements suggests that there was a shared understanding of, for example, who God is, how he relates to his people, who God's people are (or are supposed to be), what God expects of them, how God's people are to relate to the outside world, and what God's people can expect from God, specifically in the midst of hardships. It is also evident in these writings that the redactors made very little of the chronological gap that separated them from their ancestors. They saw themselves as participants of one story and understood God's word spoken centuries before as relevant for their own time.

I propose that a similar principle is at work in the way the author of 1 Peter connects his audience to Israel. Specifically, the collocation of election and suffering seen in the description of the audience (1.1, 3-6; 2.11) and the description of Jesus Christ (2.4-8, 21-25) reveal that the author is operating with categories that are analogous to the Scriptures of Israel and demonstrates an understanding of God, his audience, and their relationship with God and the outside world that is affined to what is attested in the Old Testament. My discussion of the author's description of his audience will further demonstrate the extent to which his theological analysis of the audience's situation is itself grounded in and reflective of Israel's experience in the Scriptures.

God wanted the children of Israel to think of their time in Egypt as a time of sojourning (Exod. 22.21 [22.20 LXX, MT]; 23.9). This is consistent with Deut. 7.6-8 which speaks of the patriarchs' (Jacob, specifically) sojourning in Egypt.[24] Moreover, the concept of 'being a sojourner' was to be more than a memory or a metaphor to describe the children of Israel. According to Lev. 25.23, God told the Israelites, 'The land shall not be sold in perpetuity, for the land is mine; and in my eyes you are sojourners and aliens' (προσήλυτοι καὶ πάροικοι, LXX). Although the Israelites were dwelling in the land that was given to them as an inheritance, they were considered 'not at home'. This attests to the theological reality of the situation of God's children in the world: 'not (yet) at home'. The children of Israel were urged to think of themselves in that way so that they could protect and care for the aliens and strangers who were in their midst. Israel was to treat them differently than they

---

24. Deut. 7.5-9 applies more readily to Jacob. However, the story could as well be that of Joseph, and/or that of Abraham. The audience is appropriating the story as their own and identifying themselves with the experience of the patriarchs. Propp adapts a composite picture, 'The Sojourner's Tale', that shows some of the similarities that are present in the biblical witness of the stories of the patriarchs (*Exodus 19-40*, pp. 241–2).

themselves were treated in Egypt. The memory of Egypt is one of alienness (παροικία) and of sufferings.[25] To that extent, 1 Peter's use of 'ἐκλεκτοῖς παρεπιδήμοις διασπορᾶς' (1.1), and 'παροίκους καὶ παρεπιδήμους' (2.11) in addressing his readers mirrors the reality of Israel;[26] and, therefore, warrants the claim that Israel's suffering is also part of the background of the epistle.

In 1 Pet. 2.4-8, the collocation of election and suffering is evident in the author's description of Jesus Christ in the 'living stone' metaphor. There the author brings together Ps. 118.22 [117.22, LXX] and Isa. 8.14-15; 28.16 to explain Jesus' election. The description conveys a paradox: Jesus is rejected by people, but he is chosen and precious in God's sight (2.4). The juxtaposition of rejection (suffering) and election found here is present in Ps. 118 [117, LXX] which is quoted in 1 Pet. 2.7. The psalm is a song of thanksgiving in which the psalmist celebrates with the congregation what God has done on his/her behalf and in their midst.[27] The first part of the psalm evokes God's deliverance from distress. The dangers that the psalmist is recalling can refer both to what a person faced (vv. 5-6) and to what Israel might have faced as a nation (vv. 10-12).[28] The collocation of election and suffering finds its clearest expression in Ps. 118.22 [117.22] – 'λίθον ὃν ἀπεδοκίμασαν οἱ οἰκοδομοῦντες οὗτος ἐγενήθη εἰς κεφαλὴν γωνίας' – a reference that applies either to Israel or to Israel's king.[29] There are two important points to note regarding the language of this psalm: (1) whereas suffering is remembered, the focus is on God's ability to save;[30] and (2) the celebration of past deliverance wrought by God generates acclamations/petitions to God to repeat his saving act in the future (v. 25).[31] Therefore, God's vindication of the righteous is also evident here.[32] When read this way in the context of 1 Peter, it follows, first, that the

---

25.   See Patrick D. Miller, 'Israel as Host to Strangers', *in Israelite Religion and Biblical Theology: Collected Essays* (JSOTSup, 267; Sheffield: Academic Press, 2000), pp. 548–71.

26.   See my discussion in Chapter 3.

27.   Several proposals have been put forward regarding the identity of the main speaker and the event that is being celebrated. For a discussion, see Louis Jacquet, *Les Psaumes et Le Cœur de l'Homme: Étude Textuelle, Littéraire, et Doctrinale* (3 vols; Bruxelles: Duculot, 1975), 3.304–5.

28.   Artur Weiser, *The Psalms* (OTL; Louisville: Westminster, 2000), pp. 725–7; Jacquet, *Les Psaumes*, 3.310–11.

29.   Samuel Terrien, *The Psalms: Strophic Structure and Theological Commentary* (ECC; Grand Rapids: Eerdmans, 2003), pp. 784–5; Jacquet, *Les Psaumes*, 3.314–15; Weiser, *The Psalms*, pp. 728–9. Weiser surmises, 'The interpretation of this saying in late Judaism as referring to David and to the Messiah, which also led to its application to Christ in the New Testament (Mt. 21.42; Acts 4.11; 1 Pet. 2.7), is presumably based on the correct recollection that the king appeared in the cult in the role of David (cf. Ps. 18), and that the royal cult entailed that at any given time the tradition of his ancestor was revived in the actual representative of the Davidic dynasty'.

30.   Terrien, *The Psalms*, pp. 786–7.

31.   Jacquet, *Les Psaumes*, 3.315–16; Weiser, *The Psalms*, p. 729.

32.   See my discussion in Chapter 6.

'stone metaphor' as applied to Jesus reveals that God has acted on behalf of Jesus Christ in a way that is characteristic of his actions in the Old Testament. Jesus' rejection by humans in 1 Peter is part of a larger picture that starts with election and ends with glory. The collocation of Jesus' election and suffering permeates the epistle and is implicit in the sufferings and glories (sufferings [death] and resurrection; humiliation and vindication) movement that the author uses throughout the letter (1.3, 10-12, 18-20; 2.7; 3.18). On the one hand, 1 Peter's description of Christ is rooted in the Old Testament and, on the other hand, his interpretation of the life of Israel follows a christological scheme. Thus, to speak of Christ as 'chosen' and 'rejected' implies Israel's own experience of 'chosenness' and 'rejection/suffering', and, analogously, to speak of Christ's sufferings and glories implies Israel's own suffering and vindication.[33] In 1 Pet. 1.2, the reference to 'the sprinkling of the blood of Jesus Christ' evokes both the reality of the Exodus and its implications in the context of the ratification of the covenant (Exod. 20-24) and Jesus' own suffering through the shedding of his blood (1.2, 18-20).

In 1 Pet. 2.9-10, the author uses a series of images that refer to Israel and applies them directly to the audience: elect race (Isa. 43.20); a royal priesthood, and a holy nation (Exod. 19.6); a people acquired by God (Exod. 19.5; Isa. 43.21); you who formerly were not a people, now are the people of God; who formerly had not been shown mercy, now have been shown mercy (Hos. 1.6, 9, 2.1, 23). All these designations carry the collocation of election and suffering. For example, Isaiah's description of Israel as an 'elect race' comes in the context of rehearsing God's mighty acts in the Exodus and in relation to future restoration from exile (Isa. 43.16-20). The terms 'royal priesthood' and 'holy nation' also refer to the time of the Exodus and were spoken in the context of God's deliverance of Israel from Egyptian bondage as part of the establishment of the covenant between the two parties (Exod. 19.3-6). Israel's suffering is also in the background of 1 Peter's description of the purpose of the audience's election. The phrase, 'so that you may proclaim the virtues of the one who called you out of darkness into his wonderful light' (2.9) is evocative of Isa. 43.2 – 'my people which I formed to proclaim my virtues'[34] – which, in its overall context, points to the celebration of the Exodus and anticipates the liberation from Babylonian captivity. It is clear that the author has not only Israel but Israel's own sufferings in mind when addressing the situation of his audience.

---

33.   Pearson's argument that the sufferings/glories pattern is dependent on the Old Testament concept of humiliation/vindication found in Isa. 53 (*Christological and Rhetorical Properties*, p. 43) is further support for this claim. Pearson notes that Isa. 53 and the sufferings/glories pattern are central to understanding the letter. However, Pearson focuses almost exclusively on this one Old Testament text, without recognizing that Isa. 53 participates with other Old Testament texts in shaping the background of the letter, just as 'sufferings' and 'glory' participate with the other elements of the fabula to create the narrative substructure of the letter. Naturally, some elements feature more prominently than others in the epistle and receive a more in-depth treatment. Yet, one can arrive at a much richer understanding of 1 Peter's message by paying attention to all the elements.

34.   Author's translation.

The 'stone metaphor' as applied to the audience means that they too experience suffering because of their election. And more importantly, their suffering is a passing reality that will be followed by glory (1.6; 5.10). This perspective does not diminish or trivialize the seriousness of the trials that the audience face in the present. It does help them focus on what really matters: the eternal inheritance that awaits those who live in obedience to God the Father (1.3-5). Further, the knowledge that God has vindicated Christ reassures the audience that as they now suffer as God's chosen people – as 'living stones', a 'holy priesthood', a 'holy nation', and 'God's own possession' – they can rely on the fact that God is able and will act for them in the same way he has acted in the past on behalf of Israel and Jesus.

Israel's memory was 'a memory of suffering, of powerful deliverance, and of blessing and providential care'.[35] Achtemeier rightly notes that the anticipation of future vindication prompts Christians to rejoice in the midst of their suffering (1.3-6), because 'what God has already done in and through Christ is sufficient reason for such joy'.[36] I submit that the audience have reason to rejoice also because of the realization of what God has done for Israel. Important for the author is not simply God's ability to redeem Israel, but his ability to redeem the believers from their sufferings, protect them during their sojourning, and give them an inheritance. To this he points his audience as they seek to make sense of, and respond to their hardships.

In order to substantiate the claim that the fabula of 1 Peter is common to the story of Israel, Jesus, and the audience, I have demonstrated that 'Israel's suffering' is part of the background of the letter. The author of 1 Peter discusses Jesus' sufferings in ways that highlight their uniqueness, on the one hand; and their participatory aspects, on the other hand. Certain aspects cannot be replicated by the audience. Yet, the author is able to draw some analogy from these sufferings and apply them to the audience's situation.

4.3. *1 Peter's understanding of the suffering of Christ*

The suffering of Christ plays a central role in the letter and constitutes the crux of the christology of the letter.[37] First, references to the sufferings of Christ are interspersed throughout the epistle (1.2-3, 10-12, 18-21; 2.19-20; 3.18; 4.1, 13; 5.1).[38] Second, the author locates the sufferings of Christ

---

35.   Miller, *Deuteronomy*, p. 182.

36.   Achtemeier, *1 Peter*, p. 101, n. 21.

37.   Robert W. Wall, 'Teaching 1 Peter as Scripture', WW 24 (2004), pp. 368–77 (373–4).

38.   Leonhard Goppelt argues that the christology of 1 Peter is limited to 1.18-21; 2.21-25; and 3.18-22, where the formulaic christological statements are located (*1 Peter*, p. 114; *Theology of the NT*, 2.176–8). Pearson advances that the letter's christology is located in 1.3-12, 18-22; 2.4-8, 21-25; and 3.18-22, where the sufferings/glories pattern is evident (*Christological and Rhetorical Properties*, p. 3).

at the core of his theological hermeneutic of the Old Testament (1.10-12). Third, Christ's suffering is put forth as the means by which the audience's relationship with God is established. Fourth, the author presents Christ's sufferings – more specifically, Christ's response to suffering – as exemplary for the audience.

I will discuss the author's understanding of the sufferings of Christ under three main headings: Jesus' sufferings as prelude to glory, Jesus' sufferings as exemplary, and Jesus' sufferings as redemptive. This triad provides further support for the points of contact between the stories of Israel, Jesus, and the audience. Because my discussion of the author's understanding of the suffering of Jesus and the audience follows, I will highlight here the way in which this triad is attested in the story of Israel.

This triad can be found in Israel's experience of suffering as a nation and in Old Testament accounts of righteous individuals. First, the concept 'suffering as prelude to glory' is attested, for example, in Joseph's story. When reminiscing on the events that unfolded between him and his brothers, Joseph interprets his ordeal in terms that imply that his suffering was a part of the process of God's plan to deliver the entire family (Gen. 45.4-5). Also the story itself shows that even Joseph's imprisonment was an integral part of the journey that led him to his place of prominence (Gen. 37–41). The same is evident in the story of the suffering and vindication of the servant of YHWH in Isa. 52–53. The description of the servant starts with his exaltation, thereby putting his suffering in perspective of his vindication. A similar perspective is offered in the Psalms of the Suffering Righteous (22 [21, LXX]; 31 [30, LXX]; 102 [101, LXX]), in Wis. 2.18; 4.15-17; 5, and also in Dan. 3; 6. There is the assurance that suffering will come to an end and that God will bring (or/and has brought) deliverance. Further, when God established the covenant with Abraham, he assured Abraham of the promise but also made him aware of the fact that his children will suffer for a while before experiencing God's deliverance (Gen. 15.13-14). Suffering is not the end or the primary element in the life of God's elect.

Second, 'suffering as exemplary' is evident in the sense that these stories were preserved and narrated partly because of their instructional value. In this context the focus is not on suffering *per se* but on how the righteous handled the difficult circumstances they faced. The stories of Joseph, Esther, Daniel, and Shadrach, Meshach, and Abednego, for example, would serve as guides not only for the development of other stories of steadfastness in suffering during later periods in Israel's history, but also for the formation of identity and shaping of behaviour.[39]

Third, 'suffering as redemptive' is attested in stories of righteous individuals and of Israel as a nation. Joseph's suffering made possible the preservation of his family and saved them from certain death (Gen. 45.7). As noted earlier, Ps. 118.22 [117.22, LXX] carries the implication that Israel's suffering and

39.   So also, Nickelsburg, *Resurrection*, p. 78.

subsequent vindication by God has the potential to lead other nations to God. In fact, the Exodus narrative bears witness to the fact that other ethnic groups journeyed with them out of Egypt (Exod. 12.38); undoubtedly, these groups were composed of foreigners who had witnessed God's mighty acts on behalf of Israel. Further, there is a parallel between Isa. 42.1; 49.1-3; and 52.13 which allows for understanding the 'servant of YHWH' as both an individual figure, on the one hand, and as corporate Israel, on the other hand.[40] Therefore, a case can be made for the sufferings of Israel as being redemptive in nature in the sense that they create opportunities for other nations to be drawn to God. These points of contacts will become more noticeable during my treatment of the author's understanding of the suffering of Christ, and his understanding of the suffering of the audience.

4.3.1. *Jesus' suffering as prelude to glory (1.11, 21; 3.18-22)*

One aspect of Jesus' suffering that is prominent in 1 Peter is that Jesus' suffering is not an end in itself. Jesus' suffering is only one aspect of the overall story of his relationship with God, whose scope extends from before the creation of the world until the last times, and whose end is the 'glory' that God will bestow (1.19-21). In 1 Peter, the sufferings of Christ are never discussed in isolation. For example, in 1.11, the content of the prophets' inquiry is 'the sufferings of Christ and the glories that would follow'.[41] Suffering is followed by resurrection and resurrection is followed by glory (1.19-21; 3.18-22).[42] It is worth noting that the description of the sufferings of Christ as a prelude to glory in 1 Peter is consistent with the picture and situation of the suffering servant of Isaiah (Isa. 52.13–53.12). The song shows that the sufferings of the servant of YHWH will be followed by his exaltation by YHWH (Isa. 53.11-12). It is also consistent with individual stories in the Old Testament and other Jewish literature where God's vindication of the faithful is expressed in their (earthly) exaltation following their sufferings (Dan. 11.40; 12.1-2; 2 Macc. 7). The *Similitudes* contains several references to the exaltation of the 'Elect One' (*1 En.* 45.3; 49.2; 51.3).[43] The stories of Joseph in Gen. 37–46, of Shadrach, Meshach, and Abednego in Dan. 3, and

---

40.   Childs, *Isaiah*, p. 412.

41.   Scholars (e.g., Pearson, *Christological and Rhetorical Properties*; Richard, 'Functional Christology'; Schutter, *Hermeneutic and Composition*) have spoken of the 'sufferings/glories' pattern as key to 1 Peter. It is clear that the author's language in 1.11 lends itself to this understanding. However, 1 Pet. 1.11 is only a summary statement for a richer pattern that the author is working with – election, suffering, endurance, and vindication.

42.   In 1 Pet. 3.18-22 the 'glories' that follow are expressed in terms of the submission of the angels, authorities, and powers to Christ.

43.   In the *Similitudes* the 'Elect One' does not suffer; however, the elect ones do. See, VanderKam, '1 Enoch 37-71', p. 437.

of Daniel in Dan. 6 are helpful examples.[44] In Isaiah, the servant song opens and ends with the exaltation of the righteous.[45] There, one gets a graphic picture of the humiliation and suffering of YHWH's servant; however, these are set within the larger frame of God's deliverance wrought on his behalf. Thus one finds in Isaiah an emphasis similar to that attested in Ps. 118 [117, LXX], namely, the reality and memory of suffering are supplanted by the truth of God's power to deliver. The author draws from this song the images he puts together to describe Jesus' suffering in 1 Pet. 2.22-25. Therefore, it is conceivable that this understanding has also shaped the author's discussion of Jesus' suffering. Jesus is described as one who was insulted, mistreated, and suffered a humiliating death by crucifixion (2.22-24);[46] one who in his suffering and subsequent death 'handed himself over' to the one who judges justly; and one who having suffered uttermost shame and death was made alive and exalted at the right hand of God where 'angels, authorities, and powers are in submission to him' (3.18-22).

The author's understanding of Christ's suffering as prelude to glory follows a pattern present in the Old Testament whereby the memory of suffering goes hand in hand with the recollection of God's act of salvation on behalf of the sufferer. This does not diminish the awareness of the severity of the suffering, but highlights the greatness and goodness of God who is faithful in caring for his children. In the context of the letter, Christ's suffering as prelude to glory serves to substantiate the author's claim that the audience's own trials will last only for a little while (1.6), and gives the audience the assurance of what the future holds. Since Jesus' suffering was followed with his exaltation, it follows that participation in his suffering will lead to participation in his glory – 'rejoice insofar as you are participating in Christ's sufferings in order that you may also rejoice with great joy at the revelation of his glory' (4.13). By offering the audience a glimpse of what the future has in store, the author seeks to help them put their suffering in perspective. The knowledge that one will be vindicated should affect how one interprets suffering. This, in turns, shapes how one responds to it.

44.   There is a possibility that 1 Peter's reference to 'fiery ordeals' (4.12) are an allusion to the story of Dan. 3. The fabula of 1 Peter would fit the story of Shadrach, Meshach, and Abednego because there are points of similarity between their story and the reality of 1 Peter's audience. They were part of the elect living in the diaspora of Babylon (Dan. 1.1-7), who suffered due to their display of faithfulness to God in exile (3.1-22). They endured their sufferings which involved a literal trial by fire (3.22-26) and benefited God's deliverance and vindication (3.27-30). See further, Nickelsburg, *Resurrection*, pp. 119–40.

45.   See Childs, *Isaiah*, pp. 407–23 (412).

46.   Martin Hengel explains, 'By the public display of a naked victim at a prominent place – at a crossroads, in the theater, on high ground, at the place of his crime – crucifixion also represented his uttermost humiliation, which had a numinous dimension to it' (*Crucifixion in the Ancient World and the Folly of the Message of the Cross* [Philadelphia: Fortress, 1977], p. 87).

4.3.2. Jesus' suffering as exemplary (2.21-25)

As part of his rhetoric to shape the audience's response to suffering, the author of 1 Peter presents Jesus' suffering as an example for his audience. He explains, 'Christ also suffered[47] on your[48] behalf, leaving you a pattern so that you may follow in his footsteps' (2.21). It is significant that the author uses 'suffering' rather than 'death' language here when referring to the events surrounding the passion of the Christ. This is the case, perhaps, because the audience's suffering is prominent in the author's mind.[49] The author is clearly aware of the death of Christ. This can be seen by his use of concepts like 'shedding of [his] blood' (1.2; cf. 1.18-20), 'resurrection … from the dead' (1.3), 'having been put to death …' (3.18). Yet, in setting Jesus as an example, he focuses on Jesus' suffering as a way to allow the audience to relate more readily to his experience. Even in 1 Pet. 2.24, where the author alludes to Jesus' crucifixion,[50] the 'death' language is applied not to Jesus but metaphorically to the audience, and associated with 'resurrection' language in relation to the change of behaviour that is brought about by Jesus' vicarious sufferings. For the author of 1 Peter, Jesus serves as an example in terms of the context of his sufferings and his response to them. In what way(s) do they serve as a model to the audience?

First, Christ's sufferings occur in a similar context; namely, Christ and the believers both suffer at the hands of those who are disobedient to God's will and God's word (2.4, 7-8, 19-23). The image of Jesus' (the living stone) rejection in 1 Pet. 2.4 is amplified with the author's description of Jesus being insulted and mistreated (2.23-24). The contexts of Ps. 118 [117, LXX] and Isa. 53 imply that the suffering arose from people who are not attuned to what God was/is doing in the life of the elect. The author's description of his audience suggests that the audience faces a similar predicament (1 Pet. 2.11; 3.1; 4.3-4).

---

47. Some mss read ἔπαθεν (e.g., 𝔓⁷², A, B, C, P, *Byz*, and *syr*[h]) while others offer ἀπέθανεν (e.g., 𝔓⁸¹, ℵ, *syr*[p], and ψ). The immediate context of the verse favours the first option. Those mss that read ἀπέθανεν have probably substituted ἔπαθεν in order to harmonize the author's words with traditional confessions (1 Thess. 5.10; Rom. 8.5).

48. The textual apparatus presents great difficulty at this point. Some mss read ὑμῶν, ὑμῖν (e.g., 𝔓⁷², ℵ, A, and B), others read ἡμῶν, ὑμῖν (33, 322, and *Byz*), and yet others read ἡμῶν, ἡμῖν (e.g., 1243, 1505, and *syr*[p]). This may be the result of confusion because the pronouns are very close in pronunciation. However, it is possible that the problem arose from a deliberate effort by copyists to identify (or distance) themselves with the text. A similar problem is attested in 3.18. The author of 1 Peter himself modifies the personal pronouns in his appropriation of the text of Isa. 53.

49. See Michaels, 'St. Peter's Passion', p. 392.

50. It is clear that 'he who bore our sins on the tree' is an allusion to Jesus' crucifixion. However, the language he uses is drawn from Deut. 21.23 which, in its original context, does not refer to death by crucifixion. See Hengel, *Crucifixion*, p. 85; also, Joseph A. Fitzmyer, 'Crucifixion in Ancient Palestine, Qumran Literature, and the New Testament', *CBQ* 40 (1978), pp. 493–513.

Second, the author emphasizes Christ's innocence as an aspect of his sufferings: 'he committed no sin, nor was deceit found in his mouth' (2.22); 'Christ also suffered once for all for sins, righteous for the unrighteous' (3.18). The author also underscores Christ's obedience to God in the context of his sacrifice which contributes to the audience's election (1.1-2). Further, the idea of Christ's innocence is parsed in terms of his blood being precious, as that of a lamb without defect or blemish (1.19). Because Christ was innocent, it follows that he did not deserve the mistreatment he received from his oppressors. As I will demonstrate below, the author encourages his audience repeatedly not to suffer for the wrong reason, and to consider it honourable if they suffer as righteous, because in this way they participate in Christ's sufferings and follow in his steps (2.11-12, 19-20; 3.16-17; 4.1-2, 13-16).

Third, Christ's sufferings can be seen as an example for the believers because of the way he responded to the hardships that he faced. The two main aspects of Jesus' response are (1) his non-retaliation, and (2) the expression of his dependence and trust on God (2.23). This is pivotal because one of the key issues in the letter is the author's call to the audience to demonstrate proper behaviour in the face of trials. This is significant because according to 1 Peter, it is possible to suffer for the wrong reasons (2.20; 4.15), as well as to respond to sufferings in an inappropriate fashion. Therefore, the author exhorts the audience, from 1.13 onward, encouraging them to respond to trials in an appropriate manner, as obedient children of God, à l'instar de Jesus Christ. Although the author does not deal with the alternative, it remains clear that how one responds to harassment potentially affects how one's story plays out in the end; that is why he was focused on calling forth the right kind of response from the audience. This aspect will be treated more fully in the following chapter. As I will demonstrate, the author's discussion of the audience's appropriate response to suffering can be summed up as 'faithful response' which includes steadfastness, doing good, and subordination. These are behavioural expressions from persons who have rooted their trust in God, know of God's past saving act, and depend on him to bring about salvation on their behalf.

4.3.3. Jesus' suffering as redemptive (1.2, 3-5, 10-12, 18-21; 2.21-25; 3.18-22)

The author's discussion of the redemptive nature of the sufferings of Christ permeates the epistle. In the greeting section (1.2), he uses sacrificial language borrowed from the context of covenant making of Exod. 24 to talk about the audience's election. Implicit in that context are Jesus' own sufferings and death, the liberation of Israel from slavery, and the believers' own redemption. That thought is reinforced in 1.3-5, when the author speaks of the readers' new birth as being brought about by God through the 'resurrection of Jesus Christ from the dead' (1.3). The author's emphasis on the salvation of the audience is maintained in 1.10-12, in which a connection is made between the prophets' inquiry regarding the audience's salvation, and the Spirit of

Christ's testimony about 'the sufferings of Christ and the glories what would follow' (1.11).

An explicit connection is borne out between Jesus' sufferings and the redemption of the believers in 1.18-21; 2.21-25; 3.18-22. All three passages appear in the context of the author's use of Christ's experience as grounding for an exhortation given to the audience (1.13-17; 2.19-20; 3.14-17). All three passages are followed by an additional exhortation that outflows from the fact that Jesus suffered and the responsibility the readers have because they have been redeemed (1.22–2.3; 3.1-17; 4.1-6). As such, the discussion of the suffering of Christ is structurally located at the centre of the author's exhortation to the audience. It is both the grounding and motivation for shaping their behaviour.[51]

Whereas all three passages portray the redemptive nature of Jesus' suffering, each contains a characteristic emphasis. In 1 Pet. 1.18-21, the focus is on deliverance from the futile behaviours and lifestyles that are characteristic of those who are not walking in obedience to God[52] – a reminder that the author offers within the overall context of his call to holiness. In this context, Christ's suffering becomes a warrant for the audience's demonstration of holy conduct that is characteristic of the new life they have received through the death and resurrection of Jesus Christ (1.22–2.3). Through the uses of several contrasting images, the author establishes the value of Jesus' blood and calls the audience to display behaviours that are worthy of the means of their redemption.[53] Whereas Christ's suffering was caused by people who did not believe in God's work (2.4, 8, 23), his death, implied in 1.19, subsequent resurrection and glorification by God are part of God's redemptive plan carried out on behalf of the audience (1.20-21). One gets a glimpse of the theocentric nature of the epistle. It is God the Father who has raised Jesus Christ and given him glory and in him rest the faith and hope of the audience (1.21). However, this could also be read as a warrant: because the believers are aware of God's vindication of Jesus they can trust God to do the same for them. But for that to happen, they need to continue to live in obedience to God's word.[54]

In 1 Pet. 2.21-25 Jesus' sufferings contain a nuance between his attitude in the face of sufferings (vv. 22-23), and their atoning value (vv. 24-25). There is something inherently unique about Jesus' sufferings in regard to their atoning value which can never be replicated by the audience. Yet, the author still draws an analogy between Jesus and the addressees in that aspect. As

---

51. For example, 1 Pet. 2.21-25 is structurally set as the centre of a chiasm that comprises 1 Peter's exhortations: to everybody (2.11-17), to a specific (representative) group: slaves (2.18-20); the sufferings of Christ (2.21-25); to specific (representative) groups: wives and husbands (3.1-7); to everybody (3.8-12). See Green, *1 Peter*, p. 73.

52. So also, Jobes, *1 Peter*, p. 118.

53. See my discussion of 1.18-21 in Chapter 3.

54. The author's rhetoric in 1.22 is consistent with the overall tenor of his exhortations to the audience. He does not so much offer them new advice as he encourages them to continue doing things that they have been practising already.

Jesus' suffering was effective in bringing about the audience's salvation, the audience's suffering can be effective in bringing those who were once disobedient to the place where they too may be redeemed from their futile way of life (2.11-12; 3.1-2).[55] I am not proposing that the author suggests that there is an atoning value to the audience's suffering. The efficacy of the audience's sufferings resides in their ability to point the outsider to God who through Christ will accomplish his salvific purpose in his/her life. In the *Similitudes*, there is a corporate–individual interplay at work in the description of the 'Son of Man'. The 'Son of Man' is an individual, yet, he represents the nation.[56] In Isaiah, on the one hand, the community of Israel was identified as fulfilling the role of the servant of YHWH (Isa. 49.3); on the other hand, Israel is differentiated from the servant of YHWH since the suffering of the servant brings about Israel's justification (Isa. 53.8-11).[57] As in Isaiah, the work of God in Christ brings about the audience's salvation. Yet, now that they have become God's people, his servant, he also uses them to carry out his plan of salvation. As I shall demonstrate in the following chapter, much depends on the sufferers' response to hardships. For, it is in seeing their good conduct, the way they respond to suffering, that the disobedient may come to glorify God.

The discussion of the atoning value of Christ's sufferings comes into focus in 1 Pet. 2.24 in which the author speaks about Jesus 'bearing our sins in his body on the tree'.[58] This an appropriation of Isa. 53.4, 12b with an allusion to Deut. 21.23, which the author brings together and interprets in a way that identifies Jesus with the suffering servant of Isaiah and the audience with Israel.[59] In a few words, he brings to the fore the purpose of Christ's suffering: 'in order that having died to sins we might live for righteousness' (2.24).[60] The author complements the picture of Jesus' sufferings with an appropriation of Isa. 53.5, which emphasizes the physical abuse of the suffering servant of YHWH. The picture of the atoning and redemptive nature

---

55.   It is debated whether 'the day of visitation' and the overall context of 2.12 should be understood primarily as referring to the final eschatological day of judgement (Achtemeier, *1 Peter*, 178; Jobes, *1 Peter*, pp. 171–2; Michaels, *1 Peter*, pp. 118–20), or a time in the life of the unbeliever when God visits him/her to bring salvation (Beare, *1 Peter*, p. 164; Elliott, *1 Peter*, pp. 470–1; Reicke, *1 Peter*, p. 94). I will demonstrate later in this study that the author of 1 Peter holds these two concepts (the present and the future) in tension and that the two options are not mutually exclusive.

56.   For a discussion on the identity of the 'Son of Man' in *1 Enoch*, see e.g., VanderKam, '1 Enoch 37-71'; Bock, *Blasphemy and Exaltation*, pp. 148–54; John J. Collins, 'The Son of Man in First Century Judaism', *NTS* 38 (1992), pp. 448–66.

57.   Childs, *Isaiah*, p. 418.

58.   Michaels, *1 Peter*, p. 143.

59.   So also, Jobes, *1 Peter*, p. 199.

60.   For a brief moment, the author moves from 'you' to 'we/us'. The change might be a way for the author to emphasize the universal reach and import of Christ's sacrifice on the cross. It can also be a way for him to identify with the audience (cf. 5.1). That Isa. 53 is part of the background here may suggest that the author has forgiveness of sins in mind as well. So Green, *1 Peter*, p. 88.

of Christ's sufferings is completed by yet further imagery taken in part from Isa. 53. In the process, the author moves back to the second person ('you'), but it is clear that his identification with the entire audience continues. Karen Jobes speculates whether the change from 'we/us' to 'you' in 2.24 marks the author's return to the household code so that the 'you' refers to the slaves who were thus identified in 2.20.[61] However, conceptually and structurally, the language in 2.21-25 suggests that Christ's example applies to the entire audience, and that all the different groups in the audience are liable to suffer. This fits the perspective that Christ's suffering effectively atones for the sins of the audience and restores their relationship with God. This also fits the image of the wandering sheep, which is part of the overall mural the author is painting in 2.25, which contains an allusion to Isa. 53.6 (cf. Ezek. 34.6). The LXX describes the lost, wandering, and perhaps disobedient ways of the congregation of Israel, and the fact that God caused the servant to bear their iniquity in their stead. The author of 1 Peter picks up the 'wandering' aspect and merges it with Isa. 40.10-11 (cf. Ezek. 34.11-13), which portray images of God as a shepherd, to complete the redemptive analogy:[62] 'but now you have returned to the shepherd and guardian of your lives' (2.25). Jesus' sufferings have brought about a change of behaviour, the need to live for righteousness and healing, which conveys the idea of wholeness, and a change of state, in other words, conversion.[63]

In 1 Pet. 3.18-22, the author mentions specifically that Christ suffered for our sins, but as Michaels points out, one cannot assume that he attaches any technical meaning to it until 4.1-2, when he reiterates the concept of Christ's suffering and explains the effects that Christ's sufferings should have for/on the sins of the audience.[64] The focus is on linking the audience's experience with that of Jesus while pointing out the uniqueness of Jesus' suffering. He suffered not only as a righteous person, but he did so on behalf of unrighteous people as well. As a righteous person Christ did not need to suffer, but his innocence and his righteousness allowed him to effectively suffer on behalf of the unrighteous.

The atoning value of the vicarious suffering of the righteous is also present in the servant song of Isaiah and other Jewish writings of the Second Temple period (Isa. 53.5-7; *4 Macc.* 6.26-30; 17.22). The uniqueness of Jesus' suffering is marked by the author's use of 'once and for all', which qualifies the vicarious suffering death of Christ as having effectively atoned for the sins of the unrighteous. Therefore, there should no longer be a need for such action in the future. The author probably wanted to point out the difference between Christ's unrepeatable sacrifice and the recurring nature of the Old Testament sacrifices.[65] When read together with 1 Pet. 4.1-2, it also shows that the author expects his audience to live above reproach since Christ's

61. Jobes, *1 Peter*, p. 198.
62. So Jobes, *1 Peter*, p. 198.
63. Green suggests that healing may be referring to holiness (*1 Peter*, pp. 89–90).
64. Michaels, *1 Peter*, p. 202.
65. So also, Achtemeier, *1 Peter*, pp. 246–7.

sufferings have effectively done away with sins and brought the audience into a relationship with God the Father: 'Christ suffered for sins, so that he might lead you[66] to God'.[67] On the one hand, the sacrifice need not be repeated because it is effective; on the other hand, those who have been led to God are expected to live such a life, one that is above sin, so that they will no longer have sins to be atoned for (4.1-2).

The author complements his thoughts with a description of Christ's death and resurrection. The concept of the death and resurrection of Christ has been connected with the audience's redemption since the beginning of the epistle (1.3, 18-22). Whereas the resurrection is not explicitly mentioned in 2.21-25, together these passages convey the same important idea: Jesus' suffering makes possible the relationship that exists between God and the audience. The author will eventually bring Christ's exaltation to the fore (3.22), thereby highlighting the *Christus Victor* aspect of the understanding of atonement: Christ in his suffering (death) and resurrection is victorious over evil.[68] In so doing, he also paints for his audience part of the trajectory of God's vindication of Jesus: the righteous sufferer is exalted at God's right hand.

In sum, Christ's suffering plays a prominent role in 1 Peter. It is used both as a grounding and motivation for the exhortations given to the audience. The author's understanding of Christ's suffering is multifaceted; therefore, I organized the discussion around three main headings – sufferings as prelude to glory; sufferings as example to the audience, sufferings as redemptive – in order to discuss the author's understanding of the suffering of Christ. His understanding of Christ's suffering reflects his awareness of the Old Testament as the concepts he uses to describe Jesus' experience of and response to hardships are analogous to the Old Testament and other Jewish writings of the Second Temple period. The author's discussion of Jesus in the letter is not for its own sake, but to offer the readers a lens through which they should interpret their trials. He speaks of the audience's sufferings as 'participation in Christ's sufferings'.

4.4. The audience's suffering as participation in Christ's sufferings

In his attempt to shape the behaviour of the audience, the author tries to bring them to the point of understanding that their suffering is something

---

66.   The change from 'you' to 'us' in some of the manuscripts is widely rejected, and rightly so. However, that change is a testimony that some of the people who approached this text wanted to identify with the text to the point of changing the wording. It speaks to the fact that they understood 1 Peter to be referring to them, that they were themselves part of the story. The author himself changes the 'we' from the LXX to 'you' in his text, and deliberately moves back from 'we/us' to 'you' designations in the text.

67.   The imagery of the shepherd in 2.25 drawn from Isa. 53.6 conveys in essence a similar idea to what the author is expressing here.

68.   Green, *1 Peter*, p. 121.

that they should rejoice in, because through them they are participating in Christ's own sufferings (4.13). The purpose of this statement was to guide the audience to rethink the meaning of the hardships they were going through in order to make sense of it.[69] The audience's identification with Jesus in his sufferings is attested in that they are encouraged to think of their experience in terms that are similar to Jesus' sufferings. The author seems to draw analogies between Jesus and the audience even in those aspects of Jesus' sufferings that are considered unique to Jesus' experience. As the situations of Jesus and the audience are not identical, where necessary, I will discuss the author's understanding of the sufferings of the audience in terms that put the emphasis on the audience's point of view. An inquiry of the text shows that 1 Peter encourages the believers to think of their sufferings as prelude to glory, as an effective means of redemption, and as witness.[70]

4.4.1. *Suffering as prelude to glory (1.6-7; 4.12-14)*

From the very beginning of the letter, the author puts the audience's sufferings in perspective. First Peter 1.6-7 suggests that suffering is not a normal part of life, but it is a reality that the readers face. However, 'εἰ δέον' suggests that suffering was also only a potential reality. The author does not encourage the audience to suffer, does not idealize suffering, nor sets suffering as a prerequisite to glory. He warns his readers not to suffer for what is wrong (2.20; 4.15). Rather, he is addressing a situation that is already happening (2.19-20; 4.12-14), and offering the audience ways to deal with the issue.

Further, suffering is temporary. It will last only a little while. Whereas 1 Peter repeatedly makes reference to the eschaton (1.5, 7; 4.7), it is unlikely that the author is suggesting a time frame to his audience for the duration of their trials as if he knew of an impending end to the lot that has befallen them. Rather, he encourages them to put their sufferings in the bigger perspective of who God is, what he has done for Jesus Christ, what he has done for them through Jesus Christ, and what he is able to do for them in their present circumstances (1.3-12). In the process, the author contrasts the lasting nature of the inheritance that has been bestowed upon the audience and the passing nature of the trials that audience is suffering (1.3-6). In addition, he suggests to the audience that their suffering can have a positive outcome (1.6-7). Charles H. Talbert has argued that the imagery that the author uses here is attested both in Jewish and Greek literature (Prov. 17.3; Wis. 3.6; Sir. 2.5; Plato, *Republic* 413 D).[71] He then suggests that trials in 1 Peter should be

---

69. See Bruner, *Acts of Meaning*, pp. 39–43; Cornell, 'That's the Story of Our Life', p. 45.

70. The corresponding concepts to Jesus' suffering as exemplary that apply to the audience, specifically as it relates to his response to suffering, will be dealt with in greater detail in Chapter 5.

71. Talbert, *Learning through Suffering*, pp. 42–5; see also, Achtemeier, *1 Peter*, pp. 101–2.

understood as 'an education by God which separates the pure from the dross in the Christian's life, leaving behind the genuine part'.[72] This image can also be understood as the author's way of explaining to the audience the need and benefits of endurance in the face of suffering.[73] Finally, he describes the future with an assurance that is located in the faith already at work in the audience and demonstrated in the love and belief that they have placed in the person of Jesus Christ (1.7-9).

The author of 1 Peter is as much concerned with the present as he is with the eschatological realities his audience experience and will experience (1.5, 7-9; 4.13). To speak of 'at the revelation of Jesus Christ' (ἐν ἀποκαλύψει Ἰησοῦ Χριστοῦ) encourages the audience to think of their salvation in eschatological terms. However, by pointing their attention to this event, the author reinforces the claim that God raised Christ from the dead. This is important because he will later make the connection between the sufferings of Christ and glories that follow (1.10-12, 19-21; 3.18-22), and encourage the audience to understand their own sufferings in light of Jesus' experience. Therefore, Jesus' example becomes motivation and proof to the audience that suffering is indeed a prelude to glory and assures the audience of the ultimate outcome of their own sufferings. That assurance is based on the fact that God is the one at work in the bestowal and preservation of the audience and the reward that is awaiting them (1.3, 5) in the same way he was worked in resurrecting Jesus from the dead and giving him glory (1.21). To that extent, the trials they now face are not the end of the story.

The author encourages the audience to put their sufferings in perspective in 4.12-14.[74] The parallels between the two passages (1.6-7 and 4.12-14) are striking: one can easily observe the connection between the trials and fire, the invitation to rejoice in the midst of sufferings, and the assurance that the sufferings will not last forever. There are also some differences to be noted. Whereas in 1.6-7 the 'glory' the audience will partake in is an eschatological hope that they will experience when Jesus returns, another dimension is added in 4.14. The author speaks of the audience as partaking of 'glory' in the present: 'the Spirit of glory is resting upon you'.[75] This is consistent with the author's discussion of their salvation – it is both a future reality and something that they are already experiencing (cf. 1.5 and 1.9).[76] In addition, in 1.6-7, the focus is on the transient nature of sufferings as opposed to the lasting value of the inheritance they have benefited from

72.   Talbert, *Learning through Suffering*, p. 45.

73.   See further below, Chapter 5.

74.   First Peter 4.12-14 is part of a larger pericope that ends at v. 19 where the author focuses on the eschatological nature of suffering. See further, Green, *1 Peter*, pp. 147–61; Achtemeier, *1 Peter*, pp. 304–5.

75.   This is an allusion to Isa. 11.2, which speaks of the gift of the spirit as a sign that the end of exile is near, that restoration is at hand. This implies that suffering will soon end.

76.   Feldmeier rightly notes, 'a sharp differentiation between present and future is not appropriate for 1 Peter' (*The First Letter of Peter*, p. 80).

being born again. In 4.12-14, the author encourages the audience to put their sufferings in perspective by interpreting them in light of Christ's experience. They can rejoice, because participation in Christ's sufferings is tantamount to participation in his glory. He goes so far as to suggest that the audience should expect the sufferings that have come their way.

The author contrasts the audience's reaction to suffering with the world's reaction to their change of behaviour. Whereas the pagans find it strange (ξενίζονται, 4.4) that change has occurred in the lives of those who have experienced new birth, the believers should not find it strange (μὴ ξενίζεσθε, 4.12) that they suffer as a result of their association with Christ.[77] That the audience should expect suffering should be not understood in terms that 'Christians have to suffer'; rather, they should see that the vocation of being a follower of Christ, a child of God, makes one liable to hardships from the outside world. This is analogous in part to the understanding attested both in the Old Testament and Second Temple literature regarding the collocation of election and suffering (cf. Sir. 2.1). Feldmeier also highlights the affinities between 1 Peter and Jewish wisdom literature vis-à-vis the collocation of sufferings/trials and election. He rightly notes that suffering is 'not a sign of being abandoned by God, but quite the opposite, as a test sent by God it is a sign of election'.[78] The author's rhetoric is thus crafted because suffering was already a reality for his audience. Yet, he encourages them to strive to suffer (if they must) only for the right reasons (4.15-16).

Mark Dubis has suggested that participation in Christ's suffering is to be understood as the audience's participation in the messianic woes; namely, sufferings of all kinds – famine, earthquakes, family betrayal, and the persecution of the righteous – that are a prelude to the Messiah's arrival. Although the author of 1 Peter is primarily concerned with the persecution of the elect, there are features in the way he discusses his understanding of the audience's suffering that are analogous to early Jewish literature's understanding and development of the theme of messianic woes. Dubis demonstrates the presence of a messianic woes pattern in 1 Peter, and especially in 4.12-19.[79] The author's rhetoric regarding the suffering of the audience in 4.12-19 lends itself to the claim that the sufferings of the audience should be understood as participation in the inauguration of the

77. So also, Achtemeier, *1 Peter*, p. 305; Green, *1 Peter*, p. 154.

78. Feldmeier, *The First Letter of Peter*, p. 84.

79. Mark Dubis, 'First Peter and the "Sufferings of the Messiah"', in David W. Baker (ed.), *Looking into the Future: Evangelical Studies in Eschatology* (ETSS; Grand Rapids: Baker, 2001), pp. 85–96; idem, *Messianic Woes in First Peter: Suffering and Eschatology in 1 Peter 4:12-19* (SBL, 33; New York: Peter Lang, 2002). For a discussion on 'messianic woes', see further Dale C. Allison, *The End of the Ages Has Come: An Early Interpretation of the Passion and Resurrection of Jesus* (Philadelphia: Fortress, 1985); Richard J. Bauckham, 'The Great Tribulation in the Shepherd of Hermas', *JTS* 25 (1974), pp. 27–40.

80. Achtemeier argues to the contrary, proposing that the sufferings of the Christians are the beginning of God's judgement and not part of it, and therefore should not be considered as participation in the messianic woes (*1 Peter*, p. 315). See also, Bauckham, 'Great Tribulation', p. 36.

end.[80] However, this theme is not as pervasive in 1 Peter as Dubis suggests.[81] For example, Dubis argues that the image of the gold being refined (1.6-7) is to be understood as messianic woes together with (and in light of) the 'πύρωσις' imagery found in 4.12.[82] Although the images are similar, the one conveyed in 1.6-7 applies more readily to the idea of purging as education as pointed out by Talbert.[83] Further, Dubis overstates his case by claiming that suffering is a necessity in the sense that the author believes the readers must suffer; namely, 'they must past through the woes before they can enter the consummated messianic age'.[84] The author of 1 Peter does not place suffering as the prerequisite for participation in God's eternal glory; rather, it is holiness of life and good conduct that are an outflow of one's election and new birth and demonstrated in the midst of suffering (1.13–2.4). One cannot rule out the possibility that a person can enter the messianic age without having suffered for the name of Christ. The author's rhetoric regarding suffering as necessary depends on the fact that his audience was *already* experiencing suffering. But, there is a sense in which the language implies the suffering of the audience is an abnormality because the blasphemies and abuses the audience undergo are the result of inappropriate responses from pagans who are oblivious to God's work (3.13-16; 4.4-6). As I will demonstrate in the following chapter, the response to suffering is a crucial component in 1 Peter's message that should be read together with the author's understanding of the suffering of the audience. One finds that the author repeatedly encourages the readers to *continue* 'doing good', which implies practising the very thing(s) that brought about suffering in the first place (1.14, 22; 2.1; 4.1-4). Clearly, one who suffers for the name of Christ and recants or forsakes the life of holiness as a result would have forfeited his/her inheritance. This is why it is imperative that one stands firm in the face of trials. *Didache* 16.5 reads: 'Then shall humanity[85] come to the fiery trial and many shall be offended and be lost, but they who remain steadfast in their faith shall be saved …'[86] Therefore, the behavioural qualities that are characteristic of God's children and enable the elect to endure should be viewed as the prerequisite to glory, and not suffering per se.

Another problem with Dubis' proposal is the claim that the audience's suffering comes as part of God's sovereign plan.[87] God is aware of all that is happening in the life of the elect (1.1-9) and of the unbeliever (2.8) and works out his purposes accordingly. It is possible to understand testings (πειρασμός, 1.6; 4.12) in 1 Peter to originate from God as a means of maturation or from

81.   Dubis, 'Sufferings', p. 96. He argues, 'This pattern is especially manifest in 4.12-19, but this concept also stands behind other texts within 1 Peter and, indeed, the theology of the book as a whole'.

82.   Dubis, 'Sufferings', pp. 87–9; idem, *Messianic Woes*, pp. 76–85.

83.   Talbert, *Learning Through Suffering*, p. 49.

84.   Dubis, 'Sufferings', p. 90; idem, *Messianic Woes*, pp. 85–95.

85.   Lit. 'the creation of people or men'.

86.   Author's translation.

87.   Dubis, 'Sufferings', p. 95; idem, *Messianic Woes*, pp. 94–5.

the devil as temptation (cf. 5.8-9).[88] Dubis recognizes this, but advances, 'Satan is merely an instrument in God's hand, ultimately fulfilling God's own sovereign purposes'.[89] This raises a theological question regarding whether God *needs* his people to suffer in order to act on their behalf. Further, this implies that God uses the unbelievers to blaspheme his children and holds them accountable for doing so. This runs contrary to the picture of the just judge the author of 1 Peter paints of God, one who judges each according to his/her deeds (1.17; 2.23). There is a fundamental difference between the concept that God is aware of the sufferings of his children and the one that claims God is responsible for the same.

The author of 1 Peter describes the suffering of the audience as prelude to glory. In so doing, he encourages the reader to put their experience in the perspective of what God has done on behalf of his children in the past. He sets the trajectory of Jesus' life before them as an example to show that suffering is not the end of the story. In addition, he parses their sufferings in terms of participation in Christ's own sufferings which involves identification with Christ in some other aspects of his sufferings as well.

4.4.2. *Suffering as effective (4.1-6, 15-19)*

The author draws several other analogies between Christ's sufferings and the sufferings of the audience. First, there is an analogy to the redemptive value of Christ's suffering, specifically as it relates to its atoning aspect. Christ's sufferings effectively atoned for the sins of the audience, and brought about a change of behaviour. This change of behaviour has caused the audience to be alienated from their former network of relationships and has become the source of the audience's sufferings. Perhaps the best way to understand the text here is to take into consideration the complete sentence that constitutes 4.1-2 – 'Therefore, since Christ has suffered in the flesh, arm yourselves with the same thought: that the one who has suffered in the flesh is done with sin, so as to live no longer according to human desires, but according to the will of God during the rest of one's earthly existence'. Three things should be noted here: (1) Christ's sufferings as a righteous person directly impact the way the audience ought to live. Implicit here is the notion of Christ's example. Christ suffered as a righteous person; they too should suffer as a righteous people. Because Christ's sufferings put an end to sin, their present sufferings should not be a result of sinful behaviour (4.15), nor should they respond to sufferings in ways that are not becoming to their new status as God's children (4.2). The atoning suffering of Christ was effective in bringing about their redemption, their new birth, that is, their conversion; therefore, their suffering should provide a way to demonstrate that a change has indeed

---

88. See e.g., Achtemeier, *1 Peter*, p. 306; Elliott, *1 Peter*, pp. 772–3; Green, *1 Peter*, p. 155.
89. Dubis, *Messianic Woes*, p. 95.

taken place. (2) The emphasis on 'in the flesh' (σάρξ is used three times in the sentence, and occurs elsewhere in the pericope) grounds the audience's experience in Jesus' own. This is important because it comes on the heels of Jesus' exaltation and glorification and discussion about the righteousness of Jesus – images that might cause the audience to see Jesus' example as unattainable. (3) The author is very much focused on giving the audience a perspective for life *here and now*. The audience should not be concerned only about the eschatological realities and implications of their sufferings; these should and do have an impact during their earthly existence as well (4.2).

Related to this concept is the notion that the audience's suffering is effective in ensuring victory over sins. As Christ was victorious over sin (3.18-22), so the believer is expected to live a life that is above reproach, being victorious over sin (4.1-2). In fact, their own sufferings are a result of having put to death the sinful ways that characterized their former lives (cf. 1.17-21). Characteristic of 1 Peter is the way the author describes the audience as already doing some of the very things he is exhorting them about. It means that the audience is suffering because they are displaying the kind of behaviour distinctive of those who live according to the will of God. This is clearly borne out in 4.3-4, which gives the reason behind the sufferings that the believers are facing. In this case, they are expected to continue this victorious life in the midst of suffering. This is what will enable them to demonstrate proper response to the trials that come their way.

Second, the suffering of the audience is effective in relation to the (eschatological) salvation of the righteous and judgement of unbelievers. Arguing from the perspective of messianic woes, Dubis suggests, 'First Peter's eschatological ordeal has a redemptive function for believers (1 Pet. 4.12) and punitive function for unbelievers (1 Pet. 4.18)'.[90] Irrespective of how one understands the concept of messianic woes in 1 Peter, it is clear that the author sees a connection between the suffering of the audience and their future on the one hand, and between their suffering and the fate of their detractors, on the other hand.

The author's insistence that his audience should not suffer for the wrong reasons and should glorify God if they suffer while doing good is presented to the audience in the context of being ready to stand God's judgement (4.15-17). Earlier in the epistle, the exhortation to good conduct is connected with the audience's relationship with God the Father who is also identified as judge (1.17). There, it is not clear whether the judgement is eschatological, or whether it is an on-going reality. Also, in 1.17 suffering is only implicit in the concept of παροικία as the focus is on the holiness of life that is required from those who have been given new birth (1.13-21). The suffering of the audience, if handled properly, might be effective in outfitting the believer for salvation. This is consistent with the image of suffering as refinement or maturation attested in 1.6-7 and 4.12. Further, the author also shows that those who blaspheme the believers will have to give an account to the one

90. Dubis, *Messianic Woes*, pp. 91–2.

who is ready to judge the living and the dead (4.5). He does not specify what will happen; one can only imagine that there might be retribution in store. The main point here is that the believers are informed that those who have caused hardships will be held accountable. First Peter 4.17-18 contains two rhetorical questions that parallel each other and highlight the predicament of the unbeliever. The question in 4.17b is reiterated in 4.18, which is a quotation from Prov. 11.31. The author paints a picture of the unbeliever, in order to help the audience put their own suffering in perspective to show that in the end the situation of the righteous will be better than that of the unbeliever. In addition, there is the assurance that the righteous will be vindicated. This is why the author goes on to tell the suffering audience to hand themselves to God (4.19).

4.4.3. *Suffering as witness (2.12; 3.1-2, 13-17; 4.3-6)*

This aspect of the audience's suffering contains affinities both with the effectiveness and exemplary natures of Christ's suffering. The audience's suffering can bring about the conversion of unbelievers. And, the witness is carried out in ways that are analogous to the author's understanding of the life of Jesus. The sufferings of the audience parallel those of Christ in terms of the reality expressed in the 'stone metaphor'. On the one hand, the audience suffer abuse from those who are disobedient to God (2.12, 18; 3.1, 13) in the same way the 'living stone' suffered (was rejected) by those who were oblivious to God's work (2.4, 7-8). On the other hand, as the 'living stone' was a means of stumbling for some and of belief for others (2.7-10), so are the 'living stones' in a position to cause some to stumble (4.3-5) and others, who were formerly disobedient, to come to believe (2.12; 3.1-2). The discussion about the fate of the disobedient in 2.7-8 parallels the discussion about the fate of those who reproach the audience in 4.1-6, 12-19. The reaction of the disobedient to the 'living stone' has precipitated their downfall, a form of judgement from God. First Peter 4.1-6, 12-19 suggests that the reaction of those who malign the audience will also be followed by judgement (4.5-6, 17-18). The conduct of the audience (what they no longer do, who they no longer are [4.3-4, 15], and what they do now, who they are now [4.16]) is equated with the predication of the gospel which the outside world is given an opportunity to accept or reject. For the author, those who blaspheme the Christians' good behaviour are as blind to the work of God and disobedient to the word of God as those who rejected the 'living stone'.[91]

The author's language implies that the sufferings of his audience can be effective as witness to those who are disobedient to God. This understanding is explicit in 2.12 where it is stated that the demonstration of good conduct in the midst of suffering may lead blasphemers to glorify God on the day of visitation. The author does seem to put that response in an eschatological

---

91.   See my discussion in the preceding section.

perspective.[92] However, if one takes seriously into account the effective witnessing value of the audience's suffering, it opens the possibility of outsiders being won to God *in the present* so that they can glorify God *in the eschaton*. In fact, it is imaginable that the appropriate response can also be manifest in the present (2.13-15). Although 'silencing the talk of foolish people' may not in itself be equated with faith in God, it shows that the audience's attitude has generated change in the situation to the point where the accusers are silent and confused (3.16).

The audience's suffering as witness is also conveyed in 3.1-2 in which the author explains to the wives in the audience that their conduct has the potential to gain their unbelieving husbands to Christ.[93] There, the emphasis is placed on conduct over against verbal witness. Yet, elsewhere, the readers are urged to use verbal witness when and where necessary (3.15-16). This implies that the believers have the power to point people to God in a similar fashion that Jesus' sufferings led them to God and effected a change of behaviour in them. I am not arguing that the sufferings of the audience have any atoning value; rather, I am proposing that the author of 1 Peter understands the sufferings of the audience to be as effective as those of Jesus in bringing change in the disobedient. In this manner the author is calling the audience to follow Christ's example.

The exemplary aspect is also evident in 3.18-19 and 4.1-2 because the author had just exhorted the audience that it is better for them to suffer for doing good, in other words, as a righteous person in the context of offering a verbal testimony to one's faith (3.17). Further, the words 'ὅτι καὶ Χριστὸς ... ἔπαθεν' are the same that the author used earlier in the epistle (2.21), when introducing the paradigmatic nature of Christ's sufferings. But here, that thought is complemented with 'once for sins', a thought that also occurred in 2.24. D. Edmond Hiebert proposes that the idea of *imitatio Christi* is absent in this context and that the author's purpose is not so much to present a standard for behaviour as it is to offer the objective ground and cause for salvation.[94] It is clear that the emphasis on the 'once-and-for-all' aspect of Christ's sufferings underscores its uniqueness. This is all the more the case, that the emphasis is also that he suffered for sins. However, this emphasis does not necessarily exclude *imitatio Christi*. The imitation may only go so far as 'doing good'; yet, it is implicit in the emphasis on Jesus' suffering as a 'righteous'. There was something about the believers' steadfastness in sufferings that eventually appealed to their detractors. In *Dialogue with Trypho* Justin Martyr offers a helpful insight into this situation when he writes:

> Now it is obvious that no one can frighten or subdue us who believe in Jesus throughout the whole world. Although we are beheaded and crucified, and exposed to wild beast, and chains, and flames, and every other means of torture, it is evident

92.   The 'day of visitation' generally points to the final judgement (Isa. 10.3; Jer. 6.15; Wis. 3.7-8). See Achtemeier, *1 Peter*, pp. 176–8; Michaels, *1 Peter*, pp. 119–20.

that we will not retract our profession of faith; the more we are persecuted, the more do others in ever-increasing numbers embrace the faith and become worshippers of God through the name of Jesus (110.4).[95]

One can say that the atoning nature of Jesus' sufferings corresponds to the audience's suffering as witness to unbelievers: they are both effective, and that of the audience's is patterned after that of Christ.

4.5. *Conclusion*

In this chapter, I have looked at the second element of the fabula of 1 Peter: suffering. I provided evidence to support the claim that 'suffering' as an element of the four-part fabula the author operates with is common to the story of Israel, Jesus, and the audience. First, I discussed the way the sufferings of Israel are implicit in the epistle and serve as a background to the author's treatment of the sufferings of the audience. Then, I focused on the author's understanding of the sufferings of Jesus Christ. Jesus' sufferings are understood as prelude to glory, exemplary, and redemptive. Characteristic of his theological hermeneutic, the author of 1 Peter roots these concepts in Scripture. Finally, I showed how the audience's sufferings mirror the sufferings of Jesus. Although there are aspects of Jesus' sufferings that are unique, as a whole, 1 Peter seeks to encourage the audience to suffer like Jesus suffered. They are to rejoice in their sufferings because these are only temporary and ultimately lead to glory. But to experience that inexpressible joy at the revelation of Jesus Christ, they have to demonstrate the proper response now. The next chapter will deal with 'faithful response' which has to do with how 1 Peter puts forward to the audience what is the appropriate reaction to suffering.

93.   In 1 Pet. 3.1 the verb κερδηθήσονται is a future passive which is being used with the force of a subjunctival phrase with an ἵνα clause.

94.   D. Edmond Hiebert, 'The Suffering and Triumphant Christ: An Exposition of 1 Pet. 3.18-22', *BSac* 139 (1982), pp. 146–58.

95.   St Justin Martyr, *Dialogue With Trypho* (SFC, 3; ed. Michael Slusser; trans. Thomas B. Falls; Washington: Catholic University of America, 2003), p. 165.

Chapter 5

FAITHFUL RESPONSE IN 1 PETER

5.1. Introduction

In the preceding chapter, I proposed that the way one responds to afflictions plays a key role in determining the outcome of one's experience. The author does not elaborate explicitly on what may happen if a person does not respond appropriately to hardships. He only offers some warnings (1.17; 2.20; 4.15-18). W. C. van Unnik surmises about 1 Pet. 2.20, 'The contrast underlying this verse is that between ἁμαρτάνοντες and ἀγαθοποιοῦντες. Suffering following the former is well deserved and no claim to glory; suffering following the latter is more than κλέος, it is χάρις παρὰ θεῷ',[1] The author of 1 Peter emphasizes that one should not suffer for the wrong reasons, and should meet trials, when they occur, with 'faithful response', which comprises 'steadfastness', 'doing good', and 'subordination' (2.18-20; 3.15-17).

The idea of 'steadfastness' finds its clearest expression in the use of the verb ὑπομένω (2.20). This verb conveys such responses as: to stand one's ground, to stand firm,[2] and to maintain a belief or course of action in the face of opposition.[3] W. Radl suggests that this verb can be understood as referring to 'staying as opposed to fleeing'.[4] The cognate derivative noun ὑπομονή, 'refers overwhelmingly – and positively – to independent, unyielding, defiant perseverance in the face of aggressive misfortune, and thus to a kind of courageousness'.[5] The same idea is conveyed by the use of words like ὑποφέρω (2.19); ἀνθίστημι (5.9); or concepts like 'ἕτοιμοι ἀεὶ πρὸς ἀπολογίαν παντὶ τῷ αἰτοῦντι' (3.15). For the author, there is a close connection between steadfastness and righteousness/holiness for while the sufferer remains defiant, he also continues to behave in a way that is pleasing to God.

1.   W. C. van Unnik, 'A Classical Parallel to 1 Peter ii. 14 and 20', *NTS* 1 (1954/55), pp. 198–202.
2.   See LSJ, pp. 1888–9.
3.   See BDAG, p. 1039.
4.   W. Radl, 'ὑπομένω', in *EDNT* (Vol. 3; Grand Rapids: Eerdmans, 1993), pp. 404–5.
5.   W. Radl, 'ὑπομονή', in *EDNT*, 3.405. See also, BDAG, pp. 1039–40.

The second element, 'doing good', is expressed primarily by the verb 'ἀγαθοποιέω' (2.15, 20; 3.6, 17), and its cognate noun 'ἀγαθοποιΐα' (4.19). It is also expressed conceptually through the exhortation 'μὴ ἀποδιδόντες κακὸν ἀντὶ κακοῦ ἢ λοιδορίαν ἀντὶ λοιδορίας, τοὐναντίον δὲ εὐλογοῦντες' (3.9). In 1 Peter, 'doing good' in the face of suffering involves active non-retaliation which springs from a life of holiness. This is possible precisely because the sufferer has chosen to remain steadfast. S/he is able to 'do good' to his/her detractor in view of changing the situation.

The third element, 'subordination' is expressed by the verb 'ὑποτάσσω' (2.13, 18; 3.1, 5, 22; 5.5). This verb can be translated to 'subject oneself', 'subordinate', 'be subjected', or 'obey'.[6] For the author of 1 Peter, 'ὑποτάσσω' is not about servile submission, or unquestioning obedience to another, but about acting appropriately within the context of human relationships.[7] Elliott proposes that it 'entails a recognition of respect for order manifested in the acknowledgement of one's subordinate position in relation to those in authority'.[8] Michaels suggests that 'to defer' is a more appropriate definition of 'ὑποτάσσω' and that, in 1 Peter, 'ὑποτάσσω' is 'a matter of choice, not of nature or necessity'.[9] It is worth noting that, in 1 Peter, the motivation for 'subordination' is the sufferer's dependence on God.

The collocation 'steadfastness', 'doing good', and 'subordination', as a description of faithful response contains some overlap and interconnectedness in the way these elements are treated in 1 Peter. They appear in close proximity to each other in the discussion of how the audience should respond to suffering. The collocation appears throughout, but there are instances in which all three elements are explicit (ὑποτάσσω [2.18]; ὑπομένω [2.20]; and ἀγαθαποείω [2.20]); and instances in which some of the elements are implicit. For example, in 3.15-17, 'steadfastness' and 'subordination' are implicit in 'ἕτοιμοι ἀεὶ πρὸς ἀπολογίαν παντὶ τῷ αἰτοῦντι' (3.15), while ἀγαθαποείω (3.17) is explicit. The author uses this collocation to underscore the kind of response that is characteristic of the righteous sufferer.

In this chapter, I will demonstrate that, in 1 Peter, a 'faithful response' to suffering is characterized by a decision to maintain godly conduct expressed through standing firm, non-retaliation to abuse, and peaceful behaviour in the face of hardships. This arises from a person's sense of dependence on God. It is not a passive or servile submission to abuse; rather, it is a courageous decision to bear unjust mistreatment in the sure hope that God will vindicate one's cause. Further, I will substantiate the claim that 'faithful response' is an element of the fabula of 1 Peter by demonstrating that it is a concept that is treated in a similar fashion in the life of Israel, Jesus, and 1 Peter's audience.

The author of 1 Peter has a keen interest in key episodes in Israel's life – exodus and exile, especially. This leads to further exploration of the

6. See BDAG, p. 1042.
7. See Achtemeier, *1 Peter*, p. 182.
8. Elliott, *1 Peter*, p. 487.
9. Michaels, *1 Peter*, pp. 123–4.

Old Testament narrative and Israel's faithful response to suffering. I will demonstrate that there are points of contact between the way these texts portray the way in which corporate Israel and righteous individuals respond to trials and what one finds in 1 Peter. Second, I will discuss the author's description of Jesus' attitude and response to sufferings which depends partly on Isaiah's portrayal of the suffering servant of Yahweh, and partly on the author's knowledge of the passion of Jesus which he gathers from the Jesus-tradition. Third, I will show how the author encourages his audience to respond to suffering. In his quest to shape the audience's behaviour, the author of 1 Peter sets up Jesus' experience as the ultimate paradigm for the addressees to follow. Therefore, their response to suffering is to be patterned after that of Jesus Christ.

5.2. *Israel's faithful response as background for 1 Peter (Exod. 2.23-25; Ps. 31)*

Faithful response, according to my working definition, consists of non-retaliation to abuse and peaceful behaviour in the face of hardships that arise from dependence on God's ability to bring about deliverance on one's behalf. Such characteristics are found in the life of Israel as a nation and in stories of righteous persons in the Old Testament and other Jewish writings. I have demonstrated that the epistle is replete with words and concepts that echo the Exodus narrative (1.2, 13, 18-20), and highlight God's *lovingkindness* which motivates him to act on behalf of Israel (1.3-4). In addition, the idea of new birth into an inheritance is reminiscent of the purpose of the Exodus which was to give Israel the inheritance promised to the patriarchs. This 'volume' of echoes[10] in 1 Peter leads to further consideration of the Exodus story. His description of the audience in 1.1 and 2.11 evokes Israel's exilic existence. The author casts some of his exhortations to the audience in the language drawn from Israel's own experience of sojourning (1.15-17).

The metaphor of 'exile' highlights the importance of 'faithful response'. Smith-Christopher points out that exilic discourse brings with it the central question of response – either faithful endurance or accommodation/apostasy. He suggests that the texts associated with the Babylonian exile should be read 'with the *presumption of resistance*'. He adds, 'the stories of Daniel and Esther are Hebrew tales of refusing Persian "executive privilege"'.[11] Similarly, in one breath, the author of 1 Peter talks about the suffering connected to diasporic existence, the hope of deliverance, and the kind of behaviour required in order to experience this salvation and to receive the inheritance associated with it (1.3-9).

---

10.   I am indebted to Hays for this language. Richard B. Hays, *Echoes of Scripture in the Letters of Paul* (New Haven: Yale University Press, 1989).

11.   Smith-Christopher, *Biblical Theology of Exile*, p. 24; idem, 'Impact of the Babylonian Exile', in Scott (ed.), *Exile*, pp. 7–36.

The book of Exodus treats Israel's response to suffering as key to the events that would unfold and find their culmination in Israel's departure from Egypt. The first two chapters set up the narrative and introduce the children of Israel (1.1-7), the origin of their sufferings (1.8-16, 22), and some of the ways they tried to cope with their situation initially (1.15-21; 2.1-22). At the beginning of the book, the narrator offers an assessment of the situation of the children of Israel which is congruent with God's promises to the patriarchs regarding the growth and strength of their descendents (Gen. 13.16; 26.24; 46.4). We are told: 'The Israelites were fruitful and prolific; they multiplied and grew exceedingly strong, so that the land was filled with them' (Exod. 1.7). This assessment is contrasted with that of the new king of Egypt who sees Israel's numerical strength as a threat to Egypt's existence (Exod. 1.8-10).[12] This is given as the basis of the suffering that will be inflicted on Israel by the Egyptians. The text also reveals that Israel's initial reactions, for example, the actions of the midwives and of Moses' family, seem to produce mixed results. Moses' own decision to meet violence with violence backfires and forces him to become an alien (2.22).[13] It is at this juncture that the narrative introduces another reaction of Israel to their sufferings (Exod. 2.23-25).

If the assessment of the narrator about the strength of the Israelites in Exod. 1.7 and the assessment of the king of Egypt in 1.9-10 regarding the numerical and military potential of the Israelites are well-founded, it follows that the Israelites had the option of rebelling against the slavery and mistreatment inflicted by the Egyptians. In fact, this is what Moses set out to do on a small scale. Yet, the turning point in the narrative occurs when the Israelites cry out for help (2.23-24). The narrator does not specify whether their groaning is directed toward God.[14] Propp suggests that the cries of the Israelites should be understood more in terms of cries of pain and less

---

12.   See Terrence E. Fretheim, *Exodus* (Interpretation; Louisville: John Knox, 1991), p. 27. The contrast between the narrator's point of view and that of the king of Egypt vis-à-vis the situation of Israel is consistent with the reaction of outsiders to the work of God in the life of his elect. The new king of Egypt was blind to the work of God in and through Israel. What should have been seen as God's blessing is interpreted as a personal/national threat, which resulted in the oppression of God's people. Analogously, this situation is not far removed from what is described in 1 Pet. 4.3-4.

13.   Fretheim suggests that the narrator casts Moses' actions in a good light. He points out how the language used to describe Moses' actions in 2.11-12, 17 is the same language used of God later in the narrative, and argues that Moses' action anticipates or foreshadows God's actions (*Exodus*, pp. 42–3). However, it appears that there is a subtle contrast between Moses' action, which leads to uncertainty and no apparent change in the situation of the Israelites, and the Israelites' crying out, which leads to God stepping into the situation and bringing about the needed change. In addition, the events that immediately followed Moses' actions suggest that his initial reaction to the suffering of the children of Israel was not necessarily the best course of action. See Brevard Childs, *The Book of Exodus* (OTL; Philadelphia: Westminster, 1974), pp. 38; 42–6.

14.   Fretheim, *Exodus*, p. 48.

in terms of Israel 'haling Egypt into the divine court'.[15] However, the text in itself can be understood as a three-stage process of the description of Israel's supplications: (1) they cry out, (2) the cry rises, and (3) the cry is heard by God.[16] Further, in recounting this part of Israel's story, the writer of Deuteronomy narrates it precisely in terms of the children of Israel calling out to God in the midst of their suffering (Deut. 26.7).[17] Propp proposes that this is 'the first indication that Israel's sufferings will be neither meaningless nor interminable'.[18] Walter Brueggemann adds that Israel's cry is 'the catalyst for the entire Exodus story; it is the cry that evokes God's care'.[19] The cries of the children of Israel cause God to 'take heed of' the situation, which also bring about God's remembrance of the covenant he made with Abraham, Isaac, and Jacob.[20] This understanding occupies a central part in God's introductory speech to Moses: 'I have observed the misery of my people who are in Egypt; I have heard their cry on account of their taskmasters. Indeed, I know their sufferings, and I have come down to deliver them from the Egyptians' (Exod. 3.7-8). It is also central in the context of God's assuring Moses and the children of Israel of their deliverance, their vindication (Exod. 6.5-6).

The story of the Exodus is initiated by Israel's calling out to God for help in the midst of misery. The text attests to several attempts by the Israelites to deal with their suffering. Yet, the turning point came when they expressed their dependence on God by appealing to him for help. The narrator connects the suffering inflicted on the children of Israel by the Egyptians to the king's ignorance of Joseph (1.8), but says nothing concerning the Israelites' knowledge of the patriarch. If they knew about Joseph, it can be argued that they were also aware of the promise he made regarding God's visitation that would culminate in their exodus out of Egypt (Gen. 50.24-25). This seems to be the case, because the narrator later points out: 'And Moses took with him the bones of Joseph who had required a solemn oath of the Israelites, saying, "God will surely take notice of you, and then you must carry my bones with you from here"' (Exod. 13.19). It is possible then that the Israelites had a sense of who God was and what he was able to do on their behalf. Therefore, their cry to God might have contained some of the confidence in God's ability to deliver them that resonated from Joseph's words.

15.   William H. C. Propp, *Exodus 1-18: A New Translation with Introduction and Commentary* (AB, 2; New York: Doubleday, 1999), p. 180.

16.   Umberto Cassuto, *A Commentary on the Book of Exodus* (Jerusalem: Hebrew University Press, 1967), p. 29.

17.   So also, Durham, *Exodus*, pp. 25–6; Douglas K. Stuart, *Exodus: An Exegetical Theological Exposition of Holy Scripture* (NAC; Nashville: Broadman & Holman, 2006), pp. 102–3.

18.   Propp, *Exodus 1-18*, p. 180.

19.   Walter Brueggemann, *Exodus* (NIB, 1; Nashville: Abingdon, 1994), p. 707.

20.   Here again is evidence of the fact that God's actions on behalf of Israel precede the Exodus itself. God's actions are carried out in the context of the covenant with the patriarchs.

The Old Testament contains other evidence of faithful response to suffering. For example, Ps. 31 provides a picture of the one who trusts in God and expresses one's dependence on God for vindication, and by implication, does not retaliate in the face of false accusations, threats, and harassment.[21] The psalm possibly arose from the memory of the times when David was fleeing from King Saul (1 Sam. 19-26, especially 1 Sam. 23).[22] Some of the language present in this psalm is similar to what is found in Jeremiah (cf., e.g., Ps. 31.13 [31.14, MT, LXX] and Jer. 20.10; Ps. 31.17 [31.18, MT; 30.18, LXX] and Jer. 17.18; Ps. 31.1-2 [31.2-3, MT; 30.2-3, LXX] and Jer. 17.17). This has caused some scholars to question whether this psalm is of David.[23] What is clear is that the situation of the psalmist represents a reality in which many of God's children, 1 Peter's audience included, have found themselves – bearing up sufferings inflicted by outsiders. The psalmist faced his sufferings by relying on God for deliverance. He expresses his confidence in God in a way that recalls Exod. 3.7-8 (cf. Exod. 2.23-25): 'I will exult and rejoice in your steadfast love, because you have seen my affliction; you have taken heed of my adversities, and have not delivered me into the hand of the enemy; you have set my feet in a broad place' (Ps. 31.7-8 [31.8-9, MT; 30.8-9, LXX].[24] There are four elements that are common to both the narration of the speech attributed to God in Exod. 3.7-8 and the prayer of the psalmist in Ps. 31.

- God's hearing the cry of the children of Israel (Exod. 3.7; cf. 2.23-24); and God's hearing the prayer of the psalmist (Ps. 31.2 [31.3, MT, LXX]). In both cases, the sufferer initiates the process. To hear carries the implication of 'hearing and responding to' the situation.[25] It is about 'hearing favourably', with positive results in view.[26] Whereas God is present in the situation, the prayer for deliverance implies that the righteous sufferer does not depend on her own strength to deal with the situation in which she finds herself. It is an invitation for God to step into the situation and vindicate one's cause. The statement 'into your hand I commit my life'[27] is a clear expression of the psalmist's dependence on God (31.5 [31.6, MT; 30.6, LXX]).
- God's seeing the misery of his people in Egypt (Exod. 3.7; cf. 2.25); and God's seeing the affliction of the psalmist (Ps. 31.7b [31.8b, MT;

---

21.   See John Goldingay, *Psalms* (3 vols; BCOTWP; Grand Rapids: Baker, 2006), 1.440–1.

22.   So Goldingay, *Psalms*, 1.438.

23.   See Pierre E. Bonnard, *Le Psaultier Selon Jérémie: Influence Littéraire et Spirituelle de Jérémie sur Trente Trois Psaumes* (Paris: Cerf, 1960), p. 72; Jacquet, *Les Psaumes*, 1.667–76.

24.   On the modifications of the LXX to the MT see Jacquet, *Les Psaumes*, 1.667–8.

25.   Fretheim, *Exodus*, p. 48.

26.   Bonn Rüterswörden, 'שׁמע', in *TDOT* (Vol. 15; Grand Rapids: Eerdmans, 1977), pp. 253–79 (261).

27.   Author's translation.

30.8b, LXX]. Here, 'seeing' implies 'a move toward the other with kindness and sympathy'.[28] It is more than being aware of what it is going on. It implies taking keen interest in the matter at hand.

- God's knowing the sufferings of the children of Israel (Exod. 3.7; cf. 2.25); and God's knowing[29] the adversities of the psalmist (Ps. 31.7 [31.8, MT; 30.8, LXX]). Knowing has the sense of 'being careful of', 'paying attention to'. It is often combined with 'seeing' or 'hearing' to show a sort of process from sensory perception to intellectual understanding. In that sense the 'seeing' or the 'hearing' makes the 'knowing' possible.[30] Fretheim suggests knowing here refers to 'knowledge gained through experience'.[31] To some extent God shares in the pain of his children.
- God's delivering Israel from Egypt (Exod. 3.8); and God's delivering the psalmist from his enemies (Ps. 31.8 [31.9, MT; 30.9, LXX]). The psalmist is assured of God's deliverance in the future, because God has acted on his behalf in the past, and also perhaps, because he knows of the past wonders of God on behalf of his people.

Thus far the examples from the Old Testament provide us with the ways in which God's children handle sufferings, and there is evidence of great trust in God's ability to rescue from danger and protect in times of trouble.

This radical trust in God in the midst of hardships is also attested in exilic and post-exilic literature and in other writings of the Second Temple Judaism.[32] For example, Shadrach, Meshach, and Abednego expressed their trust in God's ability to deliver them as they resolved to accept the king's verdict that they would be thrown into the fiery furnace (Dan. 3.16-18). In the case of Daniel, the narrator puts this truth in the mouth of King Darius himself: 'The king said to Daniel, "May your God, whom you faithfully serve, deliver you"' (Dan. 6.16). In the story of the martyrdom of the seven brothers, the narrator described the mother's steadfastness in these terms: 'The mother was especially admirable and worthy of honorable memory. Although she saw her seven sons perish within a single day, she bore it with good courage because of her hope in the Lord' (2 Macc. 7.20). In Sir. 2.2-6 the righteous are urged to remain steadfast and be patient in calamity, to accept trials patiently, and to hope in God because God will help. This same confidence in God's ability to uphold the righteous and keep them from falling is expressed in *1 En.* 48.4, and in 1Q471.13-16).

---

28.   Fretheim, *Exodus*, p. 48; Goldingay, *Psalms*, 1.441; Jackie A. Naulté, 'ראה', in *NIDOTE* (Vol. 3; Grand Rapids: Zondervan, 1997), pp. 1007–15.

29.   'Knowing' is the reading attested in the MT. The LXX reads 'ἔσωσας ἐκ τῶν ἀναγκῶν τὴν ψυχήν μου'.

30.   Bergman and Botterweck, 'ידע', in *TDOT* (Vol. 5; Grand Rapids: Eerdmans, 1977), p. 462.

31.   Terence E. Fretheim, 'ידע' in *NIDOTE* (Vol. 3; Grand Rapids, Zondervan, 1997), pp. 409–13.

32.   See Nickelsburg, *Resurrection*, pp. 67–77.

In all these situations, (1) suffering is initiated as a result of something the person has done or failed to do that runs contrary to the standards and expectation of the outside world. (2) The sufferer does not withdraw from the situation, but accepts (submits to) the verdict that is passed by the authority(ies) in question; (3) the sufferer continues to uphold the holy conduct that brought about the trials; and (4) there is a testimony about the person's trust in God as a basis for enduring suffering. In these we find contact points between the stories of Israel, Jesus, and 1 Peter's audience.

Faithful response is a choice of the sufferer not to withdraw from the situation but remain firm and allow God to act on his or her behalf. It is not slavish submission, or fearful silence in the face of abuse. These responses may even empower the abuser and make matters worse. The key then is not in the response itself; rather, it is whether that response is an outflow of one's dependence on God. Whereas the contexts of these stories have their peculiarities, there is a shared theological reality that runs through all; namely, the righteous sufferer's cry to God for help, and his/her decision to respond faithfully to suffering initiate God's act of deliverance/vindication on his or her behalf. Suffering *per se* does not lead to glory; suffering that is inflicted because of one's allegiance to God and is endured on account of the Lord does. In 1 Peter, Jesus is portrayed as one who 'handed over to the righteous judge' (2.23). Similarly, the audience is encouraged to 'entrust their lives to the faithful creator' (4.19).

5.3. *Jesus' attitude in suffering: a normative paradigm (2.21-25)*

The normative and exemplary aspects of Jesus' sufferings come sharply into focus in 2.21-25. Because of the christological nature of this passage, its syntax, and the author's language (e.g., the repeated use of ὅς), some have argued for the presence of a christological hymn or that hymnic material serves as the background of this passage.[33] However, Thomas Osborne has adequately shown that such an argument is difficult to maintain.[34] Irrespective of the source-critical issues, one can safely say that the text of the Old Testament, in this context Isa. 53, is congruent with the whole letter and has become integral to 1 Peter's theological rhetoric. The author's description of Jesus' behaviour and response in the face of sufferings comprises both what

---

33.   E.g., Marie-Louise Lamau, 'Exhortation aux Esclaves et Hymne au Christ Souffrant dans La «Première l'Epître de Pierre»', *MSR* 43.3 (1987), pp. 121–43; Richard, 'Functional Christology', in Talbert (ed.), *Perspectives on First Peter*, pp. 125–7; Boismard, *Quatre Hymnes Baptismales*, pp. 15–56; Eduard Lohse, *Theological Ethics of the New Testament* (Minneapolis: Fortress, 1991), pp. 179–86 (183). Pearson, *Christological and Rhetorical Properties*, pp. 117–19.

34.   Thomas P. Osborne, 'Guide Lines for Christian Suffering: A Source-Critical and Theological Study of 1 Peter 2.21-25', *Bib* 64 (1983), pp. 381–408, (388–9); see also, Achtemeier, 'Suffering Servant', pp. 177–81; Michaels, *1 Peter*, pp. 136–7.

Jesus Christ did not do and what he did do. His response was characterized by active non-retaliation which is an outflow of his dependence on God.

The author sets up Jesus' response to sufferings as the normative example that the audience should follow.[35] It has been argued that Jesus' example refers only to slaves and not 1 Peter's entire audience.[36] Further, whereas many commentators admit that Jesus' example applies to all Christians, a closer look reveals that their focus is narrowly on what 1 Peter's injunction meant for the slaves in his audience.[37] However, several indications point to the fact that the instruction in 2.21-25 is directed to the entire audience, and not just the 'household slaves'. First, it should be noted that the slaves were in a similar predicament as the other believers – they were suffering unjustly because of their allegiance to God (2.12, 19; 3.15-17; 4.3-4). Their situation was as vulnerable as the other members' of 1 Peter's audience because of their alien status vis-à-vis the outside world.[38] The exhortation to the slaves to remain steadfast in the face of unjust suffering as righteous persons who are mindful of God (2.20) is repeated in the context of the entire audience (3.13-14; 4.15-16). Second, the language seems to tear down the 'slave versus free' categories within the congregation. For example, in one breath, the author addresses all as being 'free persons' on the one hand and all as being 'slaves of God', on the other hand (2.16). The terms 'δοῦλοι' (2.16) and 'οἱ οἰκέται' (2.18) have significant overlap in meaning. In fact, if read literally, 'οἱ οἰκέται' (those of the household, they who belong to the household) would fit 1 Peter's portrayal of the audience as members of God's household, God's family (cf. 4.17), living in subordination to human authority (2.13-15), under the tutelage of the individual household masters (heads) – some of whom are good and kind, a characteristic the author attributes to believers (cf. 3.4, 16), and some of who are unscrupulous. Third, the structure of the Petrine *Haustafel* places Christ's experience as central and paradigmatic to the whole (2.21-25).

The clause 'εἰς τοῦτο γὰρ ἐκλήθητε' refers to the author's claim that if one endures sufferings inflicted unjustly, it is a commendable act before God (2.19-20). The clause also anticipates the description of the way Jesus handled his sufferings (2.22-24).[39] Therefore, it is pivotal to both what precedes it and what follows it. On the one hand, 'εἰς τοῦτο' picks up the thought

---

35.   See my discussion on the *Haustafel* in Chapter 2.

36.   See Lamau, 'Exhortation aux Esclaves', p. 125; cf., Ernst Best, *1 Peter* (NCB; London: Oliphants, 1971), pp. 118–19.

37.   For example, Osborne concludes his study by listing 'guide lines' for those slaves who suffer unjustly ('Guide Lines', pp. 406–7). See also, Achtemeier, *1 Peter*, pp. 198–9; idem, 'Suffering Servant', p. 178; Elliott, *1 Peter*, p. 524; Spicq, *Épîtres*, pp. 106–14.

38.   See Achtemeier, *1 Peter*, pp. 192–5; Elliott, *1 Peter*, pp. 486–502; idem, *Backward and Forward*, pp. 188–9.

39.   Michaels' argument that τοῦτο in v. 21 looks backward rather than forward is unnecessary (*1 Peter*, p. 142); see also Osborne, 'Guide Lines', p. 389. While it is clear that the reference is to Peter's claim in vv. 19-20, it is also obvious that Peter provides Jesus' experience, in vv. 21-25, as the grounding for the claim.

summarized by the other neuter demonstrative in τοῦτο χάρις παρὰ θεῷ (2.20); on the other hand, the causal connection with 'ὅτι καὶ' introduces the thought about the example of Christ which creates the balance between the two clauses.[40] The author encourages his audience to see steadfastness as an outgrowth of their election. Therefore, the exhortation needs to be read in tandem with the call to holiness expressed earlier in the letter.[41] Holiness of life makes possible the kind of response that is required. It is also the basis of innocent behaviour, which one should display both in the presence and absence of suffering.

Further, the clause 'Χριστὸς ἔπαθεν ὑπὲρ ὑμῶν' refers to Christ's vicarious suffering and evokes memories of the audience's regeneration (1.2, 18-21).[42] But the author is also concerned with depicting the exemplary nature of Christ's suffering specifically as it relates to how one responds to suffering. The prepositional phrase 'ὑπὲρ ὑμῶν' can be read either (1) 'on your behalf' as 'in the place of you', or (2) 'for you' as 'for your sake', 'for your benefit'.[43] In 1 Pet. 2.24 the author elaborates on the vicarious suffering of Christ and that concept is also explicit in 3.18. Whereas this (vicarious) understanding is present in 2.21, the discussion of Jesus' response to suffering (2.22-23) makes it possible to understand 'ὑπὲρ ὑμῶν' also in terms of 'for your sake', 'for your benefit'. The participle ὑπολιμπάνων functions as a resultative participle which is reinforced by the ἵνα clause: ἵνα ἐπακολουθήσητε τοῖς ἴχνεσιν αὐτοῦ (2.21). Both readings of 'ὑπὲρ ὑμῶν' fit the context here, because Jesus is an example both in terms of his vicarious suffering and in terms of his response to suffering.[44]

Through his suffering – i.e, in the way he responded to it – Christ left a pattern (ὑπογραμμός) for others to follow. This term is not used outside of 1 Peter in the New Testament.[45] It is used by Clement of Alexandria to refer to handwriting patterns that schoolboys follow as they learn to write.[46] The author of 1 Peter complements this picture with the image of the audience following in the steps of Jesus. This might have evoked the Old Testament metaphor of 'walking with God' (Gen. 17.1; Deut. 26.17-19; 28.9; Josh. 22.5; 1 Kgs 3.14; 11.38; Neh. 5.9; Ps. 119.1-3 [118.1-3, LXX]; Prov. 14.2; Jer. 13.4). It is also attested in Second Temple literature (Bar. 1.18-19; 2.9-10; Wis. 6.4-5; Tob. 3.3-5).This is consistent with the holiness of life that

40.   The phrase 'εἰς τοῦτο' is also used in 3.9 and 4.5-6. In both instances it is combined with ἵνα to offer both a warrant and a cause for Peter's injunction (3.9), or statement (4.5).

41.   On Peter's understanding of the audience's election, see above, Chapter 3.

42.   The author's discussion of the vicarious sufferings of Jesus is more sustained in v. 24. See the section '1 Peter's Understanding of the Sufferings of Christ' in Chapter 4.

43.   See Elliott, *1 Peter*, pp. 524–5.

44.   On Jesus as an example of vicarious suffering see my discussion in Chapter 4. The focus of the present chapter is on Jesus' exemplary response to suffering.

45.   It is attested in 2 Macc. 2.18, and in the writings of Clement of Alexandria (*Strom.* 5.8.49; *1 Clem.* 16.17; *Paed.* 1.9). See Michaels, *1 Peter*, p. 144; LSJ, p. 1877.

46.   *Strom.* 5.675.

undergirds the entire existence of the believer and empowers the person to live for God. The invitation then is to live before God the way Jesus did by 'following in his steps'. As a child follows the pattern created by the pedagogue he/she is both imitating the pattern and being taught how to write.[47] Similarly, looking at how Jesus lived, especially how he suffered and walking in his steps involves both imitation and discipleship. It is worth noting, however, that one of the lexical meanings for 'ὑπογραμμός' is 'outline'. In that sense, Jesus' example only offers the parameters, i.e., 'guide lines'[48] of what constitutes faithful response to suffering. How that plays out in the life of each individual may be different. What is certain, the theological summary of Christ's passion 1 Peter offers is enough to guide the suffering Christian in how to face his/her trials as a faithful child of God.[49]

5.3.1. Steadfastness and holiness

In 1 Pet. 2.22, – '[he] who committed no sin, nor was deceit found in his mouth' – the author establishes Christ's innocence, which serves as grounding for his call to his entire audience that they also must be innocent, if and when they suffer. Christ's innocence is a basis for his non-retaliatory attitude which is an outward expression of his righteousness and holiness (1.18; 3.18). Christ's steadfastness is implicit here in the fact that he did not withdraw from the situation. The author's christological appropriation of the Old Testament is attested here as well. His description of Jesus' attitude is drawn from Isa. 53.9b, 'he had done no violence, and there was no deceit in his mouth'. For the author of 1 Peter, Jesus' attitude in suffering mirrors the reality of the servant of YHWH, and vice versa, and he wants his audience to align their lives to that same reality. He quotes the LXX of Isa. 53.9b almost word for word.[50] However, there is a striking difference between the contexts of the two texts, as Lamau points out. In Isaiah, the affirmation about the innocence of the servant of YHWH comes after his death, whereas 1 Peter proclaims the innocence of Jesus during his suffering.[51] The description of Jesus' passion focuses on Jesus' sufferings and not on his death. This is so partly because the primary focus is on lifestyle in the present, partly because he has the suffering of his audience in mind. He is concerned with helping the believers determine how to live according to the will of God during the

---

47.   See Schrenk, 'ὑπογραμμός' in *TDNT*, (Vol. 1; Grand Rapids: Eerdmans, 1964) p. 773.

48.   Osborne is inconsistent on this aspect. On the one hand, he suggests that the example of Christ's suffering relates to the entire audience (pp. 388–9); but in drawing his final conclusions he refers to the guidelines as being provided for 'the Christian slaves who suffer unjustly' ('Guide Lines', pp. 406–7).

49.   So Osborne, 'Guide Lines', p. 393.

50.   He replaces the particle ὅτι with the pronoun ὅς, and the word ἀνομία with ἁμαρτία.

51.   Lamau, 'Exhortation aux Esclaves', p. 126.

rest of their earthly existence (4.2). This is important, because the author highlights the need for the audience to live in such a way that their innocence will be manifest to their detractors with the possibility that they might be won to God (2.12; 3.1, 16). Here the identification with the audience is not centred on Jesus' sinlessness, but on the fact that his suffering did not come as a result of improper behaviour or sinful conduct (cf. 3.18; 4.15-16).[52] In this way the author makes it clear to the audience that it is not enough to endure the situation; one needs to display righteousness while remaining steadfast.

5.3.2. *Doing good and active non-retaliation*

Another descriptive statement makes up the first part of 1 Pet. 2.23, 'who while being insulted did not insult in return; while suffering did not threaten'. Though there are no explicit verbal allusions to Isaiah, the text of 1 Peter shares some conceptual affinities with that book. The attitude of Jesus while being insulted is analogous to the attitude of the servant of YHWH during the maltreatment he faced (Isa. 53.7). However, in Isaiah the servant is silent, whereas in 1 Peter Jesus is not just silent; rather, his speech is not evil.[53] Although Isa. 53 is part of the background, the author is appropriating Isaiah in such a way that the picture that is presented of Jesus Christ is one that is similar to the immediate experience of the audience, i.e., their sufferings. The author's apparent knowledge of the Jesus-tradition contributes to his picture of the suffering Christ and the attitude he displayed while undergoing these hardships.[54] The description of Christ is similar to the Gospels' passion narratives, in which one finds a picture of Jesus who did not trade insults with those who were blaspheming and mocking him (Mk 15.29-32; Lk. 22.65-70; Jn 18.19-23); rather, he trusted his life into God's hand (Mk 15.34; Lk. 23.34, 46; cf. 1 Pet. 2.23; 4.19).[55] The author of 1 Peter encourages those who are suffering to have the same attitude: 'not repaying evil for evil or abuse for abuse, but blessing instead' (3.9). For the audience, the identification with Jesus is not only in what he did not do – non-retaliation, but also his disposition – complete dependence on God. Although the author speaks of Jesus' dependence on God subsequent to his description of Jesus' non-retaliatory attitude, the former seems to be the motivating factor for the latter. This assessment is consistent with the way the author describes faithful women of the Old Testament. In 1 Pet. 3.5, the

---

52. Michaels, *1 Peter*, p. 145.
53. Michaels, 'Passion Narrative', p. 391.
54. The existence of a Jesus tradition which was passed down from one person to another is evident in Paul's writings (1 Cor. 11.17-34 (23); 2 Tim. 2.2).
55. For a discussion on the use of the Jesus tradition in the Gospels see Joel B. Green, *The Death of Jesus: Tradition and Interpretation in the Passion Narrative* (WUNT, 2.33; Tübingen: Mohr Siebeck, 1988), pp. 96–101.

language suggests that dependence on God is the basis for the holy women's obedience/subordination to their husbands.

5.3.3. *Subordination and dependence on God*

Jesus is an example for the audience, because in his sufferings he displayed complete dependence on God. First Peter 2.23b reads, 'while suffering did not threaten but handed over to the one who judges justly'. The author does not specify what or whom Jesus handed over. Therefore, scholars have made several proposals arguing that the object of the verb is (1) Jesus himself, supported in part by the parallel notion the author uses – 'let those who suffer according to the will of God entrust their lives to the faithful Creator' – in 4.19;[56] (2) his cause, in the sense that the 'handing over' encompasses Jesus' life's work in its entirety;[57] or (3) his enemies, because they are the implied objects of the other two verbs 'did not revile in return' and 'did not threaten' (οὐκ ἀντελοιδόρει and οὐκ ἠπείλει) in the immediate context.[58] The ambiguity of the passage seems to be deliberate. Each of the options listed above can fit both the context of 1 Peter and the fabula that shapes the narrative substructure of the letter.

In terms of the fabula, faithful response is followed by vindication; therefore, by handing over to God, Jesus is trusting God with all that concerned his existence, his life, the work he came to accomplish, and those who opposed and oppressed him in order for God's vindication to take place. Further, God vindicated the person of Jesus by raising him from the dead, exalting him, and giving him glory (1.18-21; 3.18-22) and the resurrection is the means of the audience's new birth. Since Jesus suffered so that the believers can enjoy a new way of life (1.17-21), the life they now live is evidence of God's vindication of Christ's work. The author testifies to the fact that the audience has embodied the qualities that are required of God's children (1.22-23). Finally, the language of 1 Peter attests to the fact that those who have rejected Jesus have themselves stumbled (2.7-9). The three options are not mutually exclusive as each highlights a particular aspect (and together, the totality) of Jesus' dependence and trust in God, on the one hand and the comprehensive nature of God's vindication on the other (3.18-22). By handing over to the one who judges justly, Christ is expressing his confidence in God's ability to vindicate his person and his cause in the sight of his enemies. The handing over of 'enemies' to God can still be considered a non-retaliatory act, because one is allowing God to deal with the matter, and judgement will result in punishment only if these outsiders fail to recognize God's work in the lives of the faithful, and continue in their disobedient ways (4.4-5, 17).

---

56. Davids, *1 Peter*, p. 105; Witherington, *1 Peter*, 135; Jobes, *1 Peter*, p. 194.
57. So e.g., Elliott, *1 Peter*, p. 531; Schlosser, 'A.T. et Christologie', p. 90.
58. So e.g., Michaels, *1 Peter*, p. 147; Richard, *Reading 1 Peter*, p. 122.

The author's description of God as 'the one who judges justly' serves to ensure the audience that their cause will be dealt with in all fairness. This is important because in a world where judgement was passed based on one's status,[59] this reminder is of great encouragement to 1 Peter's audience. Their decision to follow Christ has put them in a precarious position vis-à-vis their sphere of influence. They can live for God's approval and act in a way that will please him as opposed to acting to please the world around them and the authorities before whom they may be called to give an account (3.15). Michaels, for example, seems to rule out the possibility that governing authorities might be counted among those who malign the audience. He argues that the author wants his audience to see the authorities in a positive light.[60] Yet, it is imaginable that sufferings may originate or intensify as a result of poor judgement on the part of those placed in authority to dispense judgement. For example, Joseph went to prison not simply because of the accusation brought against him, but also because Potiphar became enraged against Joseph as a result. The narrator charges Potiphar with putting Joseph in prison (Gen. 39.19-20). Joseph accepted the verdict, and continued to live uprightly while in prison and was in the end vindicated. In the story of Shadrach, Meshach, and Abednego although accusations were levelled at them by those who wanted them ill, their fate was not decided until King Nebuchadnezzar himself had ruled on their case (Dan. 3.14-20). The three Hebrew youths remained resolute in the face of the impending furnace, and 'submitted' to the king by accepting the sentence pronounced as a result of their defying action (or lack thereof). Here too, God did not allow his children to face their hardship alone (Dan. 3.26-28). It is worth noting that in this case their steadfastness led to Nebuchadnezzar singing praises to God. This mirrors the outcome, which the author of 1 Peter presents to his audience, that good conduct in suffering makes it possible for the accusers to praise God (1 Pet. 2.12, 3.1-2). In the case of Daniel, although King Darius wanted to protect Daniel and was aware of Daniel's innocence (Dan. 6.22), the events unfolded in such a way that he was not able to, and eventually condemned Daniel for his actions (Dan. 6.14-16). Daniel remained steadfast throughout the situation and enjoyed God's care and protection in the midst of his trials.

In all of these stories one gets a clear sense that these people were not leading a life of passive resignation during their sufferings. Rather, they made an active decision to trust God, while continuing to do the good things that brought trials their way in the first place. Their sufferings were not only a result of false accusations, but also of decisions by the people placed in authority to handle their case. Therefore, one cannot assume that 1 Peter's audience will (always) receive a fair hearing, or that 1 Peter's words about what the work of those in authority is intended to be will (always) intersect

59. See deSilva, *Honor, Patronage, Kinship, and Purity*, pp. 23–93.
60. Michaels, *1 Peter*, pp. 126–7; Jobes, *1 Peter*, p. 176.

with the reality. The book of *1 Enoch* provides a grim picture of the attitude of those in authority vis-à-vis the situation of righteous sufferers:

> Then, in our tribulation, we brought a charge against them before the authorities, and cried out against those who were devouring us, but they (the authorities) neither would pay attention to our cries nor wish to listen to our voice. But (on the contrary) they were assisting those who were robbing and devouring us, those who were causing us to diminish. They (the authorities) conceal their (the offenders) injustice and do not remove the yokes of those who devour us, scatter us, and murder us; (the authorities) cover up our murder, and they (the authorities) do not remember (the fact) that they (the offenders) have lifted up their hands against us. (*1 En.* 103.14-15)[61]

It is difficult to say to what extent the reality of the audience would match what is attested in the stories above. But since receiving a fair judgement is not a given, it becomes all the more important for the author to describe God as the just judge (1 Pet. 1.17; 2.21). In so doing, he is encouraging the audience to be subordinate (to obey) to human authority (lit. creature) – 'πάσῃ ἀνθρωπίνῃ κτίσει'[62] – because at the root of such behaviour is the confidence that the audience places in God, who himself is above all human authority, as he is the faithful creator (πιστῷ κτίστῃ, 4.19), will judge all – the living and the dead. Irrespective of how the governing authorities would treat the audience, the author encourages them to treat everyone with respect (2.17), because being subordinate to human authority is not done primarily for their sake, but because of the Lord.

The description of God as a judge is closely connected with the concept of God as vindicator.[63] This designation of a judge was applied to God earlier in the epistle (1.17). There the image complements 1 Peter's description of Father. Together these two images should give comfort to the audience as they are under God's care. The concept of judgement is also present in 3.12; 4.5-6, 17-19, with the implication that God is the one who will pass judgement. Both in 1 Pet. 1.17 and in 4.17 the author relates the idea of judgement not only to outsiders, but to the readers as well. This underlines the fact that the members of the audience are expected to maintain a life that is above reproach. God knows the reality the righteous are facing and looks on them favourably. He also knows and is against those who commit evil (3.12). The judge to whom Jesus entrusted his life and his enemies is the same the members of the audience call Father. Because he raised Jesus from the dead and gave him glory (1.21), they can set their hope on God, and live with the assurance that he is able to vindicate them from their own trials. Therefore, they can follow Jesus' example by leading a life that is above reproach, meeting sufferings with non-retaliation, and putting their confidence in God (4.19).

---

61.   Isaac, '1 Enoch', in *OTP*, 1.84–5.
62.   See Elliott, *1 Peter*, p. 489. On an alternative translation for 'πάσῃ ἀνθρωπίνῃ κτίσει' and its implications see, Richard, 'Honorable Conduct', pp. 417–18.
63.   On which, see further my discussion in Chapter 6.

5.4. *The audience's faithful response to suffering*

The identification of the audience with Jesus Christ reaches a crucial point here, because the author elaborates on what the audience should do in response to sufferings. He parses the audience's response in terms of 'steadfastness', 'doing good', and 'subordination'. He urges his audience to stand firm in the midst of suffering. In so doing, the only acceptable way to resist is as a righteous person. As Christ was innocent in his suffering, so the believers are to be innocent from wrongdoing (cf. 3.18; 4.1-2). Further, the proper way to respond to the sufferings is by entrusting one's life to God, the faithful creator, while doing what is good (4.19). The collocation 'steadfastness', 'subordination', and 'doing good' contains one overall motivating factor: the sufferer's mindfulness of God.

5.4.1. *Steadfastness and holiness*

Steadfastness involves standing firm in the face of opposition and suffering while maintaining holy conduct. In this matter, the author encourages the audience to follow in the steps of Jesus (2.18-20). He highlights several key factors that contribute to the understanding of 'steadfastness'. First, steadfastness meets God's approval when the sufferer is motivated by the desire to please God. The terms 'χάρις' and 'κλέος' belong to the semantic field of 'honour'. Being aware/mindful of God implies that one acts for his approval alone as he is the arbiter of honour. Second, the suffering in question is unjust suffering, it is not deserved. The author elaborates on the idea with a rhetorical question and underlines the fact that suffering should not come as a result of bad behaviour. Third, the author underscores the connection between 'steadfastness' and 'doing good'. It is not enough to resist; it is not enough to stand firm; one needs to act positively in the situation. This concept is reiterated in 3.14-17, where the idea of God as the arbiter of honour is implicitly stated with the divine passive 'καταισχυνθῶσιν' (3.16). It is also expressed by the conditional clause 'εἰ θέλοι τὸ θέλημα τοῦ θεοῦ' (3.17). This is another way of expressing the sufferer's mindfulness of God in the midst of suffering. The clause also underlines the fact that the author understands suffering to be an intrusion in the experience of the child of God. 'Steadfastness' is here complemented by a negative command: 'do not fear them, do not be troubled'. The righteous sufferer is urged to stand firm and face his/her detractors without fear. The author is borrowing the language of the prophet Isaiah to the people of Judah (Isa. 8.12-13), and casting the audience's response to suffering in language reminiscent of the Old Testament. 'Steadfastness' also comprises a positive expression: sanctify Christ as Lord. Here, the author modifies the Old Testament text in a way that puts Christ in the place of God. He continues to subvert the societal norms of the time. Although the righteous is supposed to give an account to another, presumably someone in authority, that act is carried out not because of the interrogator, but because of the sufferer's mindfulness of God and because she has acknowledged God's/Christ's lordship over her life.

To sanctify Christ as Lord is not only to acknowledge his rule over one's life, it is also to embody the holiness that is inherent to his person. This is why the emphasis is put on the way the sufferer should express his/her steadfastness: with humility and reverence, and maintaining a good conscience. In this, one finds connection between faithful response and vindication. If the righteous sufferer responds faithfully to suffering, God will vindicate him/her by shaming his/her detractors.

5.4.2. *Doing good and active non-retaliation*

'Doing good' as an expression of faithful response to suffering involves active non-retaliation which springs from a life of holiness. One of the places in the letter where the author's exhortation to non-retaliation is expressed is in 3.8-12, particularly in v. 9. The author's exhortation here is framed in a way that suggests non-retaliation needs to be carried out in a communal fashion. 'Being like-minded' is an encouragement to have the same purpose, to act together in achieving the same goal.[64] The primary concern is to highlight the need for members of his audience to relate to each other on the same playing field (cf. 1.22-23). This exhortation then is aimed at regulating relationships that would otherwise be complicated to maintain within the church.[65] It is clear that those who have been born again find themselves in a position to learn how to relate to each other within the family of God as much as they need to know how to relate to the outside world. Therefore, the roles one has/needs to play can be complex both in relating to other believers and to the outside world. For example, within the congregation, the fact that a 'slave' is now considered a 'brother' or a 'sister' changes the relationship dynamics that are established by, and practised in society at large.[66] In this case, the language about 'being compassionate', 'loving one another' (lit. loving the brotherhood), and 'humble-minded' takes on added significance. These are 'embodied qualities' that should guide the relationships within the congregation.[67] It is, perhaps, partly the reason why the author levelled the servant-versus-free-person divide in 2.16 – all are free and all are servants of God. In addition, they are all members of God's household by virtue of their new birth. Consequently, they are brothers and sisters who call on the same Father. Therefore, they now have the same status and role(s).[68] This is not to say that the author does away with notions of hierarchy and

---

64.   Achtemeier, *1 Peter*, p. 222.

65.   Goppelt concludes, 'The five adjectives express, therefore, the practice of κοινωνία that is essential for the Church' (*1 Peter*, p. 233).

66.   Bartchy, *Slavery*, pp. 62–87.

67.   I am borrowing the term 'embodied qualities' from Green (*1 Peter*, p. 104).

68.   See David G. Horrell, 'From ἀδελφοί to οἶκος θεοῦ: Social Transformation in Pauline Christianity', *JBL* 120 (2001), pp. 293–311. Although this article deals with the Pauline corpus, Horrell's discussion about how 'fictive kinship' and 'household of God'

authority. However, he subverts the concepts and proposes a new way that is congruent with the standards God has set for his children (2.17). For example, the language of shepherding and oversight that is used to describe the role and work of elders within the congregations implies that they are in a position of authority and leadership over the 'flock of God which is among you' (5.2). However, the way the relationships are lived out between leaders and followers is not by the former 'lording it over' the latter; rather, it is by being an example (5.3). Green rightly suggests, 'The result is a "household of God" the cohesion for which is a cruciform love – that is, a love that takes its content and form from the sacrificial death of Christ on the cross – that both transcends and subverts conventional concerns with status and customary lines of authority'.[69]

The wider context of 3.8-12 connects what is said here back to 2.21-25, because they are conceptually similar. The two pericopae are tied together by the concept of non-retaliation, and the author's rooting the concept in the audience's election 'εἰς τοῦτο ἐκλήθητε' (3.9). In addition, he uses a notion similar to the 'like-mindedness' of 3.8 in 4.1, i.e., 'arm yourselves with the same thought', to encourage the audience to identify with Christ. On this basis, the author is still very much concerned with telling his audience to follow Christ's example of faithful response to suffering. In fact, 1 Pet. 3.9 constitutes not only a rehearsal of the description of Jesus' attitude (cf. 2.23), but also a reminder of Jesus' own teaching to his disciples (cf. Mt. 5.38-45; Lk. 6.27-28).[70] Doing good in the midst of sufferings involves *active* non-retaliation, because it is not enough for the sufferer to refrain from responding in kind; he or she needs to act positively in the situation. The author again reminds his audience that their faithful response is an inherent outflow of their election and if they are faithful to their calling, they will inherit a blessing.[71] Taken together, the purpose of 3.8-9 is partly to help foster unity within the congregation and partly to create unity in the way they respond to suffering from outside. Active non-retaliation, like the holiness from which it springs, is as much a community endeavour as it is an individual pursuit. The sentiments and attitudes that are fostered within the family of God prepare the members of the community to deal with the challenges of the outside world.[72]

---

language works in constructing relationships within the church is helpful. Speaking of Paul's use of the term ἀδελφός, he notes, 'This kinship description would seem to imply that Paul both assumes and promotes the relationship between himself and his addressees, and among the addressees themselves, as one between equal siblings, who share a sense of affection, mutual responsibility, and solidarity' (p. 299).

69.   Green, *1 Peter*, p. 105.

70.   That this teaching was part of the Jesus tradition is evident by its attestation in the writings of Paul (Rom. 12.17; 1 Thess. 5.15). On Jesus' teaching as the source of the formulations in both Peter and Paul, see Feldmeier, *The First Letter of Peter*, p. 186; Goppelt, *1 Peter*, pp. 230–2.

71.   Blessing here may be a parallel to 'God's approval' referred to in 2.20 or to the salvation that is to be revealed (1.4, 9).

72.   Goppelt, *1 Peter*, pp. 234–5.

The author of 1 Peter grounds his exhortation in the Scriptures of Israel (3.10-12). This time he resorts to Ps. 34.12-16 [33.13-17, LXX].[73] The overall context of the psalm is congruent with many aspects of the author's discussion.[74] The psalmist is celebrating God's acts of salvation carried out on behalf of the oppressed and in the process teaches the congregation the kind of behaviour the oppressed should demonstrate in order for God to act on his/her behalf.[75] He 'wants to draw his hearers into his own experience of the reality of God's salvation'.[76] In rooting his call to non-retaliation in Ps. 34 [33, LXX], the author of 1 Peter is (1) highlighting the importance of his exhortations for the immediate present; (2) driving home the point that the audience's actions and dispositions should be guided by their concern to please God, and not the outside world; and (3) rehearsing the theological hermeneutic and narrative dynamics at work in the epistle.

First, the phrase, 'the person who wishes to love life and see good days', highlights the author's concern for the audience to thrive in their environment and ultimately overcome the situation that they are dealing with. Bo Reicke argues that the focus here is on eschatological salvation. He proposes, 'The expression "to see good days" must be understood with reference to eternal life and cannot be referred to earthly living in calm and peace'.[77] Although it is clear that 1 Peter is concerned in part with the eschatological realities that have implications on and for the lives of the believers (1.4-9; 4.5-6, 17-18), it is also clear that the epistle is very much concerned with the 'earthly existence' of the audience. For the author, Christ suffered so that each member of the audience can live 'according to the will of God, during the time that remains for him/her to conduct his/her earthly existence' (4.2). The exhortations are given to help the readers face life in the present in such a way that they would be worthy of the life to come.[78] To that extent, the language matches the concern of the psalmist regarding what to do to benefit God's blessing in the present.[79] 'Doing good' constitutes embodying the divine qualities in the same

73. The author made reference to this psalm earlier in the epistle (cf. 1 Pet. 2.3 with Ps. 34.9).

74. The author changes the second person address in the psalm to the third person and changes the opening interrogation into an affirmative sentence. Goldingay suggests that 1 Peter's focus seems to be the regulation of evil speech in relation with other people, whereas the psalmist seems to be focusing primarily on evil speech in relation to God (*Psalms*, p. 483). While this may be true, to the extent that oppression is from other people, one cannot exclude the option that the psalmist is focusing on relationships between the righteous and his/her oppressor(s). See further, Michaels, *1 Peter*, pp. 179–80; Achtemeier, *1 Peter*, pp. 225–6.

75. See further e.g., Peter C. Craigie, *Psalms 1-50* (WBC, 19; Waco, TX: Word, 1983), pp. 276–82; Goldingay, *Psalms*, pp. 475–86; Jacquet, *Psaumes*, 1.710–24; Hans-Joachim Kraus, *Psalms 1-59* (Minneapolis: Ausburg, 1988), pp. 381–8; C. H. Richards, 'Psalm 34', *Int* 40 (1986), pp. 175–9; Terrien, *Psalms*, pp. 301–6.

76. Kraus, *Psalms*, p. 387.

77. Reicke, *1 Peter*, p. 105. So also Michaels, *1 Peter*, p. 180; Best, *1 Peter*, p. 131.

78. Benedikt P. Schwank, 'L'Épître (1 P 3,8-15)', *AsSeign* 59 (1966), pp. 16–32 (20).

79. Achtemeier admits that the psalmist is concerned with life in the present, but argues that Peter's primary concern is with eschatological salvation (*1 Peter*, p. 226).

way God's children are required to embody God's holiness. The Psalmist tells the congregation of worshippers that God is good (Ps. 34.8 [33.9, LXX]; cf. 1 Pet. 2.3), then admonishes them to 'do good' (Ps. 34.14 [33.15, LXX]; cf. 1 Pet. 2.20; 3.6, 11, 17; 4.19). Similarly, the author's exhortation to good conduct is based on the fact that the audience has become aware of God's goodness (1 Pet. 2.3).[80]

Second, the use of Ps. 34 [33, LXX] underscores the fact the author wants his audience's actions and dispositions to be guided by their mindfulness of God, and not by what the outside world requires of them (2.13, 19-20; 4.1-2). In the context of oppression, refraining from acts of evil speech, doing what is good, and seeking peace constitute the proper response of the righteous (1 Pet. 3.9-11). In the context of the psalm this falls under what constitutes the 'fear of YHWH' (Ps. 34.12-15 [33.13-16, LXX]). The author of 1 Peter might have been aware of this, because he alludes to another part of the psalm (Ps. 34.8 [33.9, LXX]) earlier in the letter (1 Pet. 2.3), and the overall context of the Psalm, God's salvation/vindication of the righteous sufferer, fits the message of the letter (e.g., 2.15; 3.15-16, 18-22; 5.10). It follows, 'doing good' can be understood as being rooted in the 'the fear of YHWH'. In telling the audience not to be afraid of their accusers (3.6, 13-16), the underlying reason is the 'fear of YHWH' which causes a person to be primarily concerned with how he/she lives before God, and constitutes what shapes one's conduct in dealing with others.[81]

Third, the use of Ps. 34 [33, LXX] is further evidence of the theological hermeneutic and the narrative dynamics that are at work in 1 Peter. The text of Ps. 34.15-16 [33.16-17, LXX] contains the same anthropomorphic concepts of seeing and hearing for God that are attested in the other Old Testament texts treated above (Exod. 3.7-8; Ps. 31.2, 7 [31.3, 8 MT; 30.3, 8, LXX]). The psalmist describes God's salvation on his behalf in terms that are analogous of God's acts on behalf of Israel in the past, and the author of 1 Peter applies that reality directly to the audience (3.12). The theological reality of God's saving act transcends the chronological gaps between the beneficiaries of God's goodness. The psalmist states the truths about doing good and God's deliverance of the righteous as a matter of fact (34.16-20). The author of 1 Peter goes one step further and highlights the link between the two concepts by adding the causality marker, ὅτι (3.11-12). In so doing, he frames the audience's response to trials in a way that encourages them to put their response in perspective, the same way they put their sufferings in perspective. Refraining from evil and doing good spring from the assurance of God's presence with the sufferer in the midst of hardships and his ability to

---

However, he does not rule out the possibility that the reference in 1 Peter could be to life in the present.

80.　'εἰ ἐγεύσασθε ὅτι χρηστὸς ὁ κύριος' is a first class condition which implies that 1 Peter assumes the audience has in fact tasted that the Lord is good. So also, Jobes, *1 Peter*, pp. 138–9.

81.　Kraus, *Psalms*, p. 387.

vindicate the righteous. It is an expression of dependence on God inherent in the righteous' praying and crying to God from their precarious situation.

5.4.3. Submission to human authority and dependence on God

The call to be subordinate to human authority needs to be understood as part of the author's overall exhortation to the audience to respond faithfully to sufferings (2.13-16). In this context, it is designed to help them cope with and silence prejudice. Submission involves the idea of 'not fleeing' from the situation, but accepting the turn of events, not because one is fearful, but because one places one's hope and trust in God. That dependence on God is at the root of the exhortation to the audience to be subordinate to human authority is attested implicitly and explicitly in the expressions – διὰ τὸν κύριον (2.13), διὰ συνείδησιν θεοῦ (2.19), ἐλπίζουσαι εἰς θεὸν (3.5), εἰ θέλοι τὸ θέλημα τοῦ θεοῦ (3.17), and κατὰ τὸ θέλημα τοῦ θεοῦ (4.19) – that occur in the context of the author's discussion of how the audience should respond to trials. The invitation to trust God, i.e., to express one's dependence on God in the midst of sufferings and do what is good (3.17; 4.19) is framed in a way that highlights Jesus' own response to suffering and encourages the audience to follow in the steps of Jesus Christ (2.21-23). First, the concepts are similar because they both happen in a context of unjust suffering, and God is the one to whom the sufferer resorts. Second, the language of 2.23 parallels that of 4.19. The verbs that describe Jesus' (παραδίδωμι; 2.23) and the audience's (παρατίθημι; 4.19) trust in God contain some affinities in their meaning: entrusting for safekeeping, for care and preservation.[82] In addition, the exhortation to be subordinate to human authority should be read in light of what has been said in 2.11-12. There, the audience is reminded of their status as 'aliens and strangers' (2.11), of the need for the audience to fight against carnal desires that threaten their lives;[83] and of the need to maintain good conduct in the midst of sufferings (2.12).

In 1 Pet. 2.13 the believers are urged to submit to human authority 'on account of the Lord'. Here, 'κύριος' is ambiguous and can refer either to Jesus Christ or to God. The term is used in relation to Christ elsewhere in the epistle (1.3; 2.3; 3.15).[84] If this is the case here, 'διὰ τὸν κύριον' anticipates Jesus' example in 2.21-25 which includes his righteous suffering and expression of dependence on God in the midst of hardships. However, the fact that the author places God's will at the centre of his call to subordination (2.15, 19-20; 3.5-6) makes it possible that he has God in mind. Taken

82. See, BDAG, pp. 761–3, 772. See also W. Popkes, 'παραδίδωμι', in *EDNT* (Vol. 3; Grand Rapids: Eerdmans, 1993), pp. 18–20.
83. Peter uses war imagery to convey this concept. He uses similar imagery later in the epistle to encourage the audience to follow Jesus' example, and in the context of the believer's fight against sin (4.1-2). Battle imagery is also rehearsed in 5.9 where the believer is urged to resist the devil.
84. Elliott, *1 Peter*, pp. 489–90.

together with 2.15, subordination to human authority can be understood as springing from 'doing good', the practice of which is a sign of obedience to God, which leads to vindication, namely; the silencing of the ignorant talk of foolish people. The ambiguity may be deliberate on the author's part since both options fit the context. If 'κύριος' refers to Jesus Christ, then Jesus' experience becomes a warrant and an example for the audience. If it refers to God, it places God prominently on the mind of the audience and their trust in him becomes the motivating factor for their action.

Subordination to human authority as an expression of one's unwavering trust in God for deliverance is also attested in the author's injunction to the household slaves. In 1 Pet. 2.18, the household slaves are encouraged to show subordination both to masters who are kind and masters who are unscrupulous. The author supports it with a warrant that the entire audience can relate to because the truth it conveys is relevant to the reality they all faced and because of the proverbial manner in which it is put forward.[85] It is worth noting that there is a nuance between the exhortation offered in 2.13-16 and what is given in 2.18-20. In the former, the author presents the purpose of subordination: 'to silence the ignorance of foolish men' (2.15); in the latter, the focus is on providing a rationale, a justification for the act of subordinating oneself to human authority: 'this is commendable before God' (2.20). Taken together, these two concepts offer a better understanding of the author's exhortation to his entire audience.

The motivation for faithful response is grounded in the sufferer's mindfulness of God.[86] This means that the sufferer is aware of God's presence during the experience. One gathers from the epistle that the sufferings of the readers spring partly from outsiders' failure to understand why the audience behaves the way they do (1 Pet. 4.3-4; cf. Wis. 3.1-9). This assessment is applicable to masters whose servants have experienced new birth and now are part of God's family (1 Pet. 2.18); husbands who are still disobeying the word (1 Pet. 3.1-2); and governing authorities who fail to act justly toward the elect (1 Pet. 2.13; cf. *1 En.* 103.14-15). In addition, subordination to authority that is done because of one's mindfulness of God completely removes the desire or need to look for society's approval out of the equation.[87] Dependence on God here is expressed in terms of meeting and seeking his approval as the motivation to bear unjust sufferings.

It is clear from this context that suffering *per se* does not bring God's approval. The rhetorical question in 2.20 implies that suffering for the wrong reasons and as result of sinful behaviour has no benefits, but steadfastness in the face of unjust suffering is commendable before God. The author makes that clear in 3.17 and in 4.15-19 and warns the audience not to suffer as criminals, but reassures them that if they suffer 'as a Christian', they should not consider it shameful but glorify God instead (4.16). The audience is

---

85.   So Green, *1 Peter*, p. 78.
86.   Witherington, *1 Peter*, pp. 152–3.
87.   Bechtler, *Following in His Steps*, p. 192.

encouraged to put their suffering in perspective of what will happen in the
end. The author urges those suffering according to the will of God to 'entrust
their lives to the faithful creator while continuing to do good' (4.19). Whereas
submission to authority is not explicit in 4.19, the idea of judgement, the
language of God as faithful creator, and the call to depend on God while
doing good attest to a link between what is expressed here and what was said
in 2.13-17. Therefore, the author has come full circle and doing good in a
context of suffering is not only done for the sake of God's approval but also
because the believer/sufferer has firm assurance that God is in control, so he/
she can submit to human creature, because his/her life is being preserved by
the creator.

Whereas suffering may come as a result of doing what is good, perseverance
in doing what is good assures the righteous sufferer of God's approval. Read
in this light, submission to people in authority can be done with all respect
(2.18), not because one is afraid of the oppressor (3.14), not for their approval
but 'to silence the ignorance of foolish people' (2.15). It is also done so that
some may be gained [to God] (3.2) and glorify him on the day of visitation
(2.12), or be put to shame (3.16). The same is true of the exhortation in 3.1-7
where he explains to wives and the husbands in the congregation how they
can demonstrate steadfastness in suffering.[88] He addresses the wives first, and
sets Sarah as a model for them. He then addresses the husbands and advises
them on how to treat their spouses.

5.4.4. *Daughters of Sarah, not sons of Abraham?*

The discussion of how wives in the congregation should relate to their
husbands, some of whom might be non-Christians, is consistent with what
is expected of the entire congregation in terms of how they are supposed to
respond to suffering. The author encourages them to display good conduct
(3.1-2) and to follow the examples of holy women of the past who put their
hope in God while being subordinated to their husbands (3.5). He points
specifically to Sarah as a model of one who depended on God in the face of
hardships (3.6).[89]

---

88.   Jeannine K. Brown discusses the similarities and nuances in language between 3.1-6
and 3.14-16. See 'Silent Wives, Verbal Believers: Ethical and Hermeneutical Considerations
in 1 Peter 3:1-6 and Its Environment', WW 24 (2004), pp. 395–405.

89.   There has been much controversy regarding the interpretation of the author's
exhortation to servants and wives especially how submission to authority is to be
understood. For a survey of the discussion see, Bauman-Martin, 'Women on the Edge';
Steven Tracy, 'Domestic Violence in the Church and Redemptive Suffering in 1 Peter',
CTJ 41 (2006), pp. 279–96; Elisabeth Schüssler Fiorenza, *In Memory of Her: A Feminist
Theological Reconstruction of Christian Origins* (New York: Crossroad, 1998), pp. 260–6;
Brown, 'Silent Wives, Verbal Believers'. Jobes assesses as shortsighted the move to use 1
Peter as if it were a 'marriage manual simply addressing the relationship between husbands
and wives', and points out the irony that a word of affirmation given to servants and wives

It is worth noting that the author's language suggests that the exhortation was aimed at wives in general, and not only those with non-believing husbands.[90] In 1 Pet. 3.1-2 the term 'ὁμοίως' suggests that there is a link between the author's exhortation to the wives with what was said to the slaves. It signals the presence of a similar rhetoric that guides the author's injunction to these two representative groups. Further, the clause 'καὶ εἴ τινες ἀπειθοῦσιν' implies that the author is making an allowance for the possibility that some (τινες) husbands may be disobedient to God's word (3.1).[91] Therefore, the embodied qualities that he encourages the wives to display are to be understood not only for how a believing wife should relate to a non-believing husband, but also for the benefit of the relationships of believing couples in the congregation. This is why the author addresses the husbands as well. As the wives are called to honour their husbands by being subordinated to them (3.1), so the husbands are encouraged to honour their wives by treating them as co-heirs of the grace of life (3.7).

The language in 1 Pet. 3.3-4 seems to be a contextual way of encouraging the women to have their good conduct be motivated by their mindfulness of God, being concerned about pleasing God, and not the world around them. This is borne out by the contrast between 'visible' and 'invisible'.[92] In addition, the contrast between the two modes of adornment, perishable versus imperishable, and the language of 'purity' and 'holy conduct (3.2) are reminiscent of the description of the previous and current way of life of the audience, rehearsed in the context of the need for the believers to conduct a holy existence during their pilgrimage (1.13-21). In addition, the language 'precious in the sight of God' echoes the description of the 'living stone' in 2.4 with its implications of chosenness by God and possible rejection/suffering, on the one hand; and holiness of life, protection, and vindication by God, on the other hand (2.5-10). This holy conduct which springs from what is unseen is expected to be seen by the disobedient husbands and has the potential to win them for God.

---

is today criticized as enslaving and oppressive (*1 Peter*, p. 209). Similarly, Elliott condemns the 'centuries-long misuse of 1 Peter and related biblical texts to justify the suppression and abuse of women and to keep them in their so-called "place"' (*1 Peter*, p. 599). Yet, his claim that 1 Peter participates in the acceptance of the 'given-ness' of slavery and the 'natural' inferiority of females is not warranted. There is insufficient data provided in the letter to substantiate that claim. First Peter is certainly not a treatise on slavery. Moreover, the exhortation given in 2.18-20 comes on the heels of Peter's identifying all his audience as 'slaves' of God and as 'free people' in a single breath (2.16). Taken together with 2.17, it seems clear that the author is acknowledging the status quo only to subvert it. He is definitely aware of the social dynamics at play in his audience's world; he does not condone it, but subtly challenges it. See, Witherington, *1 Peter*, p. 23).

90. Achtemeier, *1 Peter*, p. 209; Witherington, *1 Peter*, pp. 160–2.

91. Elliott, *1 Peter*, p. 557.

92. The author is not pitting physical appearance against inward spiritual worth, or suggesting that appearance does not matter; rather he is concerned with highlighting the fact that the motivation for submission should be God-oriented. So Goppelt, *1 Peter*, p. 221.

The author's description of the 'holy women of old' provides the clue to understanding the focus of his discussion here: their hope in God was the motivation of their subordination to their husbands.[93] Of these women, Sarah is the chief example.[94]

Sarah demonstrated her dependence on God when faced with the deadly threat brought about by her being a sojourner and heightened by Abraham's questionable course of action. Yet, she did not withdraw from the situation, and experienced God's deliverance (Gen. 12; 20).[95] The Old Testament is silent about Sarah's motivation, but the author of 1 Peter suggests that Sarah was subordinated to Abraham, because she hoped in God. The motivation is primarily theological. It is consistent with other stories from the Old Testament and other Jewish writings that portray the response of the righteous in the face of sufferings. This is consistent with the attitude that the audience is encouraged to display in their dealings with kings and governors (2.13-14), that the servants are to display toward their masters, and ultimately, this is characteristic of Jesus whose example all Christians should follow. Through his christological reading of the Old Testament, the author sees in Sarah a display of Christ-like behaviour.[96] Like Christ, Sarah is a model of steadfastness in the midst of hardships expressed through subordination to human authority which arises from trusting God for deliverance.

It is helpful to read 1 Pet. 3.1-6 together with v. 7 to understand 1 Pet. 3.1-7 in light of the Genesis account of Abraham and Sarah. In this context one has not only an explicit, positive example of steadfastness in suffering in Sarah, but also the implicit, negative example in Abraham. Both Abraham and Sarah as God's elect and aliens in a strange land faced the dangers associated with their situation. The author of 1 Peter sees in Sarah's attitude the kind of dependence on God that should be characteristic of the audience, and especially of the wives who could potentially face the dangers associated with being a believing spouse in a worldly environment; or even from being the believing wife of a believing husband who has to deal with the pressures of living in a hostile environment. They are Sarah's children, through emulating her example. They are not to fear anything because, since God did deliver Sarah from her dangerous situation, they too have the assurance that God will deliver them from their predicament.

---

93.   So James R. Slaughter, 'Sarah as a Model for Christian Wives (1 Pet 3:5-6)', *BSac* 153 (1996), pp. 357-65 (357-9).

94.   By referring to Sarah, the author is grounding his exhortation to the women in the Old Testament and continuing his identification of the audience with Israel. Here, the identification is done specifically through the association with the matriarch of the people of God. See Michaels, *1 Peter*, pp. 163-4.

95.   See Mark Kiley, 'Like Sara: The Tale of Terror Behind 1 Peter 3.6', *JBL* 105 (1987), pp. 689-92; Spencer, 'Peter's Pedagogical Method', pp. 112-16.

96.   Spencer, 'Peter's Pedagogical Method', pp. 118-19. Whereas Spencer claims vicarious suffering as the point of reference, I want to emphasize the aspect of Sarah's and Jesus' dependence on God in times of hardships. The two emphases are not mutually exclusive.

The author is conspicuously silent about Abraham, but this in itself speaks volumes. The language in 3.7 is a subtle polemic against Abraham's response during his time as an alien. When 1 Pet. 3.1-7 is in view the Genesis account provides a vibrant example of what to do and what not to do in the face of hardships. The author's words to the husbands in the congregations encourage them to demonstrate an attitude that Abraham failed to demonstrate in the face of sufferings. Abraham puts Sarah's life in jeopardy in order to save his own life. In this context, 'living wisely with your wife, as a weaker vessel, showing her honor as fellow heirs of the grace of life' can be understood as an encouragement to support, protect, and defend one's spouse and face sufferings together while hoping in God, so that together, both will partake in the inheritance that is ready to be revealed.

5.5. Conclusion

In this chapter my purpose has been twofold: (1) to show the author's treatment of faithful response to suffering and (2) substantiate the claim that faithful response is an element of the fabula that shapes the narrative substructure of the epistle. I have demonstrated that for the author of 1 Peter, faithful response is an active decision on the part of the sufferer not to withdraw from unjust suffering that is brought about by one's righteous living, but continue to 'do good' because of the assurance that God's deliverance will follow. I showed how this understanding is analogous to the Old Testament through a treatment of several texts drawn from the Scriptures of Israel and other Jewish writings. Then I looked at the author's understanding of Jesus' own response to suffering especially the way in which he sets Jesus' experience as an example for the audience to follow in 2.21-25. Finally, I discussed how the author of 1 Peter elaborates on what faithful response means and looks like for the audience. Through a close reading of the text and interaction with the pertinent scholarly contribution made to the field, I provided evidence for the claim that 1 Peter parses faithful response in terms of 'steadfastness', 'doing good', and 'subordination' in the face of suffering.

It is crucial for God's elect to respond faithfully to suffering precisely because this attitude leads the way for God to carry out his act of vindication on their behalf. The end to which 1 Peter points the audience is the moment where God has brought an end to their sufferings. Since God has acted in the past to vindicate those who remained steadfast in suffering by putting their trust in him, the audience can remain confident that God will also vindicate them from their sufferings. God's vindication of the righteous sufferer constitutes the focus of the chapter that follows.

Chapter 6

Vindication in 1 Peter

6.1. Introduction

The discussion of the vindication of the audience is closely tied to the
treatment of the other characteristic aspects of their relationship with God;
namely, election, suffering, and faithful response. A preliminary inquiry into
the text of 1 Peter has revealed that these elements constitute the fabula of
1 Peter, which is the lens through which the author invites the audience to
make sense of their situation. Thus far, I have demonstrated how the other
three elements (election, suffering, and faithful response) are at work in the
narrative substructure of the epistle to create meaning. In this chapter, I will
focus on the last element, vindication, in view of explaining the author's
understanding of this concept and substantiating the claim that it constitutes
an element of the fabula of 1 Peter. First, I will look at the way this concept
is dealt with in the Old Testament and other Jewish literature. Second, I will
explain the author's understanding/description of God's vindication of Jesus.
Finally, I will attend to how he treats God's vindication of the audience.

The author uses several terms and concepts to express the idea of
vindication. One of the terms he associates with vindication is 'glory'.[1] For
example, he suggests to the audience that the genuineness of their faith might
'result in praise, glory, and honor at the revelation of Jesus Christ' (1.6-7).
The metaphor of the refining process of gold suggests that the audience will
partake in these things after having remained steadfast in the face of trials.
In addition, there is an eschatological undercurrent expressed by the phrase
'ἐν ἀποκαλύψει Ἰησοῦ Χριστοῦ' as it locates the outcome of the trials in the
future. Yet, it is clear that the author understands vindication or partaking
in glory to be something that the audience experiences also in the present.
The statement 'κομιζόμενοι τὸ τέλος τῆς πίστεως ὑμῶν σωτηρίαν ψυχῶν'
in 1.9 seems to be a reiteration of the concept introduced in 1.7 about the
end result of 'the testing of faith'. There is a conceptual parallelism at work
in the two verses. The term 'salvation' parallels the three terms 'praise',

---

1.   Pearson draws a helpful parallel between the sufferings/glories pattern of 1 Peter
and the humiliation/vindication pattern attested in Isa. 53 (*Christological and Rhetorical
Properties*, pp. 42–3).

'glory', and 'honour' as another way of expressing God's reward/vindication
of the elect for their steadfastness.[2] The parallel is further strengthened by
the fact that earlier the author referred to salvation as something that would
be revealed in the last time (1.5). But here the present participle κομιζόμενοι
is dependent on ἀγαλλιᾶσθε which is a present indicative; thus, it carries the
implication that the rejoicing is in the present. It follows, therefore, that the
reception of salvation expressed by the participle happens concurrently.[3] The
author also talks about God's vindication of Christ in terms of God raising
Jesus from the dead and giving him 'glory' following his suffering (1.21).
The summary statement of the author's theological hermeneutic highlights
the two elements: the 'sufferings' of Christ and the 'glories' that followed
(1.11). In addition, he appropriates that language to the audience: 'Rejoice
insofar as you are participating in Christ's sufferings in order that you may
also rejoice with great joy at the revelation of his glory. If you are reproached
for the name of Christ, you are blessed, because the spirit of glory; namely,
the spirit of God, is resting upon you' (4.13-14). The author's christological
reading of the Old Testament is evident here as the language of 4.14 is
reminiscent of Isa. 11.2. There, the wider context talks about the dawning of
the messianic age and God's vindication of his people: the re-establishment
of Israel and retribution against the nations that have oppressed them (e.g.,
Isa. 11–14). 'The spirit of glory' connects the Spirit of God with the concept
of 'glory' mentioned earlier. Further, the apparition of Jesus' glory implies
Jesus' resurrection and exaltation, i.e., his vindication (3.18-22). In other
words, the 'glory' that was given him, will be revealed for the sake of the
audience (cf. 1.6-9). The author, thus, locates participation in Christ's glory
in the future. Yet, the language also suggests that they are already partaking
in glory, thereby emphasizing the immediacy of their experience. In Isaiah
the Spirit's abiding is a future experience (ἀναπαύσεται); in 1 Peter, it is
something that the audience experience in the present (ἀναπαύεται). In
addition, the author continues his appropriation of the reality of Israel to
the believers by changing the 'ἐπ' αὐτὸν' of the Isaianic text to 'ἐφ' ὑμᾶς'.[4]
He holds the present and the future in tension.[5] By speaking of these future
realities in ways that highlight their availability in the present,[6] he gives the
readers the assurance that, indeed, their suffering is not the entire story, or
the end of it. In addition, the abiding presence of the Spirit of God gives the
audience the assurance of preservation and vindication. They can remain

2.   The statement about 'praise, glory, and honor' is ambiguous in that it can refer to
God bestowing these things on the righteous, and/or the righteous ascribing honour to God.
The two ideas are not mutually exclusive. See Michaels, *1 Peter*, p. 31.

3.   Michaels, e.g., admits that the evidence points to understanding the rejoicing
in the present, but argues that the eschatological tone is more prominent (*1 Peter*, p. 34).
Elsewhere, Goppelt suggests that the present be treated as a 'futuristic present' (*1 Peter*, pp.
88–9).

4.   In Isaiah, the servant of YHWH is also identified collectively as Israel (Childs,
Isaiah, p. 412).

steadfast because God is present, takes notice of their situation (3.12), and his vindication is at hand (4.7, 17).

There is a close affinity in meaning between glory and honour.[7] The author uses the two terms together with 'praise' in 1.7 to express the end result of the audience's faithful response to suffering. In that sense, vindication constitutes, in part, the glory that follows sufferings and parallels the bestowal of honour by God to those who endured ill treatment because they were mindful of God and seeking God's approval. The language suggests that 'honour' follows 'suffering' and will be bestowed at the eschaton. At the same time, 'honour' is squarely located in seeking and meeting God's approval (2.7, 13, 19-20; 3.4, 17; 5.5-7). It is something the believer experiences in her lifetime, as she trusts God with her situation and remains steadfast in the face of trials. Also, the language that describes the shaming and confusion of blasphemers, which implies the honouring of the believers, is used in a context that implies present actual circumstances in the lives of the believers (2.15; 3.16). In sum, the language that the author uses for vindication suggests that it is something the audience experience in the present while awaiting its full realization in the future, when Jesus Christ is revealed.

Another term that has affinities with the concept of vindication is the verb κρίνω (1.17; 2.23; 4.5; cf. also its cognate κρίμα [4.17-18]), which the author uses in relation to God. In 1 Peter, the righteous and the disobedient are both subject to God's judgement.[8] In 1.17-18 the author brings together the images of God as Father, judge, and redeemer and uses God's impartiality as motivation for the audience's reverent conduct. On the one hand, God is the just judge in whose hands Jesus handed over everything, including himself (2.23), and in whose hands the audience is encouraged to entrust their lives for safekeeping (3.17; 4.19). On the other hand, he is the God who is ready to judge the living and the dead, and will ask an account from those who mistreated the elect (4.5). In this way the concept of God as judge is analogous to the Old Testament concept of kinsman redeemer.[9]

---

5.   See Feldmeier, 'Wiedergeburt im 1. Petrusbrief', pp. 93–4; idem, *The First Letter of Peter*, p. 80.

6.   Similarly, that the audience's inheritance is kept in heaven implies that it is already available, already bestowed and only waiting to be actualized and enjoyed (1.4-5).

7.   Harald Hegermann, 'δόξα', in *EDNT* (Vol. 1; Grand Rapids: Eerdmans, 1990), pp. 344–8 (345); Gerhard Kittel and Gerhard von Rad, 'δόξα', in *TDNT* (Vol. 2; Grand Rapids: Eerdmans, 1971), pp. 233–55; BDAG, pp. 256–8.

8.   Mathias Rissi, 'κρίνω', in *EDNT* (Vol. 2; Grand Rapids: Eerdmans, 1991), pp. 318–21; idem, 'κρίμα', in *EDNT* (Vol. 2; Grand Rapids: Eerdmans, 1991), pp. 317–18.

9.   The Old Testament understanding of *go'el* is varied. My treatment will focus on the aspect that is pertinent to 1 Peter (see my discussion on 'The fatherhood of God as election imagery', in Chapter 3; and also below). For further discussion on the role of the 'kinsman redeemer' see, e.g., Frank M. Cross, *From Epic to Canon: History and Literature in Ancient Israel* (Baltimore: Johns Hopkins University Press, 1998), pp. 3–22. See also, Robert L. Hubbard, Jr., 'The Go'el in Ancient Israel: Theological Reflections on an Israelite Institution', *BBR* 1 (1991), pp. 3–19.

The LXX uses the verb 'κρίνω' to convey the idea of God's vindication of his people, 'ὅτι κρινεῖ κύριος τὸν λαὸν αὐτοῦ καὶ ἐπὶ τοῖς δούλοις αὐτοῦ παρακληθήσεται...' (Deut. 32.36; cf. Ps. 135.14 [134.14, LXX]).[10] The idea of judgement/vindication is also attested in the author's use of 'the day of visitation' when those who oppose God's children are expected to 'glorify him' (2.12).[11] It is evidenced in 3.18-22 as well, where the author of 1 Peter rehearses the suffering death, resurrection, and exaltation of Christ and emphasizes the honourific status bestowed to Jesus Christ following his sufferings, and God's work on behalf of the 'living stone' (2.4, 7-8), where the language is analogous to concepts present in Ps. 118 [117, LXX] and Isa. 8.14; 28.16.

Vindication is the reward that comes to those who remain steadfast in the face of hardships. It is primarily concerned with (1) God preserving/delivering and ascribing glory to (honouring) his children for remaining steadfast and putting their trust in him in times of difficulty; (2) God's judgement of those who are disobedient to his word and mistreat his children; and (3) the ascription of glory to God for his work on behalf of his children. The concept is prominent in the epistle, attested as it is at key junctures: it is an integral part of 1 Peter's theological hermeneutics of the Old Testament (1.10-12); it plays an important role in the author's christology (1.18-21; 2.4, 7-8, 21-25; 3.18-22); and it is what he encourages the audience to look forward to (1.3-9; 2.12-15; 3.1-2, 15-17; 4.5, 12-19; 5.10). God's vindication is important in the mind of the audience, because it will bring an end to the suffering that they now face. Their suffering is temporary, because God's vindication is real and imminent (1.6; 4.7).

6.2. *Vindication in the Old Testament and other Jewish literature*

One of the pictures the Old Testament offers of God is that of God carrying out acts of redemption on behalf of righteous individuals and of Israel as a nation. The image used for God in that context is that of *go'el*.[12] As kinsman redeemer, God is responsible for the welfare of his children. For example,

---

10. See, e.g., Biddle, *Deuteronomy*, pp. 479–81; Peter C. Craigie, *The Book of Deuteronomy* (NICOT; Grand Rapids: Eerdmans, 1976), p. 387; Gerhard von Rad, *Deuteronomy* (OTL; Philadelphia: Westminster, 1966), p. 199.

11. See Isa. 10.3; 1QS 3.18; 4.19. Further, 'ἐν καιρῷ ἐπισκοπῆς' (Jer. 6.15; 10.15; Wis. 3.7); and 'ἐν ὥρᾳ ἐπισκοπῆς' (Sir. 18.20).

12. The cognate verb 'גאל' is used with other 'verbs of rescuing' to describe God's deliverance on behalf of the elect (e.g. 'ישׁע', 'to save, deliver' [Isa. 60.16]; 'נצל', 'to save, rescue' [Mic. 4.10]; 'עזר', 'to help' [Isa. 41.14]; and 'פדה', 'to ransom', [Hos. 13.14]; Ps. 69.18 [69.19, MT; 68.19, LXX] which stands almost as a synonym for 'גאל'. The LXX renders 'גאל' primarily with λυτρόομαι (Exod. 6.6; Lev. 25.31; 27.27, 31); or ῥύομαι (e.g., Isa. 48.20; 49.7), but occasionally with ἐξαιρέω (Isa. 60.16). See Ringgren, 'גאל', 2.350–5; Robert L. Hubbard, Jr., 'גאל', in *NIDOTE* (Vol. 1; Grand Rapids: Zondervan, 1997), pp. 789–94.

God is portrayed as one who pleads the cause of the fatherless (Prov. 23.10-11); he is the saviour of those who cry out to him in the midst of distress (Job 19.25; Ps. 31.14-24 [31.15-25 MT, LXX]; Lam. 3.57-59); above all, he is the redeemer of Israel (Exod. 3.6-8; 6.5-6; 15.13; 43.16-21).[13] As kinsman redeemer God also passes judgement on those who oppress his people (Exod. 7–12; 14; 2 Kgs 19.32-37; Isa. 47) and receives praise for the deliverance wrought on their behalf (Exod. 15; Isa. 43.20-21). My discussion of vindication in the Old Testament and other Jewish literature will focus on vindication as God's deliverance of his children and judgement of their oppressors and this concept as ascription of praise to God for his work on behalf of his children.

6.2.1. *Vindication as deliverance of God's people and judgement of their oppressors*

The deliverance of Israel from slavery out of Egypt is, arguably, the chief example of God's vindication of Israel. God's deliverance of Israel is treated in the context of his covenant with the patriarchs and as YHWH's response to the groaning of the children of Israel (Exod. 3.6-8; cf. 6.2-8). God promises not only to free the children of Israel from Egyptian bondage, but also to give them a land that is good and spacious, 'a land flowing with milk and honey' (3.8; cf. 6.6-8). God intervenes in the situation because, first, through his promise to and relationship with Abraham, Isaac, and Jacob, Israel as a nation is already his chosen people. As such, their election places them under God's care and makes God their kinsman redeemer. Second, there is an implicit causal or resultative connection between the actions attributed to God in Exod. 3.7 'εἶδον, ἀκήκοα, οἶδα γάρ', and in 3.8 'καὶ κατέβην'. God's intervention is a result of hearing the cry of his people.

Vindication comprises both what God does in favour of the elect, and what happens to their enemies. The departure of the children of Israel from Egypt was preceded by the 'ten mighty acts'[15] (plagues) that God wrought against Pharaoh and the Egyptians (Exod. 7–12).[16] God's judgement is also evident in the destruction of the Egyptian armies at the Red Sea (Exod. 14). The relationship between faithful response and vindication is expressed through the words, 'Be of good courage, stand firm, and see the deliverance of the Lord ... The LORD will fight for you, and you have only to keep still' (Exod. 14.13-14). Implied in this statement is the truth that the elect's dispositions and attitudes in the face of danger/trials are based on the assurance that God is actively at work on their behalf. Also the imperatives

---

13.   Hubbard, 'גאל', pp. 792–3.

14.   The surrounding context implies that God's action of 'coming down' was motivated by what he saw, heard, and knew of the situation of the Israelites.

15.   I am borrowing this designation from Durham (*Exodus*, p. 89).

16.   See further, Childs, *Exodus*, pp. 162–70.

θαρσεῖτε, στῆτε, ὁρᾶτε, from the LXX, highlight the fact that the stillness, the silence, or the non-retaliation that the believer is called to display is a sign of dependence and trust on the one who fights the battle. They fit the understanding of 'steadfastness' present in 1 Peter; the idea of being courageous, standing firm, and not withdrawing from the situation (1 Pet. 2.18-20; 3.1-2, 8-9; 5.8-9). It is worth noting that 'θαρσεῖτε' (be of good courage) is a positive rendering in the LXX of what is a prohibition in the MT 'אַל־תִּירָא' (fear not). It is the same verb used in Exod. 14.31 ('יָרֵא' is rendered 'φοβέομαι' in the LXX) to describe the attitude of the Israelites toward God after witnessing the mighty acts he performed on their behalf, 'So the people feared the LORD and believed in the LORD' (Exod. 14.31). One finds an analogous understanding in 1 Peter between having the fear of God (1 Pet. 2.17, 18) on the one hand, and not being afraid, or terrified of the oppressors (1 Pet. 3.6, 14) on the other. What in the Exodus narrative comes as a result of witnessing God's vindication/salvation is in 1 Peter offered as a basis and motivation for the kind of behaviour one needs to display in order to experience God's vindication. The knowledge of the Exodus story would have served as case in point for 1 Peter's audience that God is able and surely will act on their behalf, because he is their Father and will act as their 'kinsman redeemer' (1.17-21). As the narration ends with Israel's successful crossing of the Red Sea and the annihilation of their pursuers (Exod. 14.22-31), so the author's language suggests that the audience will be honoured, and their detractors put to shame (1 Pet. 1.7; 2.15; 3.16).

That concept of accountability is explicitly presented in 1 Pet. 4.5 which states that those who malign God's children will give an account to the one who stands ready to judge the living and the dead. It is implicit in the description of human authority as 'ἀνθρωπίνος κτίσις' (2.13) and God as 'πιστός κτίστης' (4.19). When read in the context of suffering inflicted on God's children, the audience of 1 Peter has the assurance that those in authority, i.e., 'human creature', will be held accountable to God, the faithful creator, for their actions. It is in this context that the believers are encouraged to live in subordination to human authority while entrusting their lives to the faithful creator.

A similar portrayal of vindication is attested in the story of Shadrach, Meshach, and Abednego (Dan. 3), and the story of Daniel (Dan. 6). The faithful response of the three young men is followed by God's deliverance. They have expressed their assurance in God's ability to save them and are willing to taste death, if that were God's will for them, rather than worship the statue Nebuchadnezzar has made (Dan. 3.15-18). The narrator highlights the fact that (1) the preservation of the lives of the three young men were witnessed by their detractors. The narrator goes to great lengths to show the extent to which Shadrach, Meshach, and Abednego suffered no harm, 'The fire had not had any power over the bodies of those men; the hair of their heads was not singed, their tunics were not harmed, and not even the smell of fire came from them' (Dan. 3.27). Further, Nebuchadnezzar testifies to the fact that God has 'sent his angel and delivered his servants who trusted in him' (Dan. 3.28); (2) there is a reversal in the attitude toward the God of the three young men with Nebuchadnezzar ordering that no one should speak ill of their God and doing so will result in death (Dan. 3.29); and (3) Shadrach, Meshach, and Abednego are promoted/honoured in the province of Babylon (Dan. 3.30).

The story of God's deliverance of Daniel from the lions' den parallels the account in Daniel 3 in many ways. First, Daniel testifies to the king that God sent an angel to protect him and credits the preservation of his life to his righteousness in God's sight, and the fact that his behaviour is not sinful. The narrator also emphasizes that Daniel has not been harmed because he has trusted God (Dan. 6.22 [6.23, LXX; MT).[17] Second, the reversal of fortune here is the fact that Daniel's accusers now face death by order of the king. The language that describes their demise both shows the utter destruction that has befallen those who plotted against God's elect, and the extent to which Daniel's experience of preservation in the lions' den has been an act of God (Dan. 6.24 [6.25, LXX; MT]). In addition, the king orders that all his subjects should have the fear of the God of Daniel (Dan. 6.26-29 [6.27-29, LXX; MT]). Third, the narrator concludes the account with a simple, yet profound statement regarding the prosperity that Daniel has enjoyed during the reigns of Darius and Cyrus.[18]

The stories in Daniel share some conceptual affinities with the way vindication is treated in 1 Peter. First, the author's emphasis on the need for his audience to suffer as righteous individuals, on the one hand, and not to suffer for doing what is wrong, on the other (1 Pet. 3.16-17; 4.14-16), matches the point in these stories that protection from God came because of Daniel's righteousness and his innocence from wrongdoing. It anticipates the fact that vindication comes to those who live righteously in God's sight. Second, the author's call to the audience to hand over their lives to God (1 Pet. 4.19) is an invitation to demonstrate the kind of trust that Shadrach, Meshach, Abednego, and Daniel expressed in God's ability to deliver them from their predicament. Third, the author's intimation that the audience's good conduct will cause their detractors to be put to shame (1 Pet. 3.16), which implies the honouring of the audience, mirrors the outcomes of both stories. The preservation of the lives of these men was in and of itself a vindication of their stance for God. This was followed by the demise of their detractors and further promotion in the royal court. Also, 1 Peter's hint that those who oppose the elect may glorify God finds its expression in both stories. Nebuchadnezzar and Darius both offered praise to God for the salvation he brought on behalf of his children (Dan. 3.28; 6.26-28).

From these stories, one gathers that vindication takes place in the present. The downfall of those who were persecuting the righteous was

---

17.   The concept of 'the angel of the Lord' protecting and delivering the righteous from danger is also expressed elsewhere in the Old Testament (Ps. 34.7 [33.8, LXX; 34.8, MT]; 91.11 [90.11, LXX]).

18.   See Nickelsburg, *Resurrection*, pp. 71-4.

immediate, and although one cannot talk about the 'conversion' of Darius or Nebuchadnezzar in the full sense of the term, there is definitely a 'change of heart' that occurred both in terms of their attitude toward God and toward Daniel, Shadrach, Meshach, and Abednego. What is clear, these righteous individuals witnessed an end to their persecution in their lifetime. They also enjoyed honour in the face of their enemies. The same is clear in the language of 'exaltation' found in Ps. 110.1 [109.1, LXX], 'The LORD says to my lord: "Sit at my right hand until I make your enemies your footstool"'. Implied in this verse is the idea that the monarch will be ruling with God, being granted power and honour by God,[19] and the idea of God fighting the battle on his behalf. Vindication as honour/shame is also attested in *1 En.* 50.2, 95).

The concept of vindication as exaltation is also attested in other Old Testament and Jewish texts; however, the location (right hand) is not always specified (Dan. 7.9-14; *4 Macc.* 17.5; *1 En.* 118.12; *T. Job* 33.3).[20] The vindication of the suffering servant of Yahweh is expressed in terms of his exaltation in the sight of those who despised him: 'See my servant shall prosper; he shall be exalted and lifted up, and shall be very high' (Isa. 52.13). These are the same terms used in relation to God (Isa. 57.15) and his throne (Isa. 6.1). It is possible to see this as an invitation for the servant of Yahweh to sit and reign with God himself.[21]

The account of the persecution of the seven brothers and their mother by Antiochus recorded in 2 Macc. 7 offers some further insight into the understanding of vindication and also shares some affinities with 1 Peter.[22] It is worth noting that a key difference between the account in 2 Macc. 7 and the other examples treated thus far and 1 Peter is the fact that these brothers and their mother actually died whereas God preserved the lives of the elect in the other accounts treated above. While 1 Peter seems to be more concerned about the suffering of the audience as opposed to their martyrdom, the author does talk unequivocally about God's ability to vindicate the righteous beyond death. In fact, 1 Peter's discussion about God raising Jesus Christ from the dead and giving him glory (1 Pet. 1.21) is analogous to the idea of vindication present in 2 Macc. 7. Three of the brothers express the assurance that God will save them from death (2 Macc. 7.9, 11, 14).[23]

19.   Geoffrey W. Grogan, *Psalms* (THOTC; Grand Rapids: Eerdmans, 2008), p. 184; Jacquet, *Les Psaumes*, 3.214; Terrien, *Psalms*, pp. 751–2; Weiser, *The Psalms*, pp. 693–4. See also, David M. Hay, *Glory at the Right Hand: Psalm 110 in Early Christianity* (SBL, 18; Nashville: Abingdon, 1973), p. 53.

20.   Hay, *Glory at the Right Hand*, pp. 23, 55. Hay conducts an analysis of the use of the exaltation language from Ps. 110 in pagan, Jewish, and Christian literature (pp. 19–103). See also, Donald Juel, *Messianic Exegesis: Christological Interpretation of the Old Testament in Early Christianity* (Philadelphia: Fortress, 1988), pp. 135–50.

21.   Pierre E. Bonnard, *Le Second Isaïe* (Paris: Gabalda, 1972), pp. 269–70. See also Childs, *Isaiah*, p. 412; John N. Oswalt, *The Book of Isaiah Chapters 40-66* (NICOT; Grand Rapids: Eerdmans, 1998), pp. 378–9.

22.   Nickelsburg points out the similarities between the account in 2 Macc. 7 and other stories in Dan. 3; 6, and Wis. 2; 4–5 (*Resurrection*, pp. 119–40).

23.   So also Nickelsburg, *Resurrection*, pp. 120–1.

- 'You dismiss us from this present life, but the King of the universe will raise us up to an everlasting renewal of life' (2 Macc. 7.9).
- When it was demanded, he quickly put out his tongue and courageously stretched forth his hands, and said nobly, 'I got these from Heaven, and because of his laws I disdain them, and from him I hope to get them back again' (2 Macc. 7.10-11).
- 'One cannot but choose to die at the hands of mortals and to cherish the hope God gives of being raised again by him' (2 Macc. 7.14).

Further, 1 Peter and 2 Macc. 7 both share an eschatological view of vindication. The 'everlasting renewal of life' anticipates the eschatological resurrection of the righteous that will follow the time of distress spoken of in Daniel (cf. Dan. 11.40; 12.1-2). It is also reminiscent of God's promise of restoration/vindication of his people (Ezek. 37.1-14). In fact, the mother's words, 'ὁ τοῦ κόσμου κτίστης ὁ πλάσας ἀνθρώπου γένεσιν καὶ πάντων ἐξευρὼν γένεσιν καὶ τὸ πνεῦμα καὶ τὴν ζωὴν ὑμῖν πάλιν ἀποδίδωσιν' (2 Macc. 7.23), share some similarity in language and may be a claim to God's promise, 'δώσω τὸ πνεῦμά μου εἰς ὑμᾶς καὶ ζήσεσθε' (Ezek. 37.14). It follows, the concept of vindication as resurrection from death can also be understood within the larger scheme of God's restoration of the inheritance bestowed to Israel.[24] There is a subtle contrast between God who is 'creator of the world' (2 Macc. 7.23) and 'king of the world' (7.9), and Antiochus who is a mere mortal (7.14, 16, 34), and a mere king with limited authority (7.16).[25] In fact, the concept that God will hold accountable those who oppress his people is also attested here (7.17, 19). The evidence suggests that there are instances in which vindication is something that the righteous sufferer looks forward to experiencing even beyond this life.

In the book of Wisdom the vindication of the righteous is expressed through the speech of the wicked who finally realize the futility of their own ways and acknowledge God's deliverance of the righteous: 'But the righteous live for ever, and their reward is with the Lord; the Most High takes care of them. Therefore they will receive a glorious crown and a beautiful diadem from the hand of the Lord, because with his right hand he will cover them and with his arm he will shield them' (5.15-16).

Vindication involves both what God does in favour of the elect and what happens to those who oppose them. Strictly speaking, vindication is a future experience because it follows suffering. However, the believer can and does experience God's vindication in his/her lifetime. In that sense, vindication can also be understood as a present experience.

---

24.   These brothers and their mother faced death because they wanted to be faithful to the Torah. The book of 2 Maccabees is part of the literature on Second Temple Judaism where the anticipation of the restoration of Israel is evident.

25.   Nickelsburg, *Resurrection*, p. 121.

6.2.2. *Vindication as ascription of glory to God*

Another aspect of vindication that one finds in the Old Testament is the ascription of glory to God for delivering the righteous. The ascription of glory may come from the righteous themselves and/or from those who were persecuting the righteous in the first place.

For example, the preservation of the righteous by God is celebrated in Exod. 15 in the song that follows the account of the crossing of the Red Sea. Childs surmises that the song 'provides the response of faith by the people who have experienced their redemption from the hands of the Egyptians at the sea'.[26] In this song the children of Israel are celebrating God's power to deliver. Their preservation, their deliverance is God's own triumph. Through his act on behalf of Israel, God has 'glorified himself' (Exod. 15.1). This is consistent with the understanding that through the plagues God was not only making himself known to the Egyptians, but also making a statement about who he was vis-à-vis the Egyptian deities (Exod. 12.12). The song rehearses God's mighty deed against the Egyptians, and enunciates the truths about who God is to the elect: he is the author of salvation (15.2), and he is the one who fights the battle for his people (15.3),[27] he is their *go'el* (15.13). The deeds accomplished on behalf of Israel have also made God's name known to those who have become aware of them and caused them to have the fear of God. In a sense, the song not only glorifies God, but also expresses the ways in which God's acts of deliverance on behalf of his people causes his name to be honoured among his people, and among the nations.

The preservation and deliverance of the righteous from danger is celebrated in Ps. 34 [33, LXX]. The psalmist bursts out in praise for what God has done for him (34.4 [33.5, LXX; 34.5, MT]). The language of the psalmist – 'εὐλογήσω τὸν κύριον ἐν παντὶ καιρῷ διὰ παντὸς ἡ αἴνεσις αὐτοῦ ἐν τῷ στόματί μου' (34.1 [33.2, LXX; 34.2, MT]) – suggests that praising Yahweh is and will be a way of life. Through this boasting the psalmist is acknowledging God's greatness and power, and making others aware of the same.[28] He encourages the congregation to join him in 'making great' the name of Yahweh (34.3, [33.3, LXX]). Craigie rightly suggests, 'Such praise does not change the divine essence, but creates awareness of God's greatness in the perception of others. And, as an expression of awareness, it is also a personal acknowledgement of divine majesty and glory'.[29] A similar concept is attested throughout the Psalms (18 [17, LXX]; 22.19-23 [21.20-24, LXX; 22.20-24, MT]; 31 [30, LXX]; 118 [117, LXX]).

---

26. Childs, *Exodus*, p. 248.

27. Cornelius Houtman rightly points out, 'only if one does battle in his name (cf. Ps. 20.2, 6; 68.5; 1 Sam. 17.45-47; Isa. 63.16) can one confidently await the outcome' (*Exodus*, HCOT; Kampen: Kok, 1996) p. 280.

28. The term כבד conveys the meaning 'to acknowledge someone in his position of power and his claim to greatness with due formality' (Kraus, *Psalms 1-59*, pp. 383–4).

29. Craigie, *Psalms 1-50*, p. 279.

There are also instances where ascription of glory to God comes from those who opposed God's people. Daniel 3 and 6 provide us two examples of that fact. Subsequent to the deliverance of Shadrach, Meshach, and Abednego from the fiery furnace the narrator reports Nebuchadnezzar's reaction as follows: 'καὶ ἀπεκρίθη Ναβουχοδονοσορ καὶ εἶπεν εὐλογητὸς ὁ θεὸς τοῦ Σεδραχ Μισαχ Αβδεναγω ὃς ἀπέστειλεν τὸν ἄγγελον αὐτοῦ καὶ ἐξείλατο τοὺς παῖδας αὐτοῦ' (Dan 3.28 [3.95, LXX]). The language reportedly used by Nebuchadnezzar (בְּרַךְ; εὐλογέω) is the same that the psalmist used in Ps 34.1 [33.2, LXX; 34.2, MT]. Therefore, Nebuchadnezzar 'made great' the name of Yahweh after witnessing the uniqueness of his saving power. A similar situation is recorded in Dan 6. There, it takes the form of a correspondence from King Darius to his servants after God delivered Daniel from the lions (Dan. 6.26-27 [6.27, LXX; 6.27-28, MT]).[30] Although the text does not have the word 'blessed', Darius' words do constitute a eulogy to God for the salvation he has wrought on behalf of Daniel. They are an acknowledgement of God's greatness.

The concept that the steadfastness and vindication of the righteous may cause the oppressors of God's children to glorify God is attested in 2 Maccabees. However, it is not actualized. The seventh brother expresses the expectation that Antiochus will eventually acknowledge that Yahweh alone is God: 'I, like my brothers, give up body and life for the laws of our ancestors, appealing to God to show mercy soon to our nation and by trials and plagues to make you confess that he alone is God' (2 Macc. 7.37). Vindication in this context constitutes the change of disposition toward God expressed by the recognition/confession of who God is. This is brought about as a result of the sufferer's steadfastness.

From the foregoing discussion I have sought to demonstrate how the concept of vindication is put forward in the Old Testament and other Jewish literature and the points of tangents that exist between these and 1 Peter's treatment of the concept. An inquiry into these texts has shown that vindication can be both a present and future experience. This applies to the elect who benefit from God's protection and their detractors who will face God's judgement. The evidence from the Old Testament also points to the fact that God's vindication of the elect does not exclusively imply punishment of those who oppress his children. There is an evangelistic component to God's vindication by which those who once were opposed to God and his work in the lives of the elect may come to know God and be counted among his children.

The concept of God's preservation and deliverance of righteous individuals who remain steadfast in suffering finds its highest expression in the life of Jesus Christ. The author of 1 Peter cements the audience's assurance of their own preservation and deliverance by discussing God's vindication of Jesus.

---

30.   The LXX text differs from the MT here. In the LXX, Darius' letter is lengthened and his language is more pointed vis-à-vis his disposition toward God after witnessing Daniel's deliverance.

6.3. *God's vindication of Jesus in 1 Peter*

The description of God's vindication of Jesus is parsed in terms that are analogous to the treatment of the concept in the Old Testament. It comprises (1) the resurrection of Jesus from the dead and his exaltation to God's right hand, (2) the confusion and shame of those who are disobedient, and (3) ascription of glory to God for his work in and through Jesus Christ.

6.3.1. *The resurrection and exaltation as God's vindication of Jesus*

The author refers to Jesus' resurrection explicitly three times in the epistle: ἀνάστασις (1.3; 3.21), ἐγείρω (1.21). In all three instances the context is concerned with what God has achieved for the audience through his act of raising Christ from the dead. The author mentions the resurrection as the means through which the audience's new birth was made possible (1.3; 3.21);[31] the resurrection is also mentioned as the basis for the hope that the believers place or should place on God (1.3, 21).[32] One also gets the sense that the resurrection is implicit, in 1.11, because, 'the sufferings of Christ and the glory that follows' assumes the resurrection. Pearson argues that the sufferings/glory pattern, identified by Schutter,[33] derives from the humiliation/vindication pattern of Isa. 53.[34] I have demonstrated earlier in this chapter how the term 'glory' is part of 1 Peter's vindication vocabulary. Further, in 1.21 the author makes it clear that the 'glory' that was given Christ was subsequent to his resurrection by God. The resurrection is also implicit in 2.4-8 where the term ζάω is used to qualify the stone.[35] Not only, is the concept of vindication attested in that passage,[36] the verb ζάω is part

---

31.   Goppelt argues that it is not the resurrection of Jesus Christ per se that accomplishes new birth, but the message about his resurrection and baptism which links the person to the resurrected one (*1 Peter*, p. 84). Goppelt is right in highlighting the need to actualize the message of the resurrection. However, he seems to diminish the event's theological importance. The distinction between the 'resurrection' and 'the message about it' is unnecessary because the message cannot stand on its own without the event. The same can be said about baptism. It saves *only* through the resurrection. In this case, both the message of the resurrection and baptism seem to be more dependent on the resurrection and not the other way around. See Édouard Cothenet, 'La Portée Salvifique de la Résurrection d'après 1 Pierre', in Martin Benzerath (ed.), *La Pâque du Christ Mystère du Salut: Mélanges en l'Honneur du Père Durrwel* (LD, 112; Paris: Cerf, 1982), pp. 249–62; Schlosser, *Résurrection*, pp. 453–6.

32.   Michel Gourgues, *A La Droite de Dieu: Résurrection de Jésus et Actualisation du Psaume 110:1 Dans le Nouveau Testament* (Paris: Gabalda, 1978), p. 80.

33.   Schutter, *Hermeneutic and Composition*, p. 123.

34.   Pearson, *Christological and Rhetorical Properties*, p. 43. Throughout the course of this study, I am arguing that 1 Peter's hermeneutical lens comprises more than a sufferings/glory or humiliation/vindication pattern. It is the fabula that comprises election, suffering, steadfastness, and vindication.

35.   Cothenet, 'La Portée Salvifique', pp. 254–7.

36.   Pearson, *Christological and Rhetorical Properties*, p. 42.

of the semantic field of 'resurrection'. The author uses the composite verb ζῳοποιέω (3.18) to describe the antithesis of Christ's having been put to death.[37] Elliott notes that for the author of 1 Peter the resurrection is 'the quintessential demonstration of God's animating and saving power and the basis of the hope and trust in God despite all adversity'.[38]

These other aspects notwithstanding, the resurrection is 1 Peter's way of expressing God's vindication of Jesus Christ. This is evident (1) in the author's way of placing the resurrection opposite his discussion of the suffering death of Christ, and (2) in his way of discussing the resurrection in tandem with Christ's exaltation or participation in God's glory. First, in 1 Peter the resurrection is the antithesis to Christ's suffering and death (1.11, 21; 3.18). It is God's way of rewarding Jesus for his steadfastness in suffering; it is a display of God's ability to deliver Christ, the righteous sufferer par excellence who has placed his trust in God (2.23). It is also the author's way of placing in front of his audience the ultimate example of God's vindication of the righteous. The fact that Jesus Christ is alive emphasizes God's ability to preserve the life of the righteous even beyond death; therefore, 1 Peter's audience can indeed put their faith and hope in God (1.21). Second, the resurrection and ascension are integral to Christ's exaltation. Therefore, Christ's vindication starts with the resurrection and culminates in his exaltation. The author appropriates the exaltation language from the Old Testament and applies it to Jesus. The description of the exaltation follows the thought pattern of Ps. 110.1.[39] First, the language that Christ is at the right hand of God assumes participation in God's glory, the sharing of power, and bestowal of honour.[40] The language used here parallels the invitation to the king to join God at the place of honour (Ps. 110.1a [109.1a, LXX]). Second, the submission of angels, powers, and authorities to Jesus parallels the promise that God made to the king in Ps. 110.1b [109.1b, LXX].[41] What is an invitation and a promise to the monarch in Ps. 110.1 is described in 1 Peter as having been realized and

37.   Schlosser, 'Résurrection', pp. 442–6. See also, Dalton, *Proclamation*, p. 137.

38.   Elliott, *1 Peter*, p. 334.

39.   On account of the difference in language between 1 Peter and the Psalm, Michaels argues that the author of 1 Peter is not quoting or alluding to Ps. 110 but adopting a well known tradition (*1 Peter*, pp. 218–19). So also, Achtemeier, *1 Peter*, p. 273.

40.   See Jacques Dupont, '«Assis à la droite de Dieu». L'interprétation du Ps. 110, 1 dans le Nouveau Testament', in Édouard Dhanis (ed.), *Resurrexit: Actes du Symposium International sur la Résurrection de Jésus (Rome 1970)* (Vatican City: Libreria Editrice Vaticana, 1974), pp. 341–422 (417–18); Gourgues, *A La Droite de Dieu*, p. 82.

41.   The terms angels, authorities, and powers refer to cosmic powers that may be aligned or opposed to God's work. Based on the context of the Old Testament text the author of 1 Peter may be drawing this language from, and the context of the epistle itself it is likely that these are enemies of God who were hostile to his work in and through Jesus Christ. However, the main point is that Jesus Christ has been given supremacy and dominion over everything. See further e.g., Achtemeier, *1 Peter*, pp. 272–4; Elliott, *1 Peter*, pp. 686–9; Michaels, *1 Peter*, pp. 218–20.

actualized in Jesus. Conceptually, the exaltation language applied to Jesus is analogous to Isa. 52.13 in that the righteous sufferer par excellence has now been made co-regent with God and made to partake in God's glory.[42] The passive voice in θανατωθείς, ζῳοποιηθείς (3.18), and ὑποταγέντων αὐτῷ (3.22) serves to highlight Jesus' steadfastness (onto death) on the one hand,[43] and the work God accomplished on his behalf, on the other. In addition, Jesus' vindication underscores the important fact that suffering is not the end of the story.[44] By locating the audience's ultimate vindication at the time of Jesus' apparition (1.7) and by talking about Jesus' return in terms of the apparition of his glory (4.13), 1 Peter gives the audience the assurance of their own vindication through which they too will get to partake fully in God's glory.

6.3.2. *Vindication as confusion/shame of the disobedient*

God's vindication of Jesus Christ is evident in 1 Pet. 2.7-8, where the author appropriates the language of Ps. 118.22 [117.22, LXX] and Isa. 8.14-15; 28.16 to make his point. The demise and shame of those who oppose God's elect is characteristic of the understanding of vindication in the Old Testament and it is also attested in 1 Peter's treatment of that concept. Vindication as 'honour' for the righteous and 'shame' for the unrighteous is also attested in *1 Enoch*: 'Be confident, you righteous ones! For the sinners are due for a shame. They shall perish on the day of (the judgment of) oppression. Take for granted this (indisputable) matter, for the Most High shall record your destruction for you (O sinners)' (*1 En.* 97.1-2).[45] Elsewhere, it is said of the righteous, 'In those days, there will be a change for the holy and righteous ones and the light of days shall rest upon them; and glory and honor shall be given back to the holy ones, on the day of weariness' (*1 En.* 50.1).[46] The reference in Ps. 118.22 [117.22, LXX] describes the reversal of fortune of the righteous, 'he was rejected, despised, and persecuted by men, but was saved and honored by God and was entrusted by him with a particular and important task'.[47] In addition, the psalm offers us the perspective of those who acknowledge God's work on behalf of the righteous – 'παρὰ κυρίου ἐγένετο αὕτη καὶ ἔστιν θαυμαστὴ ἐν ὀφθαλμοῖς ἡμῶν' (Ps. 118.23 [117.23, LXX]). The author of 1 Peter has captured this aspect by pointing out the

42.   Dupont makes a similar observation in relation to the Early Church's understanding and appropriation of Ps. 110.1 to the person of Jesus Christ; namely, the one who has died is risen and now shares in God's sovereignty in ruling the world and history ('Le Ps. 110 dans le N. T.', p. 418).

43.   'He was put to death' is a summary statement of the passion which includes Jesus' trials, humiliation, and sufferings that are attached to it.

44.   See Green, *1 Peter*, p. 133; Cothenet, 'La Portée Salvifique', p. 262.

45.   Isaac, '1 Enoch', in *OTP*, 1.77.

46.   Isaac, '1 Enoch', in *OTP*, 1.36.

47.   Weiser, *The Psalms*, p. 728.

important role God's action on behalf of the 'stone' plays in the sight of those who are attuned to God (1 Pet. 2.7). But he goes one step further and highlights the implication of God's vindication of the 'living stone' for those who have rejected him. The honouring of the 'living stone' is itself an object of shaming for those who rejected him. To that effect he has also become an object of stumbling against which they strike and fall.

In addition, the image of the 'stone/rock' in the Old Testament is one that offers refuge and protection. It is used of God: 'my mighty rock' (Ps. 62.7 [61.8, LXX; 62.8, MT]); 'the rock of my salvation' (Ps. 89.26 [88.27, LXX; 89.27, MT]); 'my rock' (Ps. 18.31 [17.32, LXX; 18.32, MT]). But the idea of a 'rock' as a source of danger is also attested. The psalmist informs the congregation of the righteous God's angels, who 'will bear you up, so that you do not dash your foot against a stone' (Ps. 91.12 [90.12, LXX]).[48] In Isaiah, the stone is said to become a 'sanctuary',[49] a 'stone one strikes against' (Isa. 8.14). Elsewhere, in Isa. 28.16, the stone laid in Zion provides stability, confidence, and assurance for him/her who believes.[50] In 1 Peter, the stone plays the dual role of affirmation and offence.[51] It is clear that the stumbling happens not because of the 'living stone' primarily, but because of the attitude one adopts toward it. The stumbling happens as a result of a person's disobedience to the word (2.8), which the author of 1 Peter associates with the good news (1.25) and describes as a means of new birth (1.24). In that sense, the stumbling is not equated with the rejection of the good news, but it comes as a consequence of rejecting the word of God, which amounts to rejecting the Christ, 'the living stone'.[52]

6.3.3. Vindication as ascription of glory to God

The opening section of 1 Peter constitutes in and of itself a tribute to God for vindicating Christ. It celebrates what God has done for the audience through Christ, and also anticipates God's vindication of the audience.

---

48.   Hans Wildberger, *Isaiah 1-12* (CC; Minneapolis: Fortress, 1991), pp. 358–60.

49.   The text of Isaiah is ambiguous at this point and there is no consensus on whether the text should be read 'sanctuary' (MT: למקדש; supported by the LXX: ἁγίασμα), or 'difficulty', 'snare', or 'conspiracy' based on a reading of the Targum. Although the options are diametrically opposed, either choice would fit 1 Peter's overall context because taken together, the three Old Testament texts that he merges create the bigger picture which accounts for the two functions attributed to the 'living stone'. For a discussion see, e.g., Paul Auvray, *Isaïe 1-39* (SB; Paris: Gabalda, 1972), pp. 118–19; Godfrey R. Driver, 'Two Misunderstood Passages of the Old Testament', *JTS* 6 (1955), pp. 82–7; Otto Kaiser, *Isaiah 1-12* (OTL; Philadelphia: Westminster, 1972), pp. 117–19; Christopher Seitz, *Isaiah 1-39* (Interpretation; Louisville: John Knox, 1993), pp. 82–3; John D. W. Watts, *Isaiah 1-33* (WBC, 24; Nashville: Thomas Nelson, 2005), pp. 156–8; Wildberger, *Isaiah*, pp. 355–6.

50.   So also, Watts, *Isaiah*, pp. 337–41.

51.   Schlosser, 'A.T. et Christologie', p. 75.

52.   Cothenet, 'La Portée Salvifique', p. 254; Michaels, *1 Peter*, p. 106; Schlosser, 'A. T. et Christologie', pp. 68–72.

The letter opens on a note that is reminiscent of an Old Testament formula for thanksgiving (1.3). The author begins the letter by 'making great' the name of God. The words 'εὐλογητός' and 'ἔλεος' evoke memories of the congregation of Israel exalting God because of who he is and recalling the deeds he has accomplished on their behalf because of his lovingkindness and the covenant he has established with them.[53] Particularly, the language 'εὐλογητὸς ὁ θεός', where the eulogy describes God in relation to a person (people), contains several parallels in the LXX (Gen. 24.27; 1 Sam. 25.32; Ezra 7.27), one of which is Nebuchadnezzar's eulogy to God for the preservation of Shadrach, Meshach, and Abednego. In comparing the two texts, one finds that the eulogy in 1 Peter parallels that of Nebuchadnezzar both conceptually and syntactically. There is the announcement of praise *per se*, the description of God, and the narration of God's mighty acts. In 1 Peter, the resurrection of Jesus Christ from the dead is a pivotal point in what God is doing for the audience. Although the focus here seems to be on the audience's new birth and its implication, the resurrection as God's vindication of Christ is an integral part of the picture the author is painting. It makes possible the relationship the audience now enjoys with God. The resurrection is also important as it shows God's power to save from suffering, and for that, God deserves to be praised.

The eulogy anticipates the audience's own vindication by God. In praising God for what he has done for Christ, the author is also celebrating what God has done, is doing, and will do for the audience. He achieves it by bringing together the past, the present, and the future in one breath through his christological appropriation of the Old Testament. This is evident, first, in the way he describes God to the readers. For an audience that appears to have a very good knowledge of the Old Testament, God is not introduced to them as 'the God of Israel' (1 Sam. 25.32), or 'the Lord God of our fathers' (Ezra 7.27). Rather he is 'God the father of Lord Jesus Christ'. This means that God 'has now manifested himself as God no longer only through Israel's election',[54] but through Jesus Christ. As such, Jesus becomes an active participant of the story that involves God's relationship with humanity, fulfils Israel's role, and experiences the reality that fits the servant of Yahweh.[55] Through the language of new birth, the author brings the audience into that

---

53. See Goppelt, *1 Peter*, pp. 80–5; Jobes, *1 Peter*, pp. 81–2; Michaels, *1 Peter*, pp. 16–17. Goppelt writes, 'Whoever pronounces the eulogy actualizes the core of his or her faith: In a worshipful and praising manner he or she confesses God as God, namely as the One to whom one owes oneself' (*1 Peter*, p. 80).

54. Goppelt, *1 Peter*, p. 80.

55. By fulfilling Israel's role, I do not mean that Jesus has replaced Israel but that in his life God's intention of Israel is realized. From a theological standpoint, one might say, he has become Israel. From 1 Peter's perspective the reverse might also be true; namely, that Israel's existence anticipated the life and work of Christ. This is at the core of the author's theological hermeneutic of the Old Testament, through which he reads the Old Testament christologically on the one hand, and interprets the life and work of Christ through the Old Testament, on the other.

same reality as they are now part of God's family and awaits their promised inheritance (1.4) and the salvation that will be revealed (1.5). God's work on behalf of the audience comprises what he did for them in the past, their new birth; what he is doing for them currently, their preservation; what he will do for them, their vindication. Although the language locates the vindication in the future, the object through which the vindication will be made tangible, the inheritance, and that which makes them eligible for it, salvation, are already bestowed.

Thus, the author of 1 Peter praises God for his work on behalf of the audience. But this is all possible because of God's act of vindication accomplished on behalf of Jesus Christ; namely, his resurrection from the dead. The author also ascribes glory to God for the hope of vindication the audience cherishes. He exhorts the audience, as well, in the hope that their behaviour will cause their detractors to glorify God. By discussing Christ's vindication, the author gives the audience the assurance of their own vindication. The same Jesus Christ God raised from the dead will appear to bring out the fullness of the audience's own vindication by God.

6.4. God's vindication of 1 Peter's audience

The discussion of the vindication of the audience follows a similar rhetoric and portrays an understanding which is alike what is attested in the Old Testament, and analogous to 1 Peter's treatment of God's vindication of Jesus Christ. The author discusses vindication primarily as something the believers are looking forward to experiencing in the near future, but the language also suggests some immediacy as well vis-à-vis their receiving the reward of their steadfastness.

6.4.1. Vindication as participation in glory/ascription of honour

First Peter begins with a view of the vindication that will be wrought on behalf of the audience. I have demonstrated how the letter opening works as a summary statement of the overall message the author conveys throughout the epistle.[56] There are two ways in which he refers to the vindication of the audience in the opening section of the letter: (1) the bestowal of the inheritance which parallels the reception of salvation, and (2) the partaking in God's glory. First, understanding the bestowal of the inheritance as a sign of vindication is one more way in which the description of the situation of the readers mirrors the situation of Israel. The election of Israel, through the covenant with Abraham, Isaac, and Jacob, included the promise of the inheritance of the land of Canaan (Gen. 15.1-14). However, between the time the promise was made to the time of its fulfilment, the children of

56. See my discussion in Chapter 2.

Israel suffered the rigours of slavery in Egypt. But they cried out to God, and God rescued them, brought them out of Egypt, and led them to Canaan. The accomplishment of the promise is set in the context of deliverance from suffering; the bestowal of the promised inheritance becomes in and of itself an expression of God's vindication. It is a way of affirming a people who were otherwise disenfranchised.

Similarly, with the election of the audience comes the promise of an undefiled, unfading, and imperishable inheritance (1 Pet. 1.4). While they rejoice in that fact, they now face trials which could potentially damage the hope that they have. Just as God promised Abraham that he would see his offspring through the sufferings of Egyptian bondage, the author of 1 Peter assures the audience that God himself is guarding them (1.5). The assurance of their preservation goes hand in hand with the assurance that their inheritance is safe and will be provided in its fullness in due time.[57] That is why the audience is urged to respond faithfully to suffering. Only those who respond faithfully are receiving and will receive fully the outcome of their faith; in other words, their vindication. The epistle closes on a similar note,[58] 'The God of all grace who has called you into his eternal glory in Christ, after you have suffered a little while, will himself mend, establish, strengthen, and fortify' (1 Pet. 5.10).[59] The author leaves no doubt about God's ability to keep and protect his elect and to give them that which is promised.

Second, another expression of the vindication of the audience is found in 1.7. There, the language shows the way in which vindication constitutes an outcome of faithful response. The former is a direct outcome of or/and depends on the latter. More importantly, it parses vindication in terms of ascription of praise, glory, and honour. Whereas these terms can refer to the praise, glory, and honour that belong or are rendered to God and/or Jesus Christ,[60] here, the author has in mind the bestowal of honour by God to those who have remained steadfast in the face of sufferings.[61] The ambiguity

---

57. Goppelt, *1 Peter*, pp. 86–7; Michaels, *1 Peter*, p. 22.

58. On the similarity between the letter opening and closing see Goppelt, *1 Peter*, pp. 86–7. See also, Thurén, *Rhetorical Strategy*, pp. 160–2. He suggests that 5.8-14 is the peroratio whose main goal is to reiterate the main objectives of the letter and 'endue them with emotional force' (p. 162).

59. The fabula of 1 Peter is attested in this verse. The author's thought moves from election to exaltation (partaking in eternal glory), and highlights suffering and vindication. Steadfastness is not explicitly mentioned in this verse, but is certainly implied and is in fact explicit in 5.9.

60. The author uses this language for God and Jesus in the epistle. For example, δόξα: God (2.12; 4.11), Jesus (1.11, 21; 4.11; 5.1); τιμη: God (2.17; 4.11; 5.11), Jesus (1.21; 2.4, 6). The word ἔπαινος is used in 2.14 as one of the functions of governors. The overall context of 1 Peter allows for understanding God as one who 'praises', 'approves' those who do good (2.19-20), on the one hand; and receives praises from his children (εὐλογητός [1.3], τὰς ἀρετὰς ἐξαγγείλητε [2.9] on the other hand).

61. Elliott, *1 Peter*, p. 342; Goppelt, *1 Peter*, p. 92; Michaels, *1 Peter*, p. 31.

in the language may be a deliberate rhetorical decision on the part of the author.[62] More importantly, it underlines the fact that the audience will partake in God's glory, receive praise, and be ascribed honour by God. The assurance that God himself will ascribe them honour makes it possible for the audience to live in a way that challenges the status quo, and the way society bestows honour. It empowers them to live a different life. David W. Kendall correctly notes, 'Christian hope involves more than an assurance of a future better than the present. Indeed, Christian hope involves the better future intruding upon, and decisively shaping, the present'.[63]

Toward the end of the epistle the author picks up the same concepts. In his address to the elders, he tells them that their good conduct and care of the flock – by setting good examples – will earn them a 'crown of glory'. This is another way of expressing the honour that will be bestowed upon the elect (cf. Wis. 5.16). The imagery is one that is prevalent in the Greco-Roman world as a means to honour those who were victorious.[64] One may safely say that the 'crown of glory' does not apply exclusively to the elders. We have demonstrated throughout this study that the author's language in relation to a specific group can and often does apply to the entire audience. In addition, as examples to the audience, the elders are expected to lead the way in terms of how to demonstrate steadfastness in sufferings. It is imaginable, therefore, that their reward will be similar in nature.[65] Further, 1 Peter applies the language of glory to the entire audience, 'because the spirit of glory; namely, the Spirit of God, rests on you' (4.14). Further, the author uses in 5.4 the same verb (κομίζω) that was used in 1.9, in the context of the audience's reception of salvation; and qualifies the 'crown of glory' in a way that is analogous to the inheritance the audience hopes for: 'εἰς κληρονομίαν ... ἀμάραντον' (1.4); 'ἀμαράντινον τῆς δόξης στέφανον' (5.4). The parallels suggest that these are different ways used by the author to express the vindication of the believers in terms of their partaking in God's glory and being bestowed honour by him.

The use of 'exaltation' language offers a hint of the audience's vindication by God. It is cast in the form an exhortation, 'Humble yourselves, therefore, under the mighty hand of God, so that he may exalt you at the proper time' (5.6), that is part of the author's final words to the audience. It starts with the dispositions and attitudes that should guide the way the believers behave with one another: humility, dependence on God, discipline, alertness, and steadfastness (5.5b-9). This underscores the point made earlier in this book:[66] in 1 Peter, life within the community of believers prepares one for

---

62.   Thurén, *Rhetorical Strategy*, pp. 164–76. Thurén's discussion is helpful, although it has some shortcomings. For an evaluation, see Campbell's discussion of the inadequacies of Thurén's approach vis-à-vis the ambiguities of 1 Peter (*Honor, Shame, and the Rhetoric of 1 Peter*, pp. 22–5).

63.   David W. Kendall, '1 Peter 1.3-9', *Int* 41 (1987), pp. 66–71.

64.   Achtemeier, *1 Peter*, pp. 329–30; Elliott, *1 Peter*, p. 834; Green, *1 Peter*, p. 169.

65.   Michaels, *1 Peter*, p. 287.

66.   See my discussion in Chapter 5.

life within society at large. The author is not only concerned about the audience's behaviour vis-à-vis the outside world. He urges all to be clothed with humility. In a world where the motto could be summed up as 'You are what you wear', the author invites his audience to be associated with the lowly.[67] This disposition is at the root of all of their actions. It finds its basis in the Old Testament – 'The Lord opposes the arrogant, but gives grace to the humble'; (Prov. 3.34) – and finds its expression in the life of the audience through their submission to God. This puts 1 Peter's submission language into perspective. The audience can submit to human authority, because it is an expression of their submission to God, who is in control of their lives and holds human authority accountable, and who, in due time, will lift them up and honour them. The God of grace gives grace to the humble. Campbell rightly argues that 'in 1 Peter, χάρις belongs to the semantic field of honor and shame'.[68] He surveys briefly the ways in which the author uses the term and its derivative (χάρισμα) throughout the epistle, highlights the connection between χάρις and the terms δόξα, κλέος, τιμή, and ἔπαινος and concludes that 'exaltation' and 'grace' are synonymous terms through which the author expresses the vindication of the audience, 'honor divinely bestowed on those who presently suffer shameful treatment by those outside the community'.[69]

6.4.2. *Vindication as shaming/confusion/judgement of blasphemers*

At several junctures in the epistle, the author underscores the outcome of the audience's good behaviour vis-à-vis those who oppose them. For example, he suggests that the audience's faithful response to suffering will cause their detractors to be silenced (2.15), shamed (2.6; 3.16), and ultimately to face God's judgement (4.5).

In his exhortation to the audience to submit to human authorities, the author centres the audience's action in their mindfulness of God, 'ὅτι οὕτως ἐστὶν τὸ θέλημα τοῦ θεοῦ ἀγαθοποιοῦντας φιμοῦν τὴν τῶν ἀφρόνων ἀνθρώπων ἀγνωσίαν' (2.15). In so doing, he links the admonition with what he said in 2.13 – submission to authority is done on account of the Lord. In that sense the οὕτως both resumes the thought that precedes,

67. Green, *1 Peter*, p. 170.
68. Campbell, *Honor, Shame, and the Rhetoric of 1 Peter*, pp. 60–2.
69. Campbell, *Honor, Shame, and the Rhetoric of 1 Peter*, pp. 60–2. Campbell proposes that 'χάρις' may refer to the honour contest of the first-century Mediterranean world. However, an honour contest assumes that at least two parties are facing off on common grounds in view of one outlasting the other. Although 1 Peter uses the concepts of honour and shame, the categories and concepts are redefined for a believing community. For example, by calling the audience to seek God's approval (2.19-20), or to be clothed in meekness (5.6) the author moves the audience away from the need or desire to be engaged in any type of 'honour contest' that would satisfy the requirements of the Greco-Roman world order. See also, Green, *1 Peter*, p. 171.

and anticipates what follows it.[70] By urging the audience to act as an expression of their obedience to and alignment with the will of God, the author is at the same time placing God in the mind of the audience as the agent of vindication, who will put a stop to the slander that is addressed toward his people. There is a cause-effect relationship between the participle 'ἀγαθοποιοῦντας' and the infinitive 'φιμοῦν' – doing good in order to silence ... – in this way, although it is often taken that the implied subject of the infinitive is ὑμᾶς,[71] the context also allows for an understanding that God is the one doing the silencing. The silencing constitutes vindication in the sense that it assumes the end of verbal harassment or/and accusations. It involves shaming of the accusers, because it assumes that they will have been proven wrong.[72] The good behaviour of the believers is in and of itself the most effective way of bringing suffering to an end. It makes the way for God to act on their behalf.

A similar understanding is conveyed in 3.16 where the author offers a similar rationale for his admonition to the audience: '...συνείδησιν ἔχοντες ἀγαθήν, ἵνα ἐν ᾧ καταλαλεῖσθε καταισχυνθῶσιν οἱ ἐπηρεάζοντες ὑμῶν τὴν ἀγαθὴν ἐν Χριστῷ ἀναστροφήν'. There, the passive καταισχυνθῶσιν should be read as a divine passive because, in 1 Peter, God is arbiter of honour and shame (2.6-7, 13, 19-20; 3.12; 5.5-6). He is the one whose approval the believers live for and seek, and those who oppose them will be called to give an account of their actions. To the extent that the author identifies his audience as 'living stones' whose reality parallels that of the 'living stone', we can say that the language of vindication used of the 'living stone' also applies to 1 Peter's audience. In this sense, God's vindication constitutes the 'shaming' of those who fail to acknowledge God's work in the lives of the faithful (2.6).

The concept of God as judge is tied to the idea of God's vindication of the audience as judgement of those who oppress his people. The author makes it clear in 4.5 that those who blaspheme the believers 'will give an account to the one who stands ready to judge the living and the dead'. He continues to highlight the fact that those who oppress the audience are accountable to God. Those who blaspheme them will give an answer to God – 'ἀποδώσουσιν λόγον τῷ ἑτοίμως ἔχοντι κρῖναι' (4.5).[73] With this rhetoric the author helps the audience put their situation into perspective and gives them the assurance of their own vindication. At its root is the assurance that God is in control of their lives and also has jurisdiction over the lives of their oppressors. Further, it gives them a sense that what happens to them does not compare to what will happen to their oppressors (4.17-18).

---

70.   E.g., Achtemeier (*1 Peter*, p. 185) and Elliott (*1 Peter*, p. 494) argue that οὕτως is exclusively retrospective; while Michaels proposes that it is exclusively prospective (*1 Peter*, p. 127).

71.   E.g., NRSV, NIV, LSG; Achtemeier, *1 Peter*, p. 185; Elliott, *1 Peter*, p. 494.

72.   Elliott, *1 Peter*, p. 632.

73.   Though the subject of the verb is not specified, the context of the epistle suggests that God is the implied subject (1.17; 2.23; 4.17-19).

The language of judgement applied to those who oppress God's elect suggests that the author has the eschatological judgement in view (4.5, 17-18). However, he continues to keep the present and future in tension.[74] For example, in 4.5 he uses the future tense and makes no effort to qualify it (ἀποδώσουσιν); however, in 4.17-18 the language suggests that judgement is an imminent experience 'ὅτι ὁ καιρὸς τοῦ ἄρξασθαι τὸ κρίμα ἀπὸ τοῦ οἴκου τοῦ θεοῦ'.[75] Further, in 2.12 the author uses 'ἐν ἡμέρᾳ ἐπισκοπῆς' which is used in the Old Testament and other Jewish literature (e.g., Isa. 10.3; Jer. 6.15; Wis. 3.7-8) to refer to the final judgement. The mention is made in discussing one of the outcomes of the believer's good behaviour in the midst of a hostile environment; namely, it may cause the blasphemers to 'glorify God on the day of visitation'. Whereas 'ἐν ἡμέρᾳ ἐπισκοπῆς' carries a future connotation, 'to glorify God' implies that a change has occurred in the life of the person who was once in a state of disobedience to God, was slandering, and was opposed to the elect and to God's work in their lives. It has been argued that this change takes place at the time of the eschaton.[76] However, the idea that those who oppose God's children can experience a change in their disposition toward God and his elect in the present, in other words, *before* the eschaton, is also attested in the epistle (3.1-2).[77] Moreover, the language of 2.12 is set in the context of the current circumstances of the believers. The good behaviour the audience is urged to display, the slandering, and the observation of the believers' good deeds all take place in the present.[78] It is possible, therefore, for the end result of the audience's good behaviour and their good deeds – an expression of their faithful response – to take place in the present. Either way, the change in disposition of the blasphemers constitutes in itself a form of vindication of the believers. The point here is that understanding of 'ἐν ἡμέρᾳ ἐπισκοπῆς' as a *double entendre* is consistent, on the one hand, with the evangelistic aspect of God's vindication as judgement upon unbelievers for the purpose of bringing them to the place of acknowledging his work in the lives of the elect. It is consistent with the concept that the suffering and steadfastness of the audience are effective as witness to the outside world. In that sense, God's judgement leads the disobedient to the place where he or she is now part of the family of God. On the other hand, it is also consistent with vindication as judgement in the form of punishment to those who fail to change their ways in spite of what they have observed (2.7-8; 4.4-5, 17-18).

74.   Feldmeier, *The First Letter of Peter*, p. 80.

75.   Judgement here is made in reference to the 'household of God'. However, in 1 Peter judgement does also include the outsiders (4.5); it only begins with the household of God, but it will follow to include the outsiders as well.

76.   Achtemeier, *1 Peter*, p. 178; Goppelt, *1 Peter*, p. 160.

77.   Elliott, *1 Peter*, pp. 470–1; Green, *1 Peter*, pp. 69–70.

78.   The particles 'ἵνα ἐν ᾧ' connect καταλαλοῦσιν, to progressive participles ἔχοντες and ἐποπτεύοντες (and vice versa) not only in terms of a cause-and-effect relationship, but also in terms of timing. They all share the same temporal location.

6.4.3. *Vindication as ascription of glory to God by and for the believer*

Another aspect of vindication that the author discusses has to do with glory that is ascribed to God because of his work on behalf of the believer. As noted earlier, the eulogy anticipates God's vindication of the audience. The author praises God for his work on behalf of the audience (1.3-9). The election resulted in the bestowal of an inheritance (1.3-5).[79] But the suffering that ensued turned the promised inheritance into an object of vindication because the audience now needed to remain steadfast in the face of trials in order to obtain it (1.13). The author also praises God for his ability to keep and protect the believer in the midst of difficult circumstances. Included in the eulogy is thanksgiving to God for the anticipated bestowal of the promised inheritance to those who would have remained steadfast in the face of sufferings.

The author also talks about the audience glorifying God, singing the praises of the one who called them out of darkness to his wonderful light (2.9). The overall context of God's election and its implications discussed in 2.4-10 makes it possible for vindication, actualized or/and hoped for, to be part of the background. Further, similar language is used in the Old Testament to refer to Israel's deliverance from Egypt (Ps. 107.14 [106.14, LXX]) and from Babylonian captivity (e.g., Isa. 9.2). The term 'τὰς ἀρετάς' is attested in Isa. 43.21 as the LXX rendering for the Hebrew word 'תְּהִלָּתִי'.[80]

In 1 Peter, the purpose of election is not suffering; suffering is a necessary intrusion. Rather, the purpose of election is an inheritance kept in heaven (1.3-5); it is partaking in God's glory (1.7; 5.10). In this way, the proclamation of God's mighty acts may serve both as a recounting of his saving act on their behalf, and as a prayer or a way to remember and depend on his ability to save in the midst of trials.

Finally, the author wants believers to live for the purpose of glorifying God. He urges them to conduct their existence in such a way that 'God may be glorified in all things through Jesus Christ' (4.11). The author offers these words in the context of exhortation given to the audience on how they should live with one another (4.7-11). As already noted, the way he encourages the readers to relate to each other is only a microcosm of the way he expects them to relate to the outside world. In fact, the concept that the believers' good behaviour may cause observers to glorify God is also applied to their relationship with those who oppress and blaspheme them (2.11-12). The believers' holy conduct, their good behaviour, and their faithful response to suffering will ultimately lead their detractors to glorify God. The author urges consistency in the lifestyle of the elect. On the one hand, the pressures of the outside world should not burden them in such a way that it affects how they relate to one another. On the other hand, they are expected to display the characteristic behaviour of being a child of God in the midst of

---

79.   This resultative connection is evident whether εἰς is translated 'for' or 'into'.
80.   'תְּהִלָּה', *BDB*, pp. 239–40; Holladay, 'תְּהִלָּה', p. 387.

the fiery trials they encounter in their dealings with the outside world. Here, vindication *per se* applies more readily to the case in which the slanderer is now glorifying God as a result of observing the good deeds of the elect. However, there is a deeper truth that runs through this concept. Even within the household of God, the motivation for good conduct is not primarily for their own sake, or for the benefit or honour of the person, or the need to assert oneself above others. The primary motivation for all of life's actions is to bring glory to God. 'To him belong the glory and the power forever and ever. Amen.'

6.5. *Conclusion*

The purpose of this chapter has been to discuss the author's understanding of the concept of vindication in view of substantiating the claim that it constitutes an element of the fabula of 1 Peter. I have demonstrated that there are close affinities between the way the concept is treated in the Old Testament and other Jewish literature, the way the author discusses Jesus' vindication by God, and the language with which he urges the audience to anticipate their own salvation. As such, the author's theological hermeneutic of the Old Testament is evident here as well. He uses the example of Jesus Christ and language that is reminiscent of Israel's Scripture to give the audience the assurance of their own vindication by God, if they remain steadfast in sufferings. God will act on their behalf in the same manner he has acted for Israel and Jesus.

The author understands vindication to be concerned with the preservation and honouring of those who respond faithfully to suffering; God's judgement of those who are disobedient to his word and mistreat his children; and the ascription of glory to God for his work on behalf of his children. Vindication is the reward that comes to the believer who chooses not to withdraw from a difficult situation based on the assurance that God's deliverance is at hand. It is primarily something that 1 Peter's audience looks forward to. It is something they may enjoy in part in their lifetime, but will enjoy fully at the revelation of Jesus Christ. God the Father who calls is the *go᾽el* who protects, preserves, and delivers from suffering. He vindicates those who remain steadfast in the midst of fiery trials by honouring them, shaming their accusers, and demanding an account of their oppressors. He does it all for the glory and honour of his name.

Chapter 7

1 PETER AND THE STORY OF GOD'S ACTIONS
ON BEHALF OF BELIEVERS

7.1. Introduction

In the preceding chapters I have sought to substantiate the claim that the author of 1 Peter has identified a common, four-part fabula – election, suffering, faithful response, and vindication – by which he narrates the stories of Israel, Christ, and his audience on the Anatolian peninsula. I demonstrated that each element is indeed part of the fabula by discussing its significance for Israel, Christ, and 1 Peter's audience. Insofar as the author arranges, rehearses, and/or recalls these elements as an expression of his theological hermeneutic, one can say that he has narrated the stories of Israel, Christ, and his audience in the process of writing the letter. In this chapter, I will offer evidence of the way the author manipulates these elements. The manipulation of these elements happens at the second level of the narrative substructure. After this, I will provide the conclusion of the entire study.

7.2. The story of God's actions on behalf of believers

In outlining the methodological considerations that would guide this study I proposed that the threefold narrative structure that I have appropriated from Bal allows me to inquire into the narrative substructure of the essentially non-narrative text of 1 Peter. Therefore, I will focus here on the second layer – i.e., 'story', which together with the 'fabula' forms the narrative substructure of the letter. Following Bal, I defined the 'text' as the place where a narrative agent tells a story – in other words, it is where the author rehearses the story of Israel, Jesus, and his audience. I have also defined 'story' as the way the narrator orders the events of the fabula. Because the four-part fabula the author identifies and operates with is common to the experiences of Israel, Jesus, and his audience, it is possible to talk about their experiencing the same story although each story has its own peculiarities. In what follows, I will select some passages in the epistle to provide evidence for the way the author manipulates the elements of the fabula to rehearse the story of God's action on behalf of 1 Peter's audience. I will identify the presence of the elements in the text, and discuss how the author has arranged them to convey his message.

We may recall that Green had earlier applied narrative analysis to the study of 1 Peter.[1] He approaches narrative as a two-level structure – 'story' and 'narrative/discourse' – and has demonstrated pointedly how the author manipulates the story of his audience. He uses 1.13-21 as an example to show how this principle is at work in 1 Peter.[2] Green argues that, in this pericope, the author of 1 Peter is primarily concerned with 'time' because his discourse is peppered with chronological markers. For Green, this temporal map spans across:

- *Primordial Time* (1.20)
- *Time of Ignorance/Futility* (1.14, 18)
- *Revelation of Jesus at the End of the Age* (1.20)
- *Time of Liberation* (1.18-19)
- *Period of Life as Aliens* (1.17)
- *Final Revelation of Jesus Christ* (1.13)

He also suggests a plotline that guides the narrative by which the author orients the lives of his audience.[3]

Green's narrative analysis is helpful in that it suggests how one might say that the author of 1 Peter is manipulating story and text. He shows the theological implications of this ordering of events and its importance for the formation of the identity of 1 Peter's audience. The result, he argues, 'is a strong sense of continuity with the past, a secure place within the arc of God's gracious purpose, and a firm basis for projecting oneself into a future made certain in Jesus' resurrection from the dead'.[4] Green also attests to the complexity with which the author orders the events in the text. He suggests that, narratively speaking, 1 Peter has a well-developed eschatological horizon that serves to motivate the audience to remain steadfast in the face of suffering. There is 'backshadowing' involved in the sense that 'the future casts its shadow on present life, calling for conduct congruent with the way things really are, and in the End will be shown to be'.[5] At the same time, for the author, 'the present is not all there is, but points to and serves a future reality that mitigates the present's claims to ultimacy'.[6]

However, Green's work is confused methodologically since he does not account for the fabula that undergirds the 'story'. To be sure, Green acknowledges the notion of 'fabula' and even uses the concept in his discussion of the narrative analysis of the Bible. One also finds the concept

1.   Green, *1 Peter*; idem, 'Narrating the Gospel'.
2.   Green, *1 Peter*, pp. 197–202; idem, 'Narrating the Gospel', pp. 269–75.
3.   Green, *1 Peter*, pp. 200–1; idem, 'Narrating the Gospel', pp. 269–74.
4.   Green, *1 Peter*, p. 202.
5.   Green, 'Narrating the Gospel', p. 275.
6.   Green, 'Narrating the Gospel', p. 275.

of fabula implied in Green's articulation of a 'pattern' by which the author of 1 Peter orders the lives of his audience.[7] He identifies 'fabula' as the story behind the story, the underlying thread and overall theme that links biblical stories together.[8] However, this stands in tension with the two-layered narratological approach he self-consciously adopts. Hence, Green's approach would have been more effective if he had adopted a three-layered understanding of narrative that would have paved the way for him to elaborate on what this 'pattern' looks like.

Boring has also proposed a way to talk about story and text. Following Petersen, Boring argues that, like all letters, 1 Peter projects a narrative world as it presupposes the ongoing history in which both the author and his audience are involved. He adds, 'For 1 Peter this world embraces the everyday lives of the readers within the story of God's mighty acts in history'.[9] Boring identifies 157 events that make up the narrative world projected by 1 Peter. He arranges these events in 'the chronological order posited by this narrative world', and divides them into ten major periods that extend from creation to eschaton:

  I. (Before) Creation to Noah
 II. Noah to Abraham and Sarah
III. Abraham and Sarah to Birth of Jesus
 IV. Life of Jesus
  V. Death of Jesus
 VI. Resurrection/Ascension/Session of Jesus
VII. Resurrection of Jesus to Readers' Time
VIII. Readers' Time
      a. Readers' Former Life
      b. Readers' Evangelized
      c. Readers' Conversion
      d. Readers' Conversion to Time of the Letter
      e. Readers' Present
 IX. The Readers' Historical Future: From the Readers' Time to the Final Revelation of Christ
  X. The Eschatological Revelation of Christ[10]

Boring's work presents a helpful overview while at the same time paying attention to the elements that contribute in shaping the narrative. Boring explains that the linear mode of representation should not be understood 'only as uninterrupted, straight-line evolutionary development. It is not the case that each segment evolves from the preceding, but is determined by God's active incursion into history'.[11] However, one does not get a clear

 7.   Green, *1 Peter*, p. 200.
 8.   Green, *Seized by Truth*, p. 62.
 9.   Boring, *1 Peter*, p. 184.
10.   Boring, *1 Peter*, pp. 185–201.
11.   Boring, *1 Peter*, p. 200. See also, idem, 'Narrative Dynamics in 1 Peter'.

sense of the situation of 1 Peter's audience. For example, Boring makes a distinction between Referential Series (events in the narrative world projected by 1 Peter, arranged in order of chronology) and Plotted Series (events in the narrative world projected by 1 Peter, arranged in the order in which they are 'plotted' in the text), yet he only references the place(s) in 1 Peter where a particular event occurs without showing the relationship between events the author brings together (plots) in the text and their implication. It would have been helpful for Boring to give priority to the way the author actually arranges these elements in the text, and to the underlying pattern by which he has done the arranging. Further, Boring's claim that 'scenes from the life of Jesus play a minimal role in this story'[12] is potentially confusing, downplays the manifest references to Jesus in the letter, and, so, reveals a weakness in Boring's approach. The author's primary concern is not so much historical representation as it is theological reflection. The events from the life of Jesus that he rehearses are central to the way he urges the audience to make sense of their own situation. God's actions on behalf of Christ and Christ's own experience of election, suffering, faithful response to suffering, and vindication guides the way he reads the Old Testament and understands the past, and serves as paradigm for the audience's life. Their story is patterned after that of Christ.

For the author of 1 Peter, the story of God's action on behalf of the audience spans from election to vindication. This creates the framework of 1 Peter's message. This is evidenced by the fact that the author recalls these two events – the beginning and end of the story – in a single breath at the beginning and closing of the epistle (1.3-5; 5.10). In the opening eulogy, the author recalls the election of the audience in relation to its purpose/result – a living hope, an inheritance. The inheritance is spoken of as being inherently connected with election. I have shown that the inheritance promised becomes a means of vindication because only those who respond faithfully to suffering will receive it. Here, the suffering of the audience is implied in the description of the audience as being 'protected by the power of God' (1.5). But his focus is the audience's election and their vindication. This is significant because the author is making the audience aware of how the story is going to end. He takes away the element of suspense, because the audience is in a difficult situation. Knowing the end, then, will give the audience impetus to respond faithfully through steadfastness, doing good, and subordination to human authority.

Toward the end of the epistle the author brings the elements of the fabula together in a similar fashion: ὁ δὲ θεὸς πάσης χάριτος, ὁ καλέσας ὑμᾶς εἰς τὴν αἰώνιον αὐτοῦ δόξαν ἐν Χριστῷ ['Ιησοῦ] ὀλίγον παθόντας αὐτὸς καταρτίσει, στηρίχει, σθενώσει, θεμελιώσει (5.10). Three elements of the fabula are explicitly evident – election: ὁ καλέσας; suffering: παθόντας; vindication: ὁ δὲ θεὸς πάσης χάριτος ... καταρτίσει, στηρίχει, σθενώσει, θεμελιώσει. Faithful response is implied because the author has already told

12. Boring, *1 Peter*, p. 201.

the audience that vindication comes as a result of faithful response, and has urged the audience to remain steadfast (5.9). Again, he emphasizes the story's ending. By describing God as 'the God of all grace', the author puts the vindication of the audience at the forefront of their minds. The term χάρις is part of the semantic field of 'honour'. It evokes approval from the arbiter of honour. The God of all grace is the God who vindicates and gives grace to the humble (5.5). It is the same word the author used as a basis to urge the audience to respond faithfully to suffering (2.20). They should remain steadfast and 'do good' in the face of trials because this is commendable before God (τοῦτο χάρις παρὰ θεῷ).

The structure of the sentence also shows the emphasis on vindication. Taken by itself, the main clause reads: 'The God of all grace will himself mend, establish, strengthen, and fortify'. Also, the subordinate clause 'who called you into this his eternal glory in Christ' connects election and vindication, and identifies participation in God's glory as the purpose of God's call. Even then, the author does not lose sight of the audience's ordeal. He gives them assurance that God will vindicate their cause and bring their suffering to an end. It is worth noting how the author manipulates the notion of time. On the one hand, though vindication is in the future, he actualizes it in his description of God, and connects it to the audience's election. On the other hand, he speaks of the audience's present suffering in a way that highlights its transient nature and gives the audience the assurance that suffering will come to an end. Further, God is the main actor, but Christ shares centre stage with him. The clause ἐν Χριστῷ can be associated both with ὁ καλέσας ὑμᾶς – 'who called you ... in Christ' and αὐτοῦ δόξαν – 'his glory ... in Christ'. The options are not mutually exclusive and fit 1 Peter's message that Christ was the means through which God brought about the audience's election, and that it is by following his example that the audience will get to share in God's glory.

There are instances when the author rehearses the story with a shift in emphasis. For example, in 1 Pet. 2.11-12 one finds the notion of 'suffering' highlighted in the way the audience is addressed – 'παροίκους καὶ παρεπιδήμους' – and in the author's mention of the slandering the audience has been subjected to. Although the two terms may primarily evoke suffering, they are also associated with the audience's election. The author has used the collocation of election and suffering earlier in the epistle – ἐκλεκτοῖς παρεπιδήμοις (1.1) and εἰ πατέρα ἐπικαλεῖσθε...τὸν τῆς παροικίας ὑμῶν χρόνον (1.17). To call God 'Father' implies that one has been given new birth by God which is an expression of 'election' in 1 Peter. Further, 'the time of your sojourning' evokes alienness and its dangers. The concept of election is attested in 1 Pet. 2.11-12 because (1) it is precisely their election that has caused them to become aliens and strangers (παροίκους καὶ παρεπιδήμους), (2) the dispositions, the honourable conduct that the author urges the audience to display are not inherent to 'suffering' but to 'election' (cf. 1.15), and (3) the term 'ἀγαπητοί' is a term of endearment and is part of the semantic field of familial language in 1 Peter, which is connected to the concept of election – e.g., τὰς ψυχὰς ὑμῶν ἡγνικότες... ἐκ [καθαρᾶς] καρδίας ἀλλήλους ἀγαπήσατε ἐκτενῶς (1.22); τὴν ἀδελφότητα ἀγαπᾶτε (2.17). Further, the clause 'ἀπέχεσθαι τῶν σαρκικῶν ἐπιθυμιῶν αἵτινες στρατεύονται κατὰ τῆς ψυχῆς' (2.11), is an expression of 'faithful response'. In essence it is an exhortation to be steadfast and resist the pressures of the world around. 'Faithful response' is also evident in the use of 'ἐκ τῶν καλῶν ἔργων ἐποπτεύοντες' (2.12). It suggests that the audience does not and should respond in kind to the slandering, but instead act in such a way that their good deeds may be observed. 'Vindication' is evident in the change of disposition of the detractors – from slandering the audience to glorifying God. The author mentions elsewhere that outsiders slander believers because they are oblivious to God's work in the lives of the believers (4.3-4). Also, in the 'stone metaphor' they refuse to acknowledge God's work in the life of the elect.

In sum, in 1 Pet. 2.11-12, the focus is on the kind of response that the audience is urged to display. Their faithful response is necessitated on the basis of who they are. As God's elect they suffer pressure from within and from the outside. In spite of (perhaps also, because of) their election they are ostracized and have become the victim of slandering and false accusation. They have to resist the desires that could lead them back to their former ways of life. And they are to continue to display the kind(s) of behaviour that brought about the slandering in the first place. This will then lead to their vindication. The just judge will surely reward them for their good deeds, for having responded faithfully to suffering.

Another place where the author rehearses the story of God's actions on behalf of the audience and places emphasis on the audience's response is in 2.18-25. There, he rehearses the story of the audience from the perspective of how faithful response leads to vindication and links the process to their election. Suffering is attested throughout, but the author discusses it in a way that highlights its intrusive nature. In this text, subordination, as part of a faithful response, is urged whether one is in a context of suffering or not (2.18). Steadfastness in the face of unjust suffering (2.19) and doing good in spite of suffering meet God's approval. The phrase 'εἰς τοῦτο γὰρ ἐκλήθητε' (2.21) brings 'election' into the picture. Here the author links the ending and beginning of the story after instructing the audience on how to arrive at the perfect ending – i.e., how to meet God's approval, which he puts as the purpose of the audience's election. Whereas in 2.21 τοῦτο may have more than one antecedent, the closest antecedent in the text is the phrase 'τοῦτο χάρις παρὰ θεῷ' (2.20). The thought expressed here – that the purpose or end of election is to enjoy God's approval – is consistent with the author's rehearsal of the story of the life of the audience elsewhere in the epistle (e.g., 1.3-5; 5.10). The phrase 'εἰς τοῦτο γὰρ ἐκλήθητε' is pivotal in the sense that it points the audience toward an example they can follow in order for their story to have the perfect ending. The author rehearses the story of Jesus' passion in a way that highlights his faithful response to suffering. He suffered in spite of his innocence and remained innocent through suffering.

He did not respond in kind, but entrusted to the one who judges justly. With this description, which is a referent to God, he introduces by implication the notion of vindication in the story. Jesus' election is implied here in that the author's narration of Jesus' passion uses the language borrowed from the suffering servant of YHWH. In addition, he has already introduced the concept of Jesus' election earlier in the epistle (e.g., 1.20; 2.4-8). In both instances, the author retells the story of Jesus through language that is reminiscent of the Old Testament narrative of God's action on behalf of corporate Israel or/and the servant of YHWH. He uses the story of Jesus' suffering and subsequent vindication in 3.18-22 again as a way to reinforce the need for the audience to respond faithfully to suffering in order to be vindicated by God (3.14-17).

In sum, the author of 1 Peter arranges the four elements of the fabula in diverse ways to emphasize particular aspects of the story of God's actions on their behalf at different points in the letter. The way the story is rehearsed invites the kind of interpretation that would shape the audience's response to the suffering they face. He is aware of the suffering of the audience. And, in order to help them make sense of their situation he reminds them that their suffering is not contradictory to their election and encourages them to focus on the goal of their election – the eschatological salvation and an inheritance that will be received at the revelation of Jesus Christ. But for them to receive this inheritance, they are to respond faithfully to suffering by remaining steadfast, doing good, and accepting the authority of those who have been appointed as superior, while knowing that God is the ultimate judge to whom everyone will give an account. For those who respond faithfully to suffering future salvation now takes the form of vindication.

In crafting his message, the author appropriates the Old Testament, draws from instances in Israel's life that have points of contact with the situation his audience is experiencing, and invites his audience to identify with Israel. In addition he uses the story of Jesus in a way that shows its rapprochement with the Old Testament and, at the same time, reveals a christological reading of the Old Testament. Because of the common elements in the story of Israel, Jesus, and the audience, the author is able to show to his audience that (1) God's people have endured the hostility of the world around them, and (2) God is able to deliver and vindicate his people if they respond faithfully to suffering. In this way, the stories of Israel and Jesus serve as case in point for the audience, and give them the assurance that God's deliverance is at hand.

7.3. Conclusions

The goal of this book is to bring to light the significance of 1 Peter's christological understanding of God's actions on behalf of Israel for its audience vis-à-vis what is the proper response toward suffering. I surveyed the literature on 1 Peter, from 1946 to the present, focusing mainly on the way scholars have understood (1) the nature and function of the christology of 1 Peter, (2) the epistle's relationship to the Old Testament, and (3) the suitability of a narratological approach to 1 Peter. Whereas there is general agreement that the Old Testament plays a major role in the composition of the epistle, scholars differ on the primary source behind the author's christological treatment. Some scholars, e.g., Earl Richard, claimed that the author was primarily dependent on hymnic and traditional materials, while others, e.g., Leonhard Goppelt, argue for the author's primary dependence on Qumranic sources. In addition, several methods have been used in approaching the text in order to make sense of 1 Peter's message. For example, William Schutter used a literary approach, Sharon Pearson employed a tradition-historical, and Richard Bechtler had recourse to social-scientific exegesis. Although these approaches have contributed much to our understanding of 1 Peter's message, I have claimed that the scholarship on 1 Peter can benefit from other methods not yet fully explored.

To that end, I proposed that a narratological approach to the study of 1 Peter can offer fresh ways of understanding the meaning of its message because a narrative analysis demonstrates that the author has identified a common four-part fabula by which he narrates the stories of Israel, Christ, and his audience on the Anatolian peninsula – and by means of this fabula he gives theological significance to the suffering of his audience and sketches for them the nature of faithful response. I provided some examples of attempts to apply narratology to the study of Pauline epistles and suggested the way in which they provided an entrée into applying a similar approach to 1 Peter. My treatment underscored and sought to respond to the need for methodological clarifications raised by other scholars involved in the enterprise of applying narrative analysis to the study of epistles. Even though some Petrine scholars, e.g., Eugene Boring, Joel B. Green, J. Ramsey Michaels, and J. de Waal Dryden have begun to address the need to apply narratology to the study of 1 Peter, their treatments are limited in scope. The method I proposed differs from other narratological methods because I used Mieke Bal's three-layer understanding of narrative: fabula, story, and text as a starting point. This approach lends itself to the narratological study of non-narrative texts. I have demonstrated that a narratological approach is warranted for the study of 1 Peter because (1) the author is engaged in theological hermeneutics as evidenced by his appropriation of the Old Testament and his identification of the audience with Israel, (2) the author's engagement in theological hermeneutics invites our interest in the same, and (3) one way of being engaged in theological hermeneutics is through a narratological reading of 1 Peter. Further, I have shown that the author's extensive use of the Old Testament assumes a narrative substructure in the epistle which undergirds the message conveyed therein. This narrative substructure is held together by a 'fabula' that constitutes the lens through which the author wants his audience to interpret their own situation. Finally, the centrality of narrative to human experience makes this approach germane to 1 Peter because the author is very much concerned with shaping the behaviour of his audience and forming their identity.

The author structured his message in order to help his readers know that their experience is not unique. An inquiry into 1 Peter has shown that the pattern of events that the audience was experiencing, including what the author urges them to look forward to, was similar, though not identical, to a pattern of events that occurred in the lives of Israel and Jesus. This pattern comprises four main elements – election, suffering, faithful response, and vindication – that make up the fabula of 1 Peter. This concept of the fabula of 1 Peter that I submit differs, for example, from Earl Richard's proposal that the themes suffering/death and glory/right hand form the basic framework the author is dealing with. It is also different from William L. Schutter's argument that the 'sufferings/glories' pattern serves as an organizing principle for the way the author has read the Scriptures. Obviously these are helpful categories. However, they fail to take into account the overall tenor of the author's theological/christological thought by focusing only on the suffering and glorification of Christ and their implications. I have demonstrated that the language the author employs in rehearsing Jesus' experience implies that he has in view not just the suffering and glory of Jesus Christ but a wider scheme or pattern that includes the concepts of election, suffering, faithful response, and vindication.

Through a christological reading of the Old Testament and a rehearsal of events from the life of Jesus, the author is able to demonstrate to his audience that not only do God's people face similar circumstances, but also God's way of dealing with his people follows a familiar pattern. Therefore, he invites his audience to write their own story onto that of Israel and of Jesus Christ. The elect who follows in Jesus' footsteps in the way he/she responds to suffering will experience God's vindication in a like manner as Jesus did.

I demonstrated how this fabula is at work in the epistle by analysing how each element of the fabula is evident in the Old Testament, and in 1 Peter's description of the life and experience of Jesus, and the identification of the audience with Israel on the one hand, and with Jesus Christ, on the other hand. The author exhorts those who suffer because of their new found identity in Christ not to withdraw from the difficult situations they face, but to remain steadfast and entrust God with their lives so as to benefit God's vindication.

This book is a demonstration of narrative analysis at the service of theological hermeneutics. The author's practice of theological hermeneutics invites reflection on contemporary engagement in the same. Consequently, just as he was able to read the Scriptures of Israel in a way that spoke directly to the situation of his audience, I want to urge that there is a way for those who suffer for Christ in today's world and read 1 Peter to be so shaped by the text that they will find the strength to remain steadfast in the face of unjust suffering because of the firm assurance that suffering is only temporary, that God's presence is manifest in their situation, and that their vindication is at hand. Further, there is a way to read 1 Peter that may allow the righteous sufferer to transcend the chronological and cultural gaps in order to grasp the theological realities that are embedded in God's word so that he/she can respond to suffering in a manner that causes God's name to be glorified and ultimately brings about the end of suffering in the present, and the full enjoyment of God's vindication at the revelation of Jesus Christ.

It is my hope that the methodology that I offer and that has shaped this study will open new avenues to study other themes in 1 Peter that the scope of this book did not allow me to engage. For example, each of the four elements of the fabula of 1 Peter can be treated more extensively individually, using the same approach demonstrated in this study. In addition, the concepts of obedience and holiness play important roles in the author's rhetoric and are crucial for maintaining one's place in God's household. Both concepts are closely connected to the concepts of covenant, election, and faithful response. Further research in 1 Peter might pursue additional ways in which the author's appropriation of the Old Testament affects his treatment of these elements. A similar case can be made for other important concepts like 'hope' and 'grace' that are present in the letter. Further research and development of what happens at the 'story' level in 1 Peter might show, for example, the way in which narrative concepts such as process, change, and choice are at work within each element and between the elements, the complexity that exists in the way the elements are arranged, the overall similarities and differences in the way they are treated.

I want to suggest another interesting and important direction the present discussion could go. Eugene Boring has questioned the relevance of 1 Peter for a contemporary audience.[13] On the other hand, Joel Green advances that although there is a multifaceted gap between 1 Peter's first-century audience and a twenty-first century reader, the latter is not just reading someone else's mail. Green states,

> Even though we recognize that each book of the Bible was written to people and in places far removed from us in time and culture, when we approach the Bible as Scripture, we take seriously the faith statement that this book is our Book, these scriptures our Scripture. We are not reading someone else's mail – as though reading the Bible is recovering an ancient meaning intended for someone else and then translating its principles for us in our own lives.[14]

Further research might focus more pointedly, then, on the ongoing relevance of 1 Peter's message, and, if it did, it might take into account the fact that there are believers in different parts of the world today whose situation may be similar in many ways to that of 1 Peter's first century audience. If and

---

13. Eugene Boring, 'Interpreting 1 Peter as a Letter [Not] Written to Us', *QR* 13 (1993), pp. 89–111.

14. Joel B. Green, 'Scripture in the Church: Reconstructing the Authority of Scripture for Christian Formation and Mission', in *The Wesleyan Tradition: A Paradigm for Renewal* (ed. Paul W. Chilcotte; Nashville: Abingdon, 2002), pp. 38–51 (51).

when these people approach Scripture looking for encouragement, hope, and guidance on how to live as God's children in a hostile environment, there is a way to approach and appropriate the text of 1 Peter – e.g., like the author of 1 Peter and the Qumranites did for the Old Testament – that will cause God's promises to become as relevant as they were many centuries ago, and 1 Peter's words to resonate as true as ever.

Another avenue of research may be to look at the canonical implications of applying narratology to the epistolary studies. From a canonical standpoint, it is possible to inquire what 'fabula' is at work in 2 Peter, for example, and what similarities and differences exist between the two epistles. It is clear that the two epistles are different. 1 Peter seems to be more concerned about the threats the church faces from outside, while 2 Peter seems to be more wary of threats from within, the danger of apostasy, and ungodliness. Yet some points of similarity are evident. (1) There is a similar dependence on the Old Testament. The author draws from the stories of fallen angels, Noah, Lot, and Balaam to provide examples to his audience of what not to do and the existence of a false prophet from within. (2) The author uses a similar grounding for his exhortation: what God has done for or given to the audience (2 Pet. 1.3-4). (3) The readers are reminded of their election and urged to live accordingly in order to enjoy the promises received from God (2 Pet. 1.10). (4) Jesus' vindication is part of the background of the letter (2 Pet. 1.17). (5) There seems to be a similar hermeneutic at work as the author makes *rapprochement* between Israel and his audience (2 Pet. 2.1), the prophets of old, Jesus, and apostles linked by the ministry of the Holy Spirit (2 Pet. 1.20-21; 3.2-3). At least two elements of the fabula identified in 1 Peter are attested. Therefore, a case can be made that a similar hermeneutic is at work, but the purpose and message are different. Further research can inquire about the implications of these points of contact.

The author of 1 Peter sees a similar pattern at work in the way God deals with his children. He also gathered that God's elect go through similar experiences vis-à-vis their interaction with the world around them. Through a christological reading of the Old Testament, he rehearses the story of Israel's election, suffering, faithful response, and vindication and of God's actions on their behalf to shape the audience's response to their own suffering. He identifies the audience with Israel, places Jesus as the ultimate example of the righteous sufferer who responded faithfully to suffering and was vindicated by God, and urges the audience to follow in Jesus' footsteps and respond faithfully to suffering so as to be vindicated by God as he was.

BIBLIOGRAPHY

Abbott, H. Porter, *The Cambridge Introduction to Narrative* (Cambridge: Cambridge University Press, 2002).

Abernathy, C. David, *An Exegetical Summary of 1 Peter* (Dallas: Summer Institute of Linguistics, 1998).

Achtemeier, Paul J., *1 Peter* (Hermeneia; Minneapolis: Fortress, 1996).

——, 'The Christology of First Peter', in Mark Allan Powell and David R. Bauer (eds), *Who Do You Say That I Am?: Essays on Christology* (Louisville: Westminster, 1999), pp. 140–54.

——, 'Newborn Babes and Living Stones: Literal and Figurative in 1 Peter', in M. P. Horgan and P. J. Kobelski (eds), *To Touch the Text: Biblical and Related Studies in Honor of Joseph A. Fitzmyer, S.J.* (New York: Crossroad, 1989), pp. 207–36.

——, 'Suffering Servant and Suffering Christ in 1 Peter', in Abraham J. Malherbe and Wayne A. Meeks (eds), *The Future of Christology: Essays in Honor of Leander E. Keck* (Minneapolis: Fortress, 1993), pp. 176–88.

Adams, Edward, 'Paul's Story of God and Creation', in Bruce Longenecker (ed.), *Narrative Dynamics in Paul: A Critical Assessment* (Louisville: Westminster, 2002), pp. 19–43.

Agnew, Francis H., '1 Pet 1:2 an Alternate Translation', *CBQ* 45 (1983), pp. 68–73.

Allison, Dale C., *The End of the Ages Has Come: An Early Interpretation of the Passion and Resurrection of Jesus* (Philadelphia: Fortress, 1985).

Auvray, Paul, *Isaïe 1-39* (SB; Paris: Gabalda, 1972).

Bal, Mieke, *Narratology: Introduction to the Theory of Narrative* (Toronto: University of Toronto Press, 2nd edn, 1997).

——, *On Meaning-Making: Essays in Semiotics* (Sonoma, CA: Polebridge, 1994).

Balch, David L., 'Hellenization/Acculturation in 1 Peter', in Charles H. Talbert (ed.), *Perspectives on First Peter* (NABPRSS, 9; Macon, GA: Mercer University Press, 1986), pp. 79–101.

——, 'Household Codes', in David E. Aune (ed.), *Greco-Roman Literature and the New Testament* (SBLRBS, 21; Atlanta: Scholars, 1988), pp. 25–50.

——, *Let Wives Be Submissive: The Domestic Code in 1 Peter* (SBLMS, 26; Chico, CA: Scholars Press, 1981).

Bartchy, S. Scott, *First-Century Slavery and 1 Corinthians 7:21* (SBLDS, 11; Atlanta: Scholars, 1973).

Barth, Markus, and Helmut Blanke, *The Letter to Philemon* (ECC; Grand Rapids: Eerdmans, 2000).

Barton, Bruce B., *1 Peter, 2 Peter, Jude* (Wheaton: Tyndale, 1995).

Bauckham, Richard J., 'The Great Tribulation in the Shepherd of Hermas', *JTS* 25 (1974), pp. 27–40.

Bauman-Martin, Betsy J., 'Women on the Edge: New Perspectives on Women in the Petrine *Haustafel*' *JBL* 123 (2004), pp. 253–79.

Beare, Francis Wright, *The Epistle of First Peter* (repr. 1961; Oxford: Blackwell, 2nd edn, 1958).

Beasley-Murray, George Raymond, *The General Epistles: James, 1 Peter, Jude, 2 Peter* (London: Lutterworth, 1965).

Bechtler, Steven Richard, *Following in His Steps: Suffering, Community, and Christology in 1 Peter* (SBLDS, 162; Atlanta: Scholars, 1998).

Bénétreau, Samuel, 'Évangile et Prophétie: Un Texte Original (1 P 1,10-12) Peut-il Éclairer un Texte Difficile (2 P 1,16-21)?' *Bib* 8 (2005), pp. 174–91.

Berger, Peter L., and Thomas Luckmann, *The Social Construction of Reality: A Treatise in the Sociology of Knowledge* (Garden City, NY: Doubleday, 1966).

Bergman, Uppsala, and Bonn Botterweck, 'יָדַע', in *TDOT* (Vol. 5; Grand Rapids: Eerdmans, 1977), pp. 448–81.

Best, Ernst, *1 Peter* (NCB; London: Oliphants, 1971).

Black, Allen, and Mark C. Black, *1 & 2 Peter* (Joplin: College Press, 1998).

Bock, Darrell L., *Blasphemy and Exaltation in Judaism and the Final Examination of Jesus* (WUNT, 2.106; Tübingen: Mohr Siebeck, 1998).

Boismard, Marie. É., 'Une Liturgie Baptismale Dans La Prima Petri', *RB* 2 (1956), pp. 181–208.

——, *Quatres Hymnes Baptismales Dans La Première Épître De Pierre* (LD, 30; Paris: Cerf, 1961).

Bonnard, Pierre E., *Le Psaultier Selon Jérémie: Influence Littéraire Et Spirituelle De Jérémie Sur Trente Trois Psaumes* (Paris: Cerf, 1960).

——, *Le Second Isaïe* (Paris: Gabalda, 1972).

Boring, M. Eugene, *1 Peter* (ANTC; Nashville: Abingdon, 1999).

——, 'Interpreting 1 Peter as a Letter [Not] Written to Us', *QR* 13 (1993), pp. 89–111.

——, 'Narrative Dynamics in First Peter: The Function of Narrative World', in Robert L. Webb and Betsy Bauman-Martin (eds), *Reading First Peter with New Eyes: Methodological Reassessments of the Letter of First Peter* (London: T&T Clark, 2007), pp. 7–40.

Bray, Gerald Lewis, and Thomas C. Oden, *James, 1-2 Peter, 1-3 John, Jude* (ACCSNT, 11; Downers Grove, IL: InterVarsity, 2000).

Briscoe, D. Stuart, *1 Peter: Holy Living in a Hostile World* (Wheaton: H. Shaw, 1993).

Brooke, George J., 'Biblical Interpretation at Qumran', in James H. Charlesworth (ed.) *The Bible and the Dead Sea Scrolls* (Vol. 1; Waco, TX: Baylor University Press, 2006), pp. 287–319.

Brooks, Peter, 'The Law as Narrative and Rhetoric', in Peter Brooks and Paul Gewirtz (eds), *Law's Stories: Narrative and Rhetoric in the Law* (New Haven: Yale University Press, 1996), pp.14–23.

Brown, Jeannine K., 'Silent Wives, Verbal Believers: Ethical and Hermeneutical Considerations in 1 Peter 3:1-6 and Its Environment', *WW* 24 (2004), pp. 395–405.

Brown, William P., *Character and Scripture: Moral Formation, Community, and Biblical Interpretation* (Grand Rapids: Eerdmans, 2002).

Brownlee, William H., 'Biblical Interpretation Among the Sectaries of the Dead Sea Scrolls', *BA* 14 (1951), pp. 54–76.

Bruce, Frederick F., *Biblical Exegesis in the Qumran Texts* (Grand Rapids: Eerdmans, 1959).

Brueggemann, Walter, *1 & 2 Kings* (SHBC; Macon, GA: Smyth & Helwys, 2000).

——, *Exodus* (NIB, 1; Nashville: Abingdon, 1994).

Bruner, Jerome, *Acts of Meaning* (Cambridge: Harvard University Press, 1990).

Bultmann, Rudolf, 'Bekenntnis- und Liedfragmente im ersten Petrusbrief', *ConNT* 11 (1947), pp. 1–14.

Calvin, John, *Commentaries on the Catholic Epistles* (Grand Rapids: Eerdmans, 1948).

Campbell, Barth L., *Honor, Shame, and the Rhetoric of 1 Peter* (SBLDS, 160; Atlanta: Scholars, 1998).

Campbell, Douglas A., 'The Story of Jesus in Romans and Galatians', in Bruce Longenecker (ed.), *Narrative Dynamics in Paul: A Critical Assessment* (Louisville: Westminster, 2002), pp. 97–124.

Carmignac, Jean, 'Le Document de Qumran sur Melkisédeq', *RevQ* 7 (1969–71), pp. 360–1.

Carroll, Robert P., 'Deportation and Diasporic Discourses in the Prophetic Literature', in James M. Scott (ed.), *Exile: Old Testament, Jewish, & Christian Conceptions* (New York: Brill, 1997), pp. 63–85.

——, *Jeremiah* (OTL; Philadelphia: Westminster, 1986).

Cassuto, Umberto, *A Commentary on the Book of Exodus* (Jerusalem: Hebrew University Press, 1967).

Cedar, Paul A., *James, 1, 2 Peter, Jude* (Waco, TX: Word, 1984).

Chatman, Seymour, *Story and Discourse: Narrative Structure in Fiction and Film* (Ithaca, NY: Cornell University Press, 1989).

Chester, Andrew, and Ralph Martin, *The Theology of the Letters of James, Peter, and Jude* (NTT; Cambridge: Cambridge University Press, 1994).

Chevalier, M. A., 'Condition Et Vocation Des Chrétiens En Diaspora: Remarques Exégétiques Sur La 1ère Épître De Pierre', *RSR* 48 (1974), pp. 387–400.

Childs, Brevard S., *Biblical Theology of the Old and New Testament: Theological Reflection on the Christian Bible* (Minneapolis: Fortress, 1992).

——, *The Book of Exodus* (OTL; Philadelphia: Westminster, 1974).

——, *Isaiah* (OTL; Louisville: Westminster, 2001).

Christensen, Duane L., *Deuteronomy 1-11* (WBC, 6a; Dallas: Word, 1991).

Clowney, Edmund P., *The Message of 1 Peter: The Way of the Cross* (Downers Grove, IL: InterVarsity, 1988).

Collins, John J., 'The Heavenly Representative: The "Son of Man" in The Similitudes of Enoch', in George W. E. Nickelsburg and John J. Collins (eds), *Ideal Figures in Ancient Judaism* (SCS, 12; Ann Arbor: Scholars, 1980), pp. 111–34.

——, 'The Son of Man in First Century Judaism', *NTS* 38 (1992), pp. 448–66.

Cook, Michael, *Christology as a Narrative Quest* (Collegeville, MN: Liturgical, 1997).

Coppens, Joseph, and Luc Dequeker, *Le Fils de l'Homme et les Saints de Très-Haut en Daniel VII, dans les Apocryphes, et dans le Nouveau Testament* (ALBO, 3.23; Paris: Université de Louvain, 2nd edn, 1961).

Cornell, Stephen, 'That's the Story of Our Life', in Paul Spickard and Jeffrey Burroughs (eds), *We Are a People: Narrative and Multiplicity in Constructing Ethnic Identity* (Philadelphia: Temple University Press, 2000), pp. 41–53.

Cothenet, Édouard, 'Les Orientations Actuelles de l'Exégèse de la Première Lettre de Pierre', in Charles Perrot (ed.), *Études sur la Première Lettre de Pierre* (LD, 102; Paris: Cerf, 1980), pp. 13–42.

——, 'La Portée Salvifique de la Résurrection d'après 1 Pierre', in Martin Benzerath (ed.), *La Pâque du Christ Mystère du Salut: Mélanges en l'Honneur du Père Durrwel* (LD, 112; Paris: Cerf, 1982), pp. 249–62.

Craigie, Peter C., *The Book of Deuteronomy* (NICOT; Grand Rapids: Eerdmans, 1976).

Cranfield, C. E. B., *The First Epistle of Peter* (London: SCM Press, 1950).

Cross, F. L., *1 Peter, a Paschal Liturgy* (London: Mowbray, 1954).

Cross, Frank M., *From Epic to Canon: History and Literature in Ancient Israel* (Baltimore: Johns Hopkins University Press, 1998).

Crouch, James E., *The Origin and Intention of the Colossian Haustafel* (FRLANT, 109; Göttingen: Vandenhoeck & Ruprecht, 1972).

Dalton, William, *Christ's Proclamation to the Spirits: A Study of 1 Peter 3:18–4:6* (AnBib, 23; Rome: Pontifical Biblical Institute, 1965).

Davids, Peter H., *The First Epistle of Peter* (NICNT; Grand Rapids: Eerdmans, 1990).

Davies, Philip R., *Whose Bible Is It Anyway?* (JSOTSup, 204; Sheffield: Sheffield Academic Press, 1995).

Davis, Ellen F., 'Teaching the Bible Confessionally in the Church', in Ellen F. Davis and Richard B. Hays (eds), *The Art of Reading Scripture* (Grand Rapids: Eerdmans, 2003), pp. 9–26.

DeHaan, Richard W., and Herbert Vander Lugt, *Good News for Bad Times: A Study of 1 Peter* (Wheaton: Victor Books, 1975).

Deissmann, Adolf, *Light from the Ancient East: The New Testament Illustrated by Recently Discovered Texts of the Graeco-Roman World* (New York: Harper & Brothers, 1927).

Delling, Gerhard, 'τάσσω', in *TDNT* (Vol. 8; Grand Rapids: Eerdmans, 1977), pp. 27–48.

deSilva, David, *Honor, Patronage, Kinship, and Purity: Unlocking New Testament Culture* (Downers Grove, IL: InterVarsity, 2000).

Deterding, Paul E., 'Exodus Motifs in First Peter', *ConcJ* 7 (1981), pp. 58–67.

deVaux, Roland, *Ancient Israel: Its Life and Institutions* (Grand Rapids: Eerdmans, 1961).

Dibble, Mark E., *Deuteronomy* (SHBC; Macon, GA: Smyth & Helwys, 2003).

Driver, Godfrey R., 'Two Misunderstood Passages of the Old Testament', *JTS* 6 (1955), pp. 82–7.

Dryden, J. de Waal, *Theology and Ethics in 1 Peter: Paraenetic Strategies for Christian Character Formation* (WUNT, 2.29; Tübingen: Mohr Siebeck, 2006).

Dubis, Mark, 'First Peter and the "Sufferings of the Messiah"', in David W. Baker (ed.), *Looking into the Future: Evangelical Studies in Eschatology* (ETSS; Grand Rapids: Baker, 2001), pp. 85–96.

——, *Messianic Woes in First Peter: Suffering and Eschatology in 1 Peter 4:12-19* (SBL, 33; New York: Peter Lang, 2002).

Dunn, James D. G., 'The Narrative Approach to Paul: Whose Story?' in Bruce Longenecker (ed.), *Narrative Dynamics in Paul: A Critical Assessment* (Louisville: Westminster, 2002), pp. 217–30.

——, *The Theology of Paul the Apostle* (Edinburgh: T&T Clark, 1998).

Dupont, Jacques, '«Assis À La Droite De Dieu». L'interprétation Du Ps 110, 1 Dans Le Nouveau Testament', in Édouard Dhanis (ed.), *Resurrexit: Actes Du Symposium International Sur La Résurrection De Jésus (Rome 1970)* (Vatican City: Libreria Editrice Vaticana, 1974), pp. 341–422.

Durham, John I., *Exodus* (WBC, 3; Waco, TX: Word, 1987).

Eckert, J., 'ἐκλεκτός', in *EDNT* (Vol. 1; Grand Rapids: Eerdmans, 1990), pp. 417–19.

Eco, Umberto, *The Limits of Interpretation* (Bloomington: Indiana University Press, 1990).

Elliott, John Hall, *1 Peter: Estrangement and Community* (Chicago: Franciscan Herald Press, 1979).

——, *1 Peter: A New Translation with Introduction and Commentary* (AB, 37; New York: Doubleday, 2000).

——, '1 Peter, Its Situation and Strategy: A Discussion with David Balch', in Charles H. Talbert (ed.), *Perspectives on First Peter* (NABPRSS, 9; Macon, GA: Mercer University Press, 1986), pp. 61–78.

——, 'Backward and Forward "in His Steps": Following Jesus from Rome to Raymond and Beyond: The Tradition, Redaction, and Reception of 1 Peter 2:18-25', in Fernando F. Segovia (ed.), *Discipleship in the New Testament* (Philadelphia: Fortress, 1985), pp. 184–209.

——, *Conflict, Community, and Honor: 1 Peter in Social-Scientific Perspective* (Eugene, OR: Wipf & Stock, 2007).

——, *The Elect and the Holy: An Exegetical Examination of 1 Peter 2:4-10 and the Phrase Basileion Hierateuma* (Eugene, OR: Wipf & Stock, 1966).

——, *A Home for the Homeless: A Sociological Exegesis of 1 Peter, Its Situation and Strategy* (Philadelphia: Fortress Press, 1981).

——, 'The Rehabilitation of an Exegetical Step-Child: 1 Peter in Recent Research', *JBL* 95 (1976), pp. 243–54.

Evans, Craig A., 'Jesus and the Continuing Exile of Israel', in Carey C. Newman (ed.), *Jesus and the Restoration of Israel: A Critical Assessment of N. T. Wright's 'Jesus and the Victory of God'* (Downers Grove, IL: InterVarsity, 1999), pp. 77–100.

Fagbemi, Stephen Ayodeji A., *Who Are the Elect in 1 Peter?: A Study in Biblical Exegesis and Its Application to the Anglican Church of Nigeria* (SBL, 104; New York: Peter Lang, 2007).

Fee, Gordon D., *Gospel and Spirit: Issues in New Testament Hermeneutics* (Peabody, MA: Hendrickson, 1991.

Feldmeier, Reinhard, *Die Christen als Fremde: Die Metapher der Fremde in der antiken Welt, im Urchristentum und im 1. Petrusbrief* (WUNT, 64; Tübingen: Mohr Siebeck, 1992).

——, *The First Letter of Peter* (trans. Peter H. Davids; Waco, TX: Baylor University Press, 2008).

——, 'Wiedergeburt im 1. Petrusbrief', in Reinhard Feldmeier (ed.), *Wiedergeburt* (Göttingen: Vandenhoeck & Ruprecht, 2005), pp. 75–99.

Fitzmyer, Joseph A., 'Crucifixion in Ancient Palestine, Qumran Literature, and the New Testament', *CBQ* 40 (1978), pp. 493–513.

——, 'The Use of Explicit Old Testament Quotations in Qumran Literature and in the New Testament', in Joseph A. Fitzmyer (ed.), *Essays on the Semitic Background of the NT* (London: Chapman, 1971), pp. 3–58.

Fowl, Stephen, *The Story of Christ in the Ethics of Paul* (Sheffield: JSOT Press, 1990).

——, 'The Importance of a Multivoiced Literal Sense of Scripture: The Example of Thomas Aquinas', in A. K. M. Adam *et al.* (eds), *Reading Scripture with the Church: Toward a Hermeneutic for Theological Interpretation* (Grand Rapids: Baker, 2006), pp. 35–50.

Fowl, Stephen, and Gregory L. Jones, *Reading in Communion: Scripture and Ethics in Christian Life* (Grand Rapids: Eerdmans, 1991).

Fretheim, Terrence E., *Exodus* (Interpretation; Louisville: John Knox, 1991).

——, 'ידע', in *NIDOTE* (Vol. 3; Grand Rapids: Zondervan, 1997), pp. 409–13.

——, *Jeremiah* (SHBC; Macon, GA: Smyth & Helwys, 2002).

Fuller, Reginald Horace, *Hebrews, James, 1 and 2 Peter, Jude, Revelation* (Philadelphia: Fortress Press, 1977).

Gamble, Harry Y., *Books and Readers in the Early Church: A History of Early Christian Texts* (London: Yale University Press, 1995).

Genette, Gérard, *Nouveau Discours Du Récit* (Paris: Seuil, 1983).

Goldingay, John, *Old Testament Theology: Israel's Faith* (2 vols; Downers Grove, IL: InterVarsity, 2006).

——, *Psalms* (BCOTWP; 3 vols; Grand Rapids: Baker, 2006).

Goodman, Martin (ed.), *Jews in a Graeco-Roman World* (Oxford: Oxford University Press, 2006).

Goppelt, Leonhard, *Apostolic and Post-Apostolic Times* (London: Black, 1970).

——, *A Commentary on 1 Peter* (ed. Ferdinand Hahn; trans. John E. Alsup; Grand Rapids: Eerdmans, 1993).

——, *Theology of the New Testament: The Variety and Unity of the Apostolic Witness to Christ* (ed. Jürgen Roloff; 2 vols; Grand Rapids: Eerdmans, 1982).

——, *Typos: The Typological Interpretation of the Old Testament in the New* (trans. Donald H. Madvig; Grand Rapids: Eerdmans, 1982).

Gourgues, Michel, *A La Droite de Dieu: Résurrection de Jésus et Actualisation du Psaume 110:1 Dans le Nouveau Testament* (Paris: Gabalda, 1978).

Green, G. L., 'The Use of the Old Testament for Christian Ethics in 1 Peter', *TynBul* 41 (1990), pp. 276–89.

Green, Joel B., *1 Peter* (THNTC; Grand Rapids: Eerdmans, 2007).

——, *The Death of Jesus: Tradition and Interpretation in the Passion Narrative* (WUNT, 2.33; Tübingen: Mohr Siebeck, 1988).

——, 'Faithful Witness in the Diaspora', in Graham Stanton *et al.* (eds), *The Holy Spirit and Christian Origin* (Grand Rapids: Eerdmans, 2004), pp. 282–95.

——, 'Living as Exiles: The Church in the Diaspora in 1 Peter', in Kent E. Brower and Andy Johnson (eds), *Holiness and Ecclesiology in the New Testament* (Grand Rapids: Eerdmans, 2007), pp. 311–25.

——, 'Modernity, History, and the Theological Interpretation of the Bible', *SJT* 54 (2001), pp. 308–29.

——, 'Narrating the Gospel in 1 and 2 Peter', *Int* 20 (2006), pp. 262–77.

——, 'Scripture and Theology: Uniting the Two So Long Divided', in Joel B. Green and Max Turner (eds), *Between Two Horizons: Spanning New Testament Studies & Systematic Theology* (Grand Rapids: Eerdmans, 2000), pp. 23–42.

——, 'Scripture in the Church: Reconstructing the Authority of Scripture for Christian Formation and Mission', in Paul W. Chilcotte (ed.), *The Wesleyan Tradition: A Paradigm for Renewal* (Nashville: Abingdon, 2002), pp. 38–51.

——, *Seized by Truth* (Nashville: Abingdon, 2007).

Green, Joel, B., and Max Turner, 'New Testament Commentary and Systematic Theology: Strangers or Friends?', in Joel B. Green and Max Turner (eds), *Between Two Horizons: Spanning New Testament Studies & Systematic Theology* (Grand Rapids: Eerdmans, 2000), pp. 1–22.

Grieb, Katherine, *The Story of Romans: A Narrative Defense of God's Righteousness* (Louisville: Westminster, 2002).

——, 'Vindication', *CC* 29 (1999), pp. 1020–1.

Grogan, Geoffrey W., *Psalms* (THOTC; Grand Rapids: Eerdmans, 2008).

Gross, Carl D., 'Are the Wives of 1 Peter 3:7 Christians?', *JSNT* 35 (1989), pp. 89–96.

Grudem, Wayne A., *1 Peter* (TNTC; Downers Grove, IL: InterVarsity, 1988).

Gundry, Robert H., *The Old Is Better: New Testament Essays in Support of Traditional Interpretations* (WUNT, 178; Tübingen: Mohr Siebeck, 2005).

Hamilton, Victor P., *The Book of Genesis Chapters 1-7* (NICOT; Grand Rapids: Eerdmans, 1990).

Hargis, Jeffrey W., *Against the Christians: The Rise of Early Anti-Christian Polemic* (New York: Peter Lang, 2001).

Harris, William V., *Ancient Literacy* (Cambridge, MA: Harvard University Press, 1989).

Hart, Trevor, 'Tradition, Authority, and a Christian Approach to the Bible as Scripture', in Joel B. Green and Max Turner (eds), *Between Two Horizons: Spanning New Testament Studies & Systematic Theology* (Grand Rapids: Eerdmans, 2000), pp. 183–204.

Hay, David M., *Glory at the Right Hand: Psalm 110 in Early Christianity* (SBL, 18; Nashville: Abingdon, 1973).

Hays, Richard B., *Echoes of Scriptures in the Letters of Paul* (New Haven: Yale University Press, 1989).

——, *The Faith of Jesus Christ: An Investigation of the Narrative Substructure of Galatians 3:1-4:11* (Chico, CA: Scholars Press, 1983).

——, 'Is Paul's Gospel Narratable?', *JSNT* 27 (2004), pp. 217–39.

Hegermann, Harald, 'δόξα', in *EDNT* (Vol. 1; Grand Rapids: Eerdmans, 1990), pp. 344–8.

Hengel, Martin, *Crucifixion in the Ancient World and the Folly of the Message of the Cross* (Philadelphia: Fortress, 1977).

Hillyer, N., *1 and 2 Peter, Jude* (NICB; Peabody, MA: Hendrickson, 1992).

Holladay, William L., *Jeremiah* (Hermeneia; 2 vols; Minneapolis: Fortress, 1989).

Hooker, Morna D. '"Heirs of Abraham": The Gentiles' Role in Israel's Story', in Bruce Longenecker (ed.), *Narrative Dynamics in Paul: A Critical Assessment* (Louisville: Westminster, 2002), pp. 85–96.

Horrell, David G., 'From ἀδελφοί, to οἶκος θεοῦ: Social Transformation in Pauline Christianity', *JBL* 120 (2001), pp. 293–311.

——, 'The Label Χριτιανός: 1 Peter 4:16 and the Formation of Christian Identity', *JBL* 126 (2004), pp. 361–81.

——, 'Social-Scientific Interpretation of the New Testament: Retrospect and Prospect', in David G. Horrell (ed.), *Social-Scientific Approaches to New Testament Interpretation* (London: T&T Clark, 1999), pp. 3–27.

——, 'Whose Faith(Fullness) Is It in 1 Peter 1:5?', *JTS* 48 (1997), pp. 110–15.

Houtman, Cornelius, *Exodus* (HCOT; 2 vols; Kampen: Kok, 1996).

Howe, Bonnie, *Because You Bear This Name: Conceptual Metaphor and the Moral Meaning of 1 Peter* (Leiden: Brill, 2000).

Hubbard, Robert L. Jr., 'The Go'el in Ancient Israel: Theological Reflections on an Israelite Institution', *BBR* 1 (1991), pp. 3–19.

——, 'גאל', in *NIDOTE* (Vol. 1; Grand Rapids: Zondervan, 1997), pp. 789–94.

Hurtado, Larry W., 'Christology', in Ralph P. Martin and Peter H. Davids (eds), *DLNTD* (Downers Grove, IL: InterVarsity, 1997), pp. 170–84.

——, 'Jesus: One and Many – The Christological Concept of New Testament Authors', *JBL* 108 (1989), pp. 710–12.

Isaac, E., '1 (Ethiopic Apocalypse of) Enoch: A New Translation and Introduction', in James H. Charlesworth (ed.), *OTP* (Vol. 1; New York: Doubleday, 1983), pp. 5–89.

Jacquet, Louis, *Les Psaumes Et Le Cœur De L'homme: Étude Textuelle, Littéraire, Et Doctrinale* (3 vols; Bruxelles: Duculot, 1975).

Janzen, J. Gerald, 'Resurrection as Vindication of Creation', *LP* 7 (1998), pp. 24–5.

Jeremias, J., 'λίθος', in *TDNT* (Vol. 4; Grand Rapids: Eerdmans, 1979), pp. 272–3.

Jones, L. Gregory, 'Embodying Scripture in the Community of Faith', in Ellen F. Davis and Richard B. Hays (eds), *The Art of Reading Scripture* (Grand Rapids: Eerdmans, 2003), pp. 143–59.

Jobes, Karen H., *1 Peter* (BECNT; Grand Rapids: Baker, 2005).

Johnstone, Robert, *The First Epistle of Peter: Revised Text, with Introduction and Commentary* (Edinburgh: T. & T. Clark, 1888).

Juel, Donald, *Messianic Exegesis: Christological Interpretation of the Old Testament in Early Christianity* (Philadelphia: Fortress, 1988).

Kaiser, Otto, *Isaiah 1-12* (OTL; Philadelphia: Westminster, 1972).

Kaminsky, Joel, 'Chosen', in *NIDB* (Vol. 1; Nashville: Abingdon, 2006), pp. 594–600.

Keith, Yandell (ed.), *Faith and Narrative* (Oxford: Oxford University Press, 2001).

Kendall, David W., '1 Peter 1:3-9', *Int* 41 (1987), pp. 66–71.

——, 'The Literary and Theological Function of 1 Pet 1:3-12', in Charles H. Talbert (ed.), *Perspectives on First Peter* (NABPRSS, 9; Macon, GA: Mercer University Press, 1986), pp. 103–20.

Kesley, David, *The Uses of Scripture in Recent Theology* (Philadelphia: Fortress, 1975).

Kiley, Mark, 'Like Sara: The Tale of Terror Behind 1 Peter 3:6', *JBL* 105 (1987), pp. 689–92.

Kittel, Gerhard, and Gerhard von Rad, 'δόξα', in *TDNT* (Vol. 2; Grand Rapids: Eerdmans, 1971), pp. 233–55.

Kleinknecht, Karl T., *Der leidende Gerechtfertigte: Die alttestamentlich-judische Tradition vom leidenden Gerechten und ihre Rezeption bei Paulus* (WUNT, 2.13; Tübingen: Mohr Siebeck, 2nd edn, 1998).

Knibb, M. A., 'The Exile in the Literature of the Intertestamental Period', *HeyJ* 17 (1976), pp. 253–72.

Kornfeld, Walter, and Helmer Ringgren, 'קדשׁ', in *TDOT* (Vol. 12; Grand Rapids: Eerdmans, 2003), pp. 521–45.

Lakoff, George, 'How the Body Shapes Thought: Thinking with an All-Too-Human Brain', in Anthony J. Sanford (ed.), *The Nature and Limits of Human Understanding* (The 2001 Gifford Lectures. London: Clark, 2003), pp. 49–73.

——, 'How to Live with an Embodied Mind: When Causation, Mathematics, Morality, the Soul, and God Are Essentially Metaphorical Ideas', in Anthony J. Sanford (ed.), *The Nature and Limits of Human Understanding* (The 2001 Gifford Lectures. London: Clark, 2003), pp. 75–108.

Lakoff, George, and Mark Johnson, *Metaphors We Live By* (Chicago: University of Chicago Press, 1980).

Lamau, Marie-Louise, *Des Chrétiens dans le Monde: Communautés Pétriniennes au 1er Siècle* (LD, 134; Paris: Cerf, 1988).

——, 'Exhortation aux Esclaves et Hymne au Christ Souffrant dans La «Première l'Epître de Pierre»', *MSR* 43.3 (1987), pp. 121–43.

Langkammer, H., 'Jes 53 und 1 Petr 2,21-25. Zur chirstologischen Interpretation der Leidenstheologie von Jes 53', *Blit* 60 (1987), pp. 90–8.

Lenski, Gerhard, *Power and Privilege: A Theory of Social Stratification* (Chapel Hill: University of North Carolina, 2nd edn, 1984).

Lepelley, Claude, 'Le Contexte Historique de la Première Lettre de Pierre', in Charles Perrot (ed.), *Études sur la Première Lettre de Pierre* (LD, 102; Paris: Cerf, 1980), pp. 43–65.

Lim, Jit-Fong, *Suffering as the Controlling Motif in the First Epistle of Peter* (TREN, 36; Philadelphia: Westminster Theological Seminary, 1994).

Lim, Timothy H., *Holy Scriptures in the Qumran Commentaries and Pauline Letters* (Oxford: Clarendon, 1997).

Lincoln, Andrew T., 'The Stories of Predecessors and Inheritors in Galatians and Romans', in Bruce Longenecker (ed.), *Narrative Dynamics in Paul: A Critical Assessment* (Louisville: Westminster, 2002), pp. 172–203.

Lindars, Barnabas, *New Testament Apologetic: The Doctrinal Significance of the Old Testament Quotations* (Philadelphia: Westminster, 1961).

Lohse, Eduard, 'Die Heiden: Juden, Christen und das Problem des Fremden source', *TR* 60 (1995), pp. 227–8.

——, 'Parenesis and Kerygma in 1 Peter', in Charles H. Talbert (ed.), *Perspectives on First Peter* (NABPRSS, 9; Macon, GA: Mercer University Press, 1986), pp. 37–59.

——, *Theological Ethics of the New Testament* (trans. M. Eugene Boring; Minneapolis: Fortress, 1991).

Longenecker, Bruce, 'Narrative Interest in the Study of Paul', in Bruce Longenecker (ed.), *Narrative Dynamics in Paul: A Critical Assessment* (Louisville: Westminster, 2002), pp. 11–16.

Longenecker, Richard, *Biblical Exegesis in the Apostolic Period* (Grand Rapids: Eerdmans, 1975).

Loughlin, Gerard, *Telling God's Story: Bible, Church and Narrative Theology* (Cambridge: Cambridge University Press, 1996).

Maartens, Pieter J., 'The Vindication of the Righteous in Romans 8:31-39: Inference and Relevance', HTS, 51 (1995), pp. 1046–87.

Malina, Bruce, *New Testament World: Insights from Cultural Anthropology* (Louisville: John Knox, 1981).

Mantey, J. R., 'On Causal *eis* Again', *JBL* 70 (1951), pp. 309–11.

——, 'The Causal Use of *eis* in the New Testament', *JBL* 70 (1951), pp. 45–8.

——, 'Unusual Meanings for Prepositions in the Greek New Testament', *Expositor* 25 (1923), pp. 453–60.

Marcus, Ralph, 'The Elusive Causal *eis*', *JBL* 71 (1952), pp. 43–4.

——, 'On causal *eis*', *JBL* 70 (1951), pp. 129–30.

Marshall, I. Howard, *1 Peter* (IVPNTC; Downers Grove, IL: InterVarsity, 1991).

——, 'How Do We Interpret the Bible Today?', *Them* 5.2 (1980), pp. 4–12.

Martin, Clarice J., 'The *Haustafeln* (Household Codes) in African American Biblical Interpretation: "Free Slaves" and "Subordinate Women"', Cain Hope Felder (ed.), in *Stony the Road We Trod: African American Biblical Interpretation* (Minneapolis: Fortress, 1991), pp. 206–31.

Martin, Ralph P., 'The Composition of 1 Peter in Recent Study', in Ralph P. Martin (ed.), *Vox Evangelica: Biblical and Historical Essays by Members of the Faculty of the London Bible College* (London: Epworth, 1962), pp. 29–42.

Martin, Troy W., *Metaphor and Composition in 1 Peter* (SBLDS, 131; Atlanta: Scholars Press, 1992).

——, 'The Test Abr and the Background of 1 Pet 3,6', *ZNW* 90 (1999), pp. 139–46.

Martin, Wallace, *Recent Theories of Narrative* (London: Cornell University Press, 1986).

Martyr, Justin, St, *Dialogue With Trypho* (SFC, 3; ed. Michael Slusser; trans. Thomas B. Falls; Washington: Catholic University of America, 2003).

Masterman, John Howard Bertram, *The First Epistle of St. Peter* (London: Macmillan, 1912).

Matlock, R. Barry, 'The Arrow and the Web', in Bruce Longenecker (ed.), *Narrative Dynamics in Paul: A Critical Assessment* (Louisville: Westminster, 2002), pp. 44–57.

McKnight, Scot, *1 Peter* (NIVAC; Grand Rapids: Zondervan, 1996).

Mendenhall, George E., 'Election', in *IDB* (Vol. 2; Nashville: Abingdon, 1962), pp. 76–82.

Metzger, Bruce M., 'The Formulas Introducing Quotations of Scripture in the New Testament and the Mishnah', *JBL* 70 (1951), pp. 297–307.

Michaels, J. Ramsey, *1 Peter* (WBC, 49; Waco, TX: Word, 1988).

——, 'Catholic Christologies in the Catholic Epistles', in Richard N. Longenecker (ed.), *Contours of Christology in the New Testament* (Grand Rapids: Eerdmans, 2005), pp. 268–91.

——, 'St. Peter's Passion: The Passion Narrative in 1 Peter', *WW* 24 (2004), pp. 387–94.

Miller, Patrick D., *Deuteronomy* (Interpretation; Louisville: John Knox, 1990).

——, 'Israel as Host to Strangers', in *Israelite Religion and Biblical Theology: Collected Essays* (JSOTSup, 267; Sheffield: Sheffield Academic Press, 2000), pp. 548–71.

Morgan, Maurya P., *Pesharim: Qumran Interpretations of Biblical Books* (CBQMS, 8; Washington: The Catholic Biblical Association of America, 1979).

Mounce, Robert H., *A Living Hope: A Commentary on 1 and 2 Peter* (Grand Rapids: Eerdmans, 1982).

Moyise, Steve, 'Isaiah in 1 Peter', in Steve Moyise and Maaten J. J. Menken (eds), *Isaiah in the New Testament: The New Testament and the Scriptures of Israel* (New York: T&T Clark, 2005), pp. 175–88.

Mueller, Art, 'Testament of Abraham', in *ABD* (Vol. 1; New York: Doubleday, 1992), p. 44.

Muilenburg, James, 'The Linguistic and Rhetorical Usages of the Particle כִּי in the Old Testament', *HUCA* 32 (1961), pp. 135–60.

Munro, Winsome, *Authority in Paul and Peter : The Identification of a Pastoral Stratum in the Pauline Corpus and 1 Peter* (SNTS, 45; Cambridge: Cambridge University Press, 1983).

Murray, J. O. F., 'Election' in *DB* (Vol. 1; Paris: Letouzey et Ané, 1895), pp. 678–81.

Naulté, Jackie A., 'רֵאָה', in *NIDOTE* (Vol. 3; Grand Rapids: Zondervan, 1997), pp. 1007–15.

Nickelsburg, George W. E. Jr., *Resurrection, Immortality, and Eternal Life in Intertestamental Judaism and Early Christianity* (HTS, 56; Cambridge: Harvard University Press, exp. edn, 2006).

Nicole, Emile, 'בָּחַר', in *NIDOTE* (Vol. 1; Grand Rapids: Zondervan, 1997), pp. 638–42.

Niskanen, Paul, 'Yhwh as Father, Redeemer, and Potter in Isaiah 63:7-64:11', *CBQ* (2006), pp. 397–407.

Osborne, Thomas P., 'Guide Lines for Christian Suffering: A Source-Critical and Theological Study of 1 Peter 2,21-25', *Bib* 64 (1983), pp. 381–408.

——, 'L'Utilisation de l'Ancient Testament dans la Première Épître de Pierre', *RTL* 12 (1981), pp. 64–77.

Oswalt, John N., *The Book of Isaiah Chapters 40-66* (NICOT; Grand Rapids: Eerdmans, 1998).

Parker, J. I., 'Election', in *NBD* (Downers Grove, IL: InterVarsity, 2nd edn, 1982), pp. 306–9.

Patrick, Dale, 'Election', in *ABD* (Vol. 2; New York: Doubleday, 1992), pp. 435–41.

Patte, Daniel, *Early Jewish Hermeneutic in Palestine* (SBLDS, 22; Missoula: Scholars, 1975).

——, 'One Text: Several Structures', *Semeia* 18 (1980), pp. 3–22.

Pearson, Sharon Clark, *The Christological and Rhetorical Properties of 1 Peter* (SBEC, 45; Lewiston: Edwin Mellen, 2001).

Perdelwitz, Richard, *Die Mysterienreligion und das Problem des I. Petrusbriefes: Ein literarischer und religionsgeschichtlicher Versuch* (RVV, 11.3; Giessen: Töpelmann, 1911).

Perkins, Pheme, *First and Second Peter, James, and Jude* (Interpretation; Louisville: John Knox, 1995).

Perrot, Charles, *Etudes Sur La Première Lettre De Pierre: Congrès De L'acfeb, Paris 1979* (LD, 102; Paris: Cerf, 1980).

Petersen, Norman, *Rediscovering Paul: Philemon and the Sociology of Paul's Narrative World* (Philadelphia: Fortress, 1985).

Phelan, James, *Living to Tell About It: A Rhetoric and Ethics of Character Narration* (Ithaca, NY: Cornell University Press, 2004).

Popkes, W., 'παραδίδωμι', in *EDNT* (Vol. 3; Grand Rapids: Eerdmans, 1993), pp. 18 20.

Powell, Mark A., *What Is Narrative Criticism?* (Minneapolis: Fortress, 1990).

Prasad, Jacob, *Foundations of the Christian Way of Life According to 1 Peter 1, 13-25: An Exegetico-Theological Study* (AnBib, 146; Rome: Pontificio Istituto Biblico, 2000).

Proctor, John, 'Judgement or Vindication? Deuteronomy 32 in Hebrews 10:30', *TynBul* 55 (2004), pp. 65–80.

Propp, William H. C., *Exodus 1-18: A New Translation with Introduction and Commentary* (AB, 2; New York: Doubleday, 1999).

——, *Exodus 19-40: A New Translation with Introduction and Commentary* (AB, 2a; New York: Doubleday, 2006).

Radl, W., 'ὑπομένω', in *EDNT* (Vol. 3; Grand Rapids: Eerdmans, 1993), pp. 404–5.

——, 'ὑπομονή', in *EDNT* (Vol. 3; Grand Rapids: Eerdmans, 1993), p. 405.

Reicke, Bo, *The Epistles of James, Peter, and Jude* (AB, 37; New York: Doubleday, 1980).

Resseguie, James, *Narrative Criticism of the New Testament: An Introduction* (Grand Rapids: Baker, 2005).

Rhoads, David, 'Narrative Criticism and the Gospel of Mark', *JAAR* 50 (1982), pp. 411–34.

Richard, Earl J., 'Honorable Conduct among the Gentiles: A Study of the Social Thought of 1 Peter,' *WW* 24 (2004), pp. 412–20.

——, *Reading 1 Peter, Jude, and 2 Peter: A Literary and Theological Commentary* (RNTS; Macon, GA: Smyth & Helwys, 2000).

——, 'The Functional Christology of First Peter', in Charles H. Talbert (ed.), *Perspectives on First Peter* (NABPRSS, 9; Macon, GA: Mercer University Press, 1986), pp. 121–39.

Richards, C. H., 'Psalms 34', *Int* 40 (1986), pp. 175–9.

Richardson, Robert L., 'From "Subjection to Authority" to "Mutual Submission": The Ethic of Subordination in 1 Peter', *FM* 4 (1987), pp. 70–80.

Rimmon-Kenan, Shlomith, *Narrative Fiction: Contemporary Poetics* (London: Routledge, 1983).

Ringgren, Helmer, 'גאל', in *TDOT* (Vol. 2; Grand Rapids: Eerdmans, 1977), pp. 350–5.

Rissi, Mathias, 'κρίμα', in *EDNT* (Vol. 2; Grand Rapids: Eerdmans, 1991), pp. 317–18.

——, 'κρίνω' in *EDNT* (Vol. 2; Grand Rapids: Eerdmans, 1991), pp. 318–21.

Rosenthal, L. A., 'Die Josephgeschichte, mit den Büchern Ester und Daniel verglichen', *ZAW* 15 (1895), pp. 278–84.

——, 'Nochmals der Vergleich Ester, Joseph-Daniel', *ZAW* 17 (1897), pp. 125–8.

Rupper, Lothar, *Jesus als der leidende Gerechte? Der Weg Jesus im Lichte eines alt-und zwischentesttamentlichen Motivs* (SBS, 5; Stuttgart: Katolisshes Biblelwek, 1972).

Rüterswörden, Bonn, 'שׁמע', in *TDOT* (Vol. 15; Grand Rapids: Eerdmans, 1977), pp. 253–79.

Sanders, E. P., *Jesus and Judaism* (London: SCM, 1985).

——, 'Testament of Abraham', in James H. Charlesworth (ed.), *OTP* (Vol. 1; New York: Doubleday, 1983), pp. 874–5.

Sanders, Jack T., 'The Transition from Opening Epistolary Thanksgiving to Body in the Letters of the Pauline Corpus', *JBL* 81 (1962), pp. 348–62.

Sanders, James, 'The Exile and Canon Formation', in James M. Scott (ed.), *Exile: Old Testament, Jewish, and Christian Conceptions* (New York: Brill, 1997), pp. 37–61.

Sandys-Wunsch, John and Laurence Eldredge, 'J. P. Gabler and the Distinction between Biblical and Dogmatic Theology: Translation, Commentary, and Discussion of His Originality', *SJT* 33 (1980), pp. 133–58.

Schlosser, Jacques, '1 Pierre 3:5b-6', *Bib* 64 (1983), pp. 409–10.

——, 'Ancient Testament Et Christologie Dans La Prima Petri', in Charles Perrot (ed.), *Études sur la Première Lettre de Pierre* (LD, 102; Paris: Cerf, 1980), pp. 65–96.

——, 'La Résurrection De Jésus D'après La *Prima Petri*', in R. Bieringer *et al.* (eds), *Resurrection in the New Testament: Festschrift J. Lambrecht* (BETL, 165; Leuven: Leuven University Press, 2002), pp. 441–56.

Schrenk, Gottlob, 'ὑπογραμμός', in *TDNT* (Vol. 1; Grand Rapids: Eerdmans, 1964), pp. 772–3.

Schüssler Fiorenza, Elisabeth, *In Memory of Her: A Feminist Theological Reconstruction of Christian Origins* (New York: Crossroad, 1998).

Schutter, William L., *Hermeneutic and Composition in 1 Peter* (WUNT, 2.30; Tübingen: Mohr Siebeck, 1989).

Schwank, Benedikt P., 'L'épître (1 P 3,8-15)', *AsSeign* 59 (1966), pp. 16–32.

Schweizer, Eduard, 'Traditional Ethical Patterns in the Pauline and Post-Pauline Letters and their Development Lists of Vices and House-Tables', in E. Best and R. Wilson (eds), *Text and Interpretation: Studies in NT Presented to Matthew Black* (Cambridge: Cambridge University Press, 1979), pp. 195–209.

Seebass, Horst, 'בחר', in *TDOT* (Vol. 2; Grand Rapids: Eerdmans, 1977), pp. 73–87.

Seitz, Christopher R., *Isaiah 1-39* (Interpretation; Louisville: John Knox, 1993).

——, *Zion's Final Destiny: The Development of the Book of Isaiah: A Reassessment of Isaiah 36-39* (Minneapolis: Fortress, 1991).

Seland, Torrey, *Strangers in the Light: Philonic Perspectives on Christian Identity in 1 Peter* (BIS, 76; Leiden: Brill, 2005).

Selwyn, Edward Gordon, *The First Epistle of St. Peter* (London: Macmillan, 1946).

Senior, Donald P., *1 Peter, Jude and 2 Peter* (SP, 15; Collegeville, MN: Liturgical, 2003).

Shafer, Byron E., 'The Root *Bhr* and Pre-Exilic Concepts of Chosenness in the Hebrew Bible', *ZAW* 89 (1977), pp. 20–42.

Shiell, William D., *Reading Acts: The Lector and the Early Christian Audience* (BIS, 70; Leiden: Brill, 2004).

Skaggs, Rebecca, *The Pentecostal Commentary on 1 Peter, 2 Peter, Jude* (Cleveland: Pilgrim, 2004).

Slaughter, James R., 'Sarah as a Model for Christian Wives (1 Pet 3:5-6)', *BSac* 153 (1996), pp. 357–65.

Sly, Dorothy, '1 Peter 3:6b in the Light of Philo and Josephus', *JBL* 110 (1991), pp. 127–9.

Smith-Christopher, Daniel L., *A Biblical Theology of Exile* (Minneapolis: Fortress, 1989).

——, 'Reassessing the Historical and Sociological Impact of the Babylonian Exile (597/587-539 BCE)', in James M. Scott (ed.), *Exile: Old Testament, Jewish, & Christian Conceptions* (New York: Brill, 1997), pp. 7–36.

Snyder, Scot, 'Participles and Imperatives in 1 Peter: A Re-Examination in the Light of Recent Scholarly Trends', *FilNT* 8 (1995), pp. 187–98.

Sohn, Seock-Tae, *The Divine Election of Israel* (Grand Rapids: Eerdmans, 1991).

Spencer, Aìda B., 'Peter's Pedagogical Method in 1 Peter 3:6', *BBR* 10 (2000), pp. 107–19.

Spicq, Ceslas, *Les Épîtres De Saint Pierre* (SB; Paris: Gabalda, 1966).

Staples, Peter, 'Rev 16:4-6 and Its Vindication Formula', *NovT* 14.4 (1972), pp. 280–93.

Stendahl, Krister, 'Biblical Theology, Contemporary', in *IDB* (Vol. 1; Nashville: Abingdon, 1962), pp. 418–32.

Strecker, Georg, *Theology of the New Testament* (Louisville: Westminster, 2000).

Stuart, Douglas K., *Exodus: An Exegetical Theological Exposition of Holy Scripture* (NAC; Nashville: Broadman & Holman, 2006).

Sweeney, Marvin A., *1 & 2 Kings* (OTL; Louisville: Westminster, 2007).

Talbert, Charles H., *Learning through Suffering: The Educational Value of Suffering in the New Testament and in Its Milieu* (Collegeville, MN: Liturgical, 1991).

——, 'Once Again: The Plan of 1 Peter', in Charles H. Talbert (ed.), *Perspectives on First Peter* (NABPRSS, 9; Macon, GA: Mercer University Press, 1986), pp. 141–51.

Tàrrech, Armand P., 'Le Milieu De La Première Épître De Pierre', *RCT* 5 (1980), pp. 95–129.

Terrien, Samuel, *The Psalms: Strophic Structure and Theological Commentary* (ECC; Grand Rapids: Eerdmans, 2003).

Theisohn, Johannes, *Der auserwählte Richter* (SUNT, 12; Göttingen: Vandenhoeck & Ruprecht, 1975).

Thomas, John Christopher, 'Reading the Bible from within Our Traditions: A Pentecostal Hermeneutic as Test Case', in Joel B. Green and Max Turner (eds), *Between Two Horizons: Spanning New Testament Studies and Systematic Theology* (Grand Rapids: Eerdmans, 2000), pp. 108–22.

Thompson, Marianne Meye, *The Promise of the Father: Jesus and God in the New Testament* (Louisville: Westminster, 2000).

Thurén, Lauri, *Argument and Theology in 1 Peter: The Origins of Christian Paraenesis* (JSNTSup, 114; Sheffield: Sheffield Academic Press, 1995).

——, *The Rhetorical Strategy of 1 Peter with Special Regard to Ambiguous Expressions* (Åbo: Pargas, 1990).

Tite, Philip L., *Compositional Transitions in 1 Peter: An Analysis of the Letter-Opening* (San Francisco: Scholars, 1997).

Toolan, Michael, *Narrative: A Critical Linguistic Introduction* (London: Routledge, 1988).

Tracy, Steven, 'Domestic Violence in the Church and Redemptive Suffering in 1 Peter', *CTJ* 41 (2006), pp. 279–96.

Truex, Jerry, 'God's Spiritual House: A Study of 1 Peter 2:4-5', *Direction* 33 (2004), pp. 185–93.

VanderKam, James C., 'Exile in Jewish Apocalyptic Literature', in James M. Scott (ed.), *Exile: Old Testament, Jewish, and Christian Conceptions* (New York: Brill, 1997), pp. 89–109.

——, 'Righteous One, Messiah, Chosen One, and Son of Man in 1 Enoch 35-71' in *From Revelation to Canon: Studies in the Hebrew Bible and Second Temple Literature* (Boston: Brill, 2002), pp. 413–38.

Vanhoozer, Kevin, 'Four Theological Faces of Biblical Interpretation', in A. K. M. Adam *et al.* (eds), *Reading Scripture with the Church: Toward a Hermeneutic for Theological*

Interpretation (Grand Rapids: Baker, 2006), pp. 135-7.

——, 'What Is Theological Interpretation of the Bible?', in *DTIB* (Grand Rapids: Baker Academic, 2005), pp. 19-25.

van Rensburg, Fika J., and Steve Moyise, 'Isaiah in 1 Peter 3:13-17: Applying Intertextuality to the Study of the Old Testament in the New', *Scriptura* 80 (2002), pp. 275-86.

Van Unnik, W. C., 'A Classical Parallel to 1 Peter ii. 14 and 20', *NTS* 1 (1954/55), pp. 198-202.

——, 'The Teaching of Good Works in 1 Peter', *NTS* 1 (1954/55), pp. 92-110.

Vermès, Geza, 'Bible Interpretation at Qumran', *ErIsr* 20 (1989), pp. 184-91.

——, *The Complete Dead Sea Scrolls in English* (London: Penguin, 2004).

Vögtle, A., 'Le Règne de Dieu Dans les Dits de Jésus', *BZ* 27.1 (1983), pp. 125-8.

Volf, Miroslav, 'Soft Difference: Theological Reflections on the Relation between Church and Culture in 1 Peter' *ExAud* 10 (1994), pp. 15-30.

von Rad, Gerhard, *Deuteronomy* (OTL; Philadelphia: Westminster, 1966).

——, *Genesis* (OTL; Philadelphia: Westminster, 1972).

Wall, Robert W., 'Teaching 1 Peter as Scripture', *WW* 24 (2004), pp. 368-77.

Warden, Duane, 'The Prophets of 1 Peter 1:10-12', *ResQ* 31 (1989), pp. 1-12.

Watson, Francis, 'Are There Still Four Gospels? A Study in Theological Hermeneutics', in A. K. M. Adam *et al.* (eds), *Reading Scripture with the Church: Toward a Hermeneutic for Theological Interpretation* (Grand Rapids: Baker, 2006), pp. 95-8.

——, 'Authors, Readers, Hermeneutics', in A. K. M. Adam *et al.* (eds), *Reading Scripture with the Church: Toward a Hermeneutic for Theological Interpretation* (Grand Rapids: Baker, 2006), pp. 120-3.

——, 'Bible, Theology and the University: A Response to Philip Davies', *JSOT* 71 (1996), pp. 3-16.

——, 'Is There a Story in These Texts?', in Bruce Longenecker (ed.), *Narrative Dynamics in Paul: A Critical Assessment* (Louisville: Westminster, 2002), pp. 231-9.

——, *Paul and the Hermeneutics of Faith* (New York: T&T Clark, 2004).

——, *Text, Church and World: Biblical Interpretation in Theological Perspective* (Edinburgh: T&T Clark, 1994).

Watts, John D. W., *Isaiah 1-33* (WBC, 24; Nashville: Thomas Nelson, 2005).

Weiser, Artur, *The Psalms* (OTL; Louisville: Westminster, 2000).

Wells, Jo Bailey, *God's Holy People: A Theme in Biblical Theology* (JSOTSup, 305; Sheffield: Sheffield Academic Press, 2000).

Westermann, Claus, *Genesis 12-36* (Minneapolis: Ausburg, 1985).

White, John L., *Light from Ancient Letters* (Philadelphia: Fortress, 1986).

——, 'New Testament Epistolary Literature in the Framework of Ancient Epistolography', *ANRW* II, 25.2 (1984), pp. 1730-56.

Windish, Hans, *Die katholischen Briefe* (HNT, 15; Tübingen: Mohr Siebeck, 2nd edn, 1930).

Winter, Bruce, 'The Public Honouring of Christian Benefactors: Romans 13.3-4 and 1 Peter 2.14-15', *JSNT* 34 (1988), pp. 87-103.

——, 'Seek the Welfare of the City', *Them* 13 (1988), pp. 91-4.

Witherington III, Ben, *Paul's Narrative Thought World: The Tapestry of Tragedy and Triumph* (Louisville: Westminster, 1994).

——, *A Socio-Rhetorical Commentary on 1-2 Peter* (LHHC, 2; Downers Grove, IL: InterVarsity, 2007).

Wright, David P., 'Holiness', in *ABD* (Vol. 3; New York: Doubleday, 1992), pp. 237-49.

Wright, N. T., *The New Testament and the People of God* (Minneapolis: Fortress, 1992).

Young, Kay, and Jeffrey Shaver, 'The Neurology of Narrative', *Substance* 30 (2001), pp. 72-84.

Zimmerli, Walther, *Old Testament Theology in Outline* (Atlanta: John Knox, 1978).

Index of References

Index of Authors